The New Management Read

CW00321491

The business environment in which managers work and the internal structure of organizations are both undergoing rapid change. This collection identifies the circumstances and ideas that are shaping the new management.

Part I of the collection covers the ways in which the world is changing that will have a lasting impact on management. Six chapters explore major areas of societal change that have a direct impact on management: demographics; gender issues; the post-modern society; green and ethical awareness; information technology and the 'shrinking world'.

Part II discusses the emerging issues and concepts that will shape future management thinking and practice, such as information management; networking and collaboration across internal and external boundaries; new models of management; and 'high-involvement organization'.

Designed to support the graduate entry course in the Open University MBA programme, the collection offers an indispensable framework for any management course, whether at executive or advanced undergraduate level, that aims to prepare managers for tomorrow's business realities.

The editors are members of the academic staff of the Open University Business School with diverse management, international consultancy and research experience.

The New Management Reader

This reader has been prepared as part of the Open University graduate entry course B800, *Foundations of Senior Management*. It is part of an integrated teaching system; the selection is therefore related to other material available to students and is designed to evoke critical understanding. Opinions expressed are not necessarily those of the course team or of the University.

If you would like to study the course to which this reader relates or receive further information about Open Business School courses, please write to **The Customer Service Centre,** The Open University, PO Box 222, Walton Hall, Milton Keynes MK7 6YY or telephone 01908 653473/655182.

The New Management Reader

Edited by Rob Paton and Greg Clark,
Geoff Jones, Jenny Lewis,
Paul Quintas at The Open University

London and New York
in association with
The Open University

First published 1996
by Routledge
11 New Fetter Lane, London EC4P 4EE

Simultaneously published in the USA and Canada
by Routledge
29 West 35th Street, New York, NY 10001

© 1996 Selection and editorial matter The Open University

Phototypeset in Garamond by Intype, London
Printed and bound in Great Britain by
Biddles Ltd, Guildford and King's Lynn

All rights reserved. No part of this book may be reprinted or
reproduced or utilized in any form or by any electronic,
mechanical, or other means, now known or hereafter
invented, including photocopying and recording, or in any
information storage or retrieval system, without permission in
writing from the publishers.

British Library Cataloguing in Publication Data
A catalogue record for this book is available from the British
Library

Library of Congress Cataloging in Publication Data
A catalogue record for this book has been requested

ISBN 0–415–13986–4 (hbk)
ISBN 0–415–13987–2 (pbk)

Contents

Part II Emergent concepts and issues

Figures

Tables

Exhibits

Introduction

Rob Paton

Organizations are changing and so is management. Some of these changes are already familiar: we are used to the de-layered organization, change management, TQM, excellence and culture building, the globalization of industries, flexible production and business process re-engineering.

But there is no let-up. We drive headlong into the future looking into a rear-view mirror (as McLuhan used to say). And the danger for management schools is that, like generals preparing to fight the last war, they find themselves generalizing about forms of organization that no longer exist, and addressing problems that are no longer a salient part of their students' perplexing experience.

So what are the *circumstances*, for organizations and management have always been shaped by the economies and societies of which they are a part, and what are the *challenges and ideas* that are re-shaping management?

It is difficult in any field to tell which differences will make a difference, which ideas will last and which will prove ephemeral. The challenge is particularly severe in management – it seems the life-cycle of a new idea or technique is becoming steadily shorter. Often, too, 'new' ideas are a matter of re-discovering particular approaches: for example, the current notions of Performance Management are clearly reminiscent of 'Management by Objectives', popular for a decade, some 25 years ago.

But there were never many certainties in management, whatever the textbooks said. And there is no avoiding a judgement about what will prove significant and what will fade. This collection represents our judgements about, in Part I, those ways in which the world is changing that will have a lasting impact on management; and in Part II the emerging issues and concepts that will shape management thinking and practice as we enter the new millenium.

Hence, the first part of the book explores some of the major social changes that are affecting organizations and our understanding of management. The six topics – demographics, gender issues, a post-modern society, green and ethical issues, information technology, and a shrinking world – all represent major societal challenges whose ramifications for managers remain unclear. The articles chosen do not (and cannot) offer a final statement or prediction on the implications for managers. But in their different ways they all pose significant questions, or challenge old certainties.

Choosing topics for the second part of the book – those issues and concepts of increasing significance for management – was more difficult. Some, like information management, and the cluster of challenges we have called interdependence (involving networking and collaboration across internal and external boundaries), were fairly obvious. Others will be less familiar, though still involving, we suggest, significant shifts in thinking and practice: for example, the greater appreciation of the huge diversity of evolving management systems (Models of management); and the spread of more intense relationships between the individual and the organization (High-Involvement Organization).

None of these issues and ideas are pristine formulations. Brands, for example, have been around for years; it is the increasing power and subtlety of brands and of the meanings attributed through and to them, that is new. What we have sought are recent, clear statements presenting a perspective, or addressing important aspects of topics, that are attracting attention and helping frame our understanding of the new business realities. Hence most of the articles were published in the last two years, the earliest five years ago; and we have edited some of them to sharpen their focus.

They were selected to accompany *Foundations of Senior Management*, the graduate-entry course in the Open University MBA programme, and we are grateful to colleagues for the assistance they have given us, both through discussion and in dedicated operational support.

Part I

Management in a changing world

Chapter 1

Demographics

Historically unprecedented changes in the size and age structure of the population – demographic changes – are happening slowly but inexorably. As the population of western economies ages, there will be fewer young workers available for employment and a bigger retired population for them to support. Many of the implications of these changes are still hard to discern. For example, although an ageing population increases demand for certain products and services, the distribution of income and resources across the age-range remains uncertain and will depend on evolving social norms, public policy and employment practices. Johnson's article sketches the demographic factors at work in advanced economies and argues that one clear consequence will be a far-reaching reappraisal of employment practices. This will be brought about by heightened competition for a vital but increasingly scarce resource: skilled labour.

Population ageing and employment policies

Paul Johnson

INTRODUCTION

Human resources – workers, managers, customers and consumers – are the driving force behind the growth of modern economies. In the developed world we are used to thinking of these human resources as being readily, almost automatically available. Economic expansion in the twentieth century has been promoted by a consistent but moderate increase in the population, which has allowed just enough restocking of the labour market and just enough increase in consumer demand to provide a continuing stimulus to economic activity. But changes in the stock of human resources do not always have such benign effects, as the link between rapid population growth and endemic malnutrition in many third world countries shows. And over the next three to four decades demographic trends will also cause grave economic problems for the advanced economies. The problem will not be too many people but too few.

Between 1990 and 2040 the working population of the European Community is projected to fall by 20 per cent – there will be forty-five million fewer workers, forty-five million fewer taxpayers – while the number of pensioners and infirm elderly people will increase significantly. This ageing and shrinking of the populations of Western Europe (already underway) is historically unprecedented, and so all predictions about its economic effects must be qualified by some degree of uncertainty. Yet we can be sure that the economic impact will be profound, with major changes occurring in the labour market, in social security mechanisms and fiscal burdens, and in the structure of demand.

This chapter examines the impact of this inexorable demographic change for business, and suggests how companies will have to change their attitudes and policies towards employment, training and retirement. First, let us explain briefly why our population is ageing and declining in size.

WHAT IS POPULATION AGEING?

The demographic facts are quite straightforward: in industrial societies the proportion of old people in the population is increasing and the proportion of people of normal working age is falling. This shift is a consequence of two complementary processes, an increase in life expectancy and a decrease in fertility.

Improvements in life expectancy have been one of the major social achievements of the developed economies since the Second World War – the result of better nutrition, housing, public health and medical services. Between 1950 and 1980 average life expectancy at birth in the OECD countries rose by more than eight years for women and almost six years for men; life expectancy has also increased at higher ages, so that more seventy-year-olds now survive to eighty, and more eighty-year-olds live to ninety. However, these gains are not the primary cause of population ageing, which rather results from our failure to produce enough children.

Since 1950 the birth rate has been falling throughout Western Europe and North America. After the post-war *baby boom* came the *baby bust* of the late 1960s, 1970s and 1980s, when having children went out of fashion. Today in the European Community only the Republic of Ireland is increasing its population, while German, Italian and Danish birth rates have slumped so dramatically that on average every three couples now produce only four children altogether. Although fertility rates are not expected to remain this low indefinitely, few demographers believe they will return to the replacement level in the near future. The projections used in this chapter are taken from a recent OECD study which adopts mid-range estimates of future fertility and mortality rates, and so are a *best guess* at population trends in developed countries up to the year 2050.

Even if these projections turn out to be too pessimistic, and fertility does return to something approaching the replacement rate by the year 2000 or shortly after, there will nevertheless be an enormous transitional problem by the third decade of the next century as the post-war *baby boom* generation enters retirement and turns to the small cohorts of working age adults for economic support. One measure of the costs today's children may have to bear is given by the old age dependency ratio: the number of persons aged sixty-five and above to every hundred people aged fifteen to sixty-four. As Figure 1.1 shows, this dependency ratio is already rising rapidly in Japan, will soon start upwards in Germany, and will accelerate from the second decade of the next century in Britain and the United States. As a result, the sixty-five and over age group will represent more than 20 per cent of the population in the developed countries by 2040, up from about 10 per cent in 1980. This rise in the proportion of elderly people will inevitably increase the economic demands that retired people place on those in work, which means that the tax contributions from

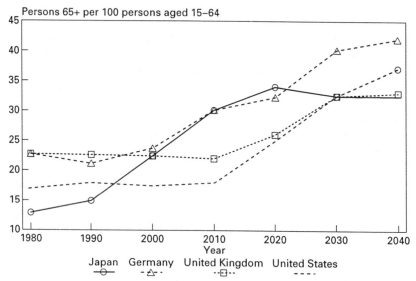

Figure 1.1 Old age dependency ratios

workers and employers will need to rise sharply if the pension and welfare systems are to be sustained in their present forms. In Britain, the extra pension bill will increase the national insurance costs for each worker by around a half, so that total national insurance contributions will have to rise from the present level of 12.5 per cent of the wage bill to 18 per cent by 2030. In 1989 it was projected that the payroll tax needed to sustain the West German pension system would have to rise from 18.5 per cent to around 42 per cent by 2030 (Schmahl, 1989, p. 143).

In all European countries employers directly bear a substantial proportion of these pension costs through their taxes. Thus this demographic change will sharply increase taxes on employment and production in the industrialised countries.

THE ECONOMIC COSTS OF POPULATION AGEING

This fiscal burden of an ageing population is only one small part of the overall economic cost. As Figure 1.2 shows, the leading industrialised countries will have to adjust to very significant changes in their labour force over the next half century.

For each country, the working population in 1990 has been set equal to 100 so that future populations can be compared with this benchmark figure. In each of these countries the working population increased over

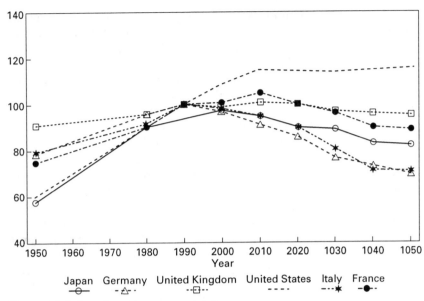

Figure 1.2 Index of working age population

the period 1950–90, at rates between 10 per cent (in Britain) and 80 per cent (in Japan). Three trends are apparent in the future:

1 In the United States the working population will continue to grow for the next twenty years, after which it will stabilise at a level 15 to 18 per cent above the 1990 figure;
2 In France and Britain the number of people of working age will be stable until 2020, after which it will fall fairly slowly;
3 In Germany, Italy and Japan the working population is already declining and by 2050 these countries will have a potential workforce far smaller than that of today. In the case of unified Germany the fall will be truly precipitate, from 53.5 million in 1990 to 36.9 million by 2050. This projected decline is greater than the *total* population of the former East Germany.

All developed countries will need to adjust both labour and product markets to the novel conditions of stable or declining populations. Higher real incomes will partly offset the effects of fewer consumers, but in some market sectors, such as housing, demographic pressures will clearly have a depressive effect. In countries such as Germany and Italy the population is projected to decline substantially faster than the housing stock depreciates. In other market sectors, the change in the age structure of the population, together with an increase in the wealth of older people, will alter the age distribution of consumer demand. The booming teenage and young adult market of the 1960s and 1970s is a thing of the past, and the new growth area will be people in later middle age, a segment hitherto seldom targeted in marketing campaigns.

This change in the age structure of people under retirement age will also profoundly affect the workings of the labour market. In 1988 there were 800,000 sixteen-year-olds in the British population. At the end of 1992 there were barely 600,000 people of school leaving age. Meanwhile, the number of workers in their late forties and fifties will rise sharply as the *baby-boomers* move into mature middle age. This shift is of potential importance since it is generally believed that younger workers are more flexible and have better and more recent training than older workers.

Not all people between fifteen and sixty-four are in employment. More young people are spending longer in higher education, and many women leave the labour force because of child-care and other family responsibilities. As a result, the actual labour force is considerably smaller than the working age population. A recent development in retirement practice – the concept of *early retirement* – has further reduced the size of the workforce. As Figure 1.3 shows, the labour force participation rates for men aged fifty-five to sixty-four have fallen sharply since the mid 1960s in all the leading industrial countries except Japan (Guillemard, 1989, p. 168).

Since the fifty-five to sixty-four age group will become a larger share of

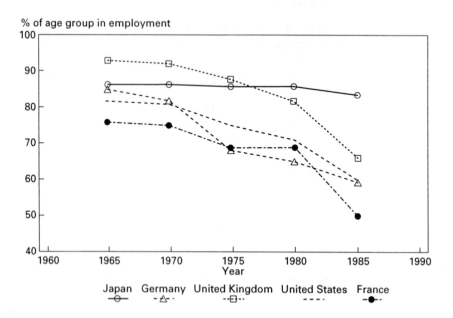

Figure 1.3 Labour force participation: males 55–64 years old

the population over the next ten to fifteen years, the decline in its labour force participation will mean that the actual labour force will decline more rapidly in many countries than will the overall working-age population. Labour in industrial countries will become an increasingly scarce resource, a change that will require new attitudes and practices on the part of both governments and employers.

EMPLOYER RESPONSES TO POPULATION AGEING: THE NEED FOR RADICAL NEW THINKING IN PERSONNEL MANAGEMENT PRACTICES

How *new* will these attitudes and practices need to be? Can the problem be solved by limited wage increases, juggling with bonus schemes and the offer of more tax-free perks? Will human resource managers be able to continue with *business as usual*? This seems unlikely.

Since the first oil price shock of 1974, the Western economies have experienced a prolonged period of general labour surplus, but demographic change will reverse these labour market conditions. This unprecedented demographic shock cannot be accommodated simply by tinkering with existing personnel management practices. What is needed is a new way of thinking, a paradigm shift, in human resource management. The most obvious example will be in the area of early retirement.

Over the last fifteen years, early retirement schemes have enabled employers to shed older workers with minimal political or trade union protest, while giving relatively well-off older workers a chance to opt for increased leisure at a younger age. Little effort has been put into providing training for older workers. Although industrial psychologists have known for thirty years or more that the productivity of older workers is in most occupations not significantly different from that of younger workers, many employers continue to assume that older workers are less productive.

The British government has already launched efforts to raise the pension entitlement age, which will tend to discourage companies from promoting early retirement. Labour shortage may be an even more important influence in this regard. Service sector companies, such as the supermarket chain Tesco in Britain and the Travelers Insurance Company in the United States, are already actively recruiting older people to fill the part-time and temporary vacancies formerly taken by juvenile or casual workers.

But such examples are exceptional; it will not be easy to reverse deeply entrenched personal and corporate attitudes to the employment of older workers. In Britain, as shown in Figure 1.4, the decline in labour force participation in men over sixty-five, which has been particularly rapid in recent years, is part of a long-run trend stretching back 100 years. Even in the period of acute labour shortage after the Second World War, older men withdrew from employment in ever increasing numbers despite intensive propaganda from the government to persuade both employers and workers that retirement should be postponed. Why are these patterns of retirement behaviour so difficult to change?

To manage their internal labour markets and secure the long-term loyalty of essential staff, many employers have established an earnings gradient in which pay is related to age. Since the marginal product of most workers does not seem to increase much above the age of fifty and in some cases declines, the profitability of workers tends to fall beyond middle age, and the incentive for the employer to remove the worker, usually by means of an early retirement deal, is strong. Rapid clear-out of older workers also ensures that promotion prospects for younger workers can be maintained. Although this is perhaps a caricature of the logic behind current personnel management practices, it is not a wholly fanciful description. Earnings gradients and early retirement are an important part of personnel policy today, and their removal would necessitate a major reconsideration of the way in which labour forces are managed.

For the individual, earnings gradients and early retirement also seem to make sense. Because so many occupational pension-schemes define their benefits in relation to final salary (rather than life-time contributions), many workers do best when their salary is maximised in their final years of employment. This pattern can be achieved by a remuneration system based upon an age-related earnings gradient, and a labour contract that

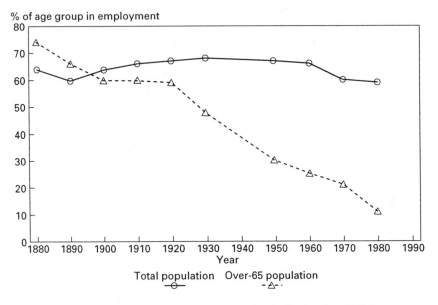

Figure 1.4 Labour force participation rates: males in England and Wales

offers early retirement rather than demotion to a lower-paid job. At present it is not in the interest of either employers or workers to alter this system.

However, general labour shortage, and intense competition for skilled younger workers will make the continued employment of older workers essential. If employers are to make use of older workers' skills, and if the employees are to be willing to go on working, it will not be enough to offer minor cash incentives for the over fifty-fives. Instead there must be a major re-organization of the promotion and remuneration structures by which large employers today organize their internal labour markets.

Furthermore, if older workers are to be encouraged to continue in employment (though not necessarily in their prime career job), they will need to be trained and retrained throughout their working life. The provision of training, even for juveniles, is hardly one of British industry's success stories, and almost no attention has been given to the particular problems of training older workers. Perhaps the promise of continual retraining throughout an extended working life can be used as an incentive to preserve employee loyalty and restrict labour turnover at a time when competition among employers for labour will become more intense.

Increasingly this competition will occur on a Europe-wide basis, which does not bode well for low-wage British employers. The generally low level of skill among the British workforce, which is compounded by a lack of in-service training, will be exacerbated as skilled staff are poached away by high-wage industries on the continent. As the pace of technological change quickens, constant retraining of the workforce will become more necessary. However, British employers will have scant incentive to bear the private cost of such training if the workers then carry their enhanced human capital to Germany or Italy where, because of a declining population, they can command much higher wages.

This combination of demographic pressure and technological change should encourage employers to reverse the move towards flexible labour contracts which has been so pronounced over the last decade. Businesses now need to consider how to develop effective long-term labour contracts that will guarantee a suitable return on the employer's investment in training. In Germany a return to formal apprenticeships for juveniles is already being discussed, as a means to prevent hectic labour mobility and wage inflation in the juvenile labour market. But since labour shortages will increase the demand for older workers, new ways need to be found to tie the middle-aged worker to the firm, so that mid-career retraining will be fully capitalised by the employer.

Here we should perhaps look at employment practices in Japan, where long-term (often life-time) welfare and housing benefits are used to tie the worker to the firm, and so ensure both employee loyalty and wage stability. A move towards long term employment contracts would be a fundamental challenge to current Western personnel management policies, which are geared to maximising labour force flexibility. Under conditions of abundant labour, flexible labour contracts are the least cost option, but they impose enormous public and private costs when workers, particularly skilled workers, are scarce.

CONCLUSION

In the relatively near future, labour shortages in the developed economies, particularly of skilled younger workers, will increase the bargaining power of labour, drive up labour costs and force employers to adjust their employment practices, particularly in relation to older workers and retirement. These adjustments will require a good deal of thought and planning, and some conscious re-orientation of the expectations of both employers and employees. If the adjustments are not made, the rising costs of labour among the shrinking populations of Western Europe and Japan will intensify the competitive advantage of third world economies, which will experience an expansion of their workforce and a decline in the relative size of their dependent child population in the early years of the next century. In the developed economies labour is a declining resource; we can no longer afford to waste it.

NOTES

1 OECD, 'Ageing populations: the social policy implications', Paris, 1988.
2 Author's calculations based on Dept of Health and Social Security, Population, Pensions Costs and Pensioners' Incomes, HMSO, London 1984.

REFERENCES

Guillmard, A. (1989) 'The trend towards early labour force withdrawals and the reorganisation of the life course: a cross-national analysis', in Johnson et al.
Schmahl, W. (1989) 'Labour force participation and social insurance systems', in P. Johnson, C. Conrad, and D. Thomson (eds): Workers versus Pensioners: Intergenerational Justice in an Ageing World, Manchester: Manchester University Press.

Chapter 2

Gender issues

In the world our parents grew up in, the 'normal' roles, occupations and social networks of men and women were clearly differentiated. Since the Second World War these separations have been eroding irreversibly and at a quickening pace. There are new ways of being women and men, new patterns of relationship between them, new career choices, and more equal social status. The substantial efforts now made by major companies in the areas of harassment and equal opportunity policies indicate both the increased acceptance of the new realities and how far there is still to go. The new generation of managers are living these social changes, both in their personal lives and in navigating the shifting and conflicting expectations of staff, colleagues and superiors. The changes do not just mean the men's club atmosphere of senior management is being eroded. They call in question fundamental assumptions about 'good management' and 'leadership'. So, for example, it is now being argued that women have different strengths and styles as managers which are just as, or more, effective than men's – but which have not so far been recognized or valued. But are such claims simplistic and misleading – do they, indeed, reinforce familiar (and restrictive) stereotypes of women?

Of stereotypes and differences: the debate about the ways women lead

Donna Dickenson

Look like a woman,
Act like a lady,
Think like a man,
Work like a horse!

Martin (1990) has drawn up two lists of qualities which are valued and downgraded in large organisations. Bureaucracies value such characteristics as 'rational', 'objective', 'impersonal', 'unemotional' and 'expert'. Under the devalued heading come qualities such as 'subjective', 'irrational', 'involved', 'personal' and 'emotional'. 'Inspection of these [lists] reveals the hidden assumptions; the devalued characteristics are all traditionally more likely to be associated with women than with men.'

The links between the male stereotype and the values that dominate many ideas about the nature of organisations are striking. Organisations are often encouraged to be rational, analytical, strategic, decision-oriented, tough and aggressive, and so are men. But when women try to present themselves this way, they may be condemned as overly assertive, pushy and 'unfeminine'.

Virginia Schein, who coined the phrase 'think manager, think male', has discovered that 20 years of equal opportunities law in the anglophone world have had little impact on this stubborn association of management with maleness, particularly among men. In research done during the 1970s, she had asked 300 male middle managers and 167 female middle managers to rate 92 descriptive items by whether they were or were not typical of women in general, men in general, and successful middle managers. She found that men gave a mean rating of zero to the resemblance between women and managers; in other words, none of the traits they thought necessary for successful managers were those they associated with women in general. Women gave a slightly higher rating to the resemblance between their sex and successful managers, but still lower than for that between men and managers. By 1989 women's perceptions had altered substantially, but men's were similar.

Schein performed a similar exercise with German management students, again yielding a correlation between the characteristics associated with maleness and those seen as necessary for success in management. Again, there was a mean zero rating between 'female' characteristics and managerial ones (Schein and Mueller, 1990). So it seems arguable that, in cultures other than English-speaking ones, an 'effective' manager is also likely to be associated with a male manager.

But do people have to conform to the 'masculine' norm to be effective as managers – or are there other ways of being a manager? Interest in gender difference and management styles has been intense over the past decade, after a long period in which the male was the norm in management theory. Reacting against the assumption that a woman had to 'think like a man' to advance, many psychologists and management theorists have recently begun to explore the idea that women can be different without disadvantaging themselves.

In this they have also questioned the earlier view that there was one objective management style. Even recently a course for women managers advised, 'Don't let other people's attitudes affect your management style. Try and behave as if there is no difference between you and the male manager . . . the qualities you need to succeed are objective, not sexual' (The Open University, 1986, p. 80). The problem with this view, to advocates of 'difference', is that it leaves women trying to conform to a 'male' model. This model makes no allowance for many women's dislike of – confrontation, exerting authority of/for its own sake, of playing 'power games' – all the possible negative aspects of 'masculinity'.

Instead, say the 'difference' disciples, women should view their femininity as a plus, and so should their employers. 'Female' virtues in negotiation, teamworking and human resource management are vital with the comparative decline of old hierarchical styles of management such as Taylorism and the mass production industries for which they were devised. The newer types of service industry that now dominate most European economies call for a different model of management, one which extols and uses 'feminine' virtues.

'WAYS WOMEN LEAD': THE ARGUMENT. . . .

One influential advocate of 'difference' is Judy B. Rosener of the University of California at Irvine. In an article published in 1990 the *Harvard Business Review* published her article, 'Ways Women Lead'. There Rosener claims that:

Women managers who have broken the glass ceiling in medium sized, non-traditional organizations have proven that effective leaders don't come from one mold. They have demonstrated that using the command-

and-control style of managing other, a style generally associated with men in large, traditional organizations, is not the only way to succeed.

(Rosener, 1990, p. 119)

Many female managers have found Rosener's message extremely positive because it means they needn't choose between the management style they find comfortable and the style that succeeds in traditionally male-dominated organisations. However, others have criticised Rosener for merely reinforcing stereotypes about women's 'caring' nature.

Although the first women into management positions were obliged to conform to male models, Rosener says, there is now a sufficient critical mass of female executives for feminine styles of leadership to be acceptable. Rosener thinks that many organisations have been hit by what the American writer Naomi Wolf might call the 'genderquake' (Wolf, 1993): women are gaining power, and increasingly on their own terms.

Organisations are beginning to see very direct and tangible benefits from employing more women in management positions, and in permitting a mix of management methods. Indeed, in certain sectors a non-traditional leadership style is a positive advantage to an organisation, Rosener thinks:

The women's success shows that a non-traditional leadership style is well suited to the conditions of some work environments and can increase an organization's chances of surviving in an uncertain world. It supports the belief that there is strength in a diversity of leadership styles.

(Rosener, 1990, p. 120)

What sorts of organisation does Rosener mean? Organisations in which women have successfully challenged traditional command-and-control models of leadership tend to be medium-sized, fast-growing, and rapidly changing. Typically, they are staffed by an unusually high proportion of workers with professional qualifications. Success in a job is measured by performance rather than adherence to hierarchical norms.

In such a fluid environment traditional hierarchies can be 'dinosaurs', and the most successful model of leadership the one which Rosener calls 'transformational' rather than 'transactional'. Rather than viewing job performance as a series of reward and punishment transactions with subordinates, as Rosener suggests male managers are more likely to do, the women executives whom she surveyed thought in terms of 'getting subordinates to transform their own self-interest into the interest of the group, through concern for a broader goal ... Moreover, they ascribe their power to personal characteristics like charisma, interpersonal skills, hard work, or personal contacts rather than to organizational stature. More specifically, the women encourage participation, share power and information, enhance other people's self-worth, and get others excited about their work' (Rosener, 1990, p. 120).

What specific methods of leadership did these women executives find fruitful? Rosener's interview subjects frequently referred to inclusion – trying to make people feel part of the organisation – rather than exclusion – reminding employees that they do not share the manager's status. They encouraged democracy in setting performance goals and determining strategy. They used a conversational style which implied a certain equality and invited involvement. They avoided accusations of hypocrisy by acting on the suggestions they received, and sometimes changing particular decisions in response to staff input.

Although such tactics may look risky, Rosener's women executives felt that they had protected themselves by involving their colleagues and subordinates in this way:

> Participation also increases support for decisions ultimately reached and reduces the risk that ideas will be undermined by unexpected opposition. Getting people involved also reduces the risk associated with having only one person handle a client, project or investment.
>
> (Rosener, 1990, p. 122)

The women managers surveyed by Rosener recognised limitations to participatory styles of leadership: 'Soliciting ideas and information from others takes time, often requires giving up some control, opens the door to criticism, and exposes personal and turf [territorial] conflicts. In addition, asking for ideas and information can be interpreted as not having answers' (Rosener, 1990, p. 122). This could be particularly threatening for a woman manager, who may need to be seen as twice as competent as a comparable man. Appearing indecisive or ignorant could be very damaging to these female managers. Rosener admits calmly that 'When participation doesn't work, they act unilaterally' (Rosener, 1990, p. 122).

However, rather than viewing knowledge solely as power or proof of their competence, the interviewees in Rosener's study did prefer to share information whenever possible – and power with it. Open disclosure, they felt, enhanced the general communication flow within the organisation and benefited managers directly, by increasing the likelihood that problems would be voiced before they became overwhelming. Again, there were dangers in sharing information: 'It allows for the possibility that people will reject, criticize or otherwise challenge what the leader has to say, or, more broadly, her authority ... Because information is a source of power, leaders who share it can be seen as naive or needing to be liked' (Rosener, 1990, p. 123). But among the highly educated workforce typically found in the women managers' sorts of organisation, the expectation of sharing information was well-nigh impossible to resist. Furthermore, it was seen as encouraging a sense of self-worth in staff and raising morale.

The female managers interviewed by Rosener thought it particularly crucial to 'refrain from asserting their own superiority, which asserts the inferiority of others. All those I interviewed expressed clear aversion to behaviour that sets them apart from others in the company – reserved parking places, separate dining facilities, pulling rank' (Rosener, 1990, p. 123.) Instead, these women based their managerial authority on achieving measurable results. This was particularly crucial to those female managers working in conservative professions like merchant banking, where their egalitarian and enthusiastic management style might otherwise be 'interpreted as cheerleading [which] can undermine credibility' (Rosener, 1990, p. 124).

Rosener believes that the fast-moving employment world of the late twentieth century has created opportunities for new managerial styles, and opportunities for women executives through the very crises which have often typified the corporate world. 'When change is rampant, everything is up for grabs, and crises are frequent. Crises are generally not desirable, but they do create opportunities for people to prove themselves. Many of the women interviewees said they got their first break because their organizations were in turmoil' (Rosener, 1990, p. 125).

Survival of the fittest in this rapidly evolving environment requires organisations to adopt whatever management style works. Rosener claims that interactive or transformational leadership, as practised by the women managers in her survey, has taken root because it suits firms in these new circumstances. However, she adds a final warning: 'The fact that women are more likely than men to be interactive leaders raises the risk that these companies will perceive interactive leadership as 'feminine' and automatically resist it' (Rosener, 1990, p. 125). However, some male managers are already coming to accept this model, she claims.

... AND THE CRITIQUE

I think Rosener is well-advised to add her last qualification – that many men are picking up 'female' management styles. In fact, I wonder whether men really are (or ever were) any less likely than women to use interactive leadership styles. A Greek study bears out my doubts.

In a survey of 300 respondents from both private and public-owned companies, Dimitris Bourantas and Nancy Papalexandris (1990) set out to test two hypotheses:

1 that female managers use more democratic leadership styles than male managers
2 that subordinates would be more satisfied with female managers as a result.

The survey subjects comprised abut 100 employees with female managers and 200 with men at the helm. Bourantas and Papalexandris asked them to classify their managers' leadership style in one of four categories: 'autocratic', 'paternalistic', 'consultative' or 'participative'. They actually found that a slightly higher percentage of male managers followed democratic styles (consultative or participative). A far higher percentage of women than men adopted a 'paternalistic' style, according to their subordinates. Nor were employees any more (or less) content with female managers: the 'happy family' which Rosener pictures was no more likely to be found in organisations with women in control.

Perhaps the difference is that Rosener's subjects were managers evaluating their own style of leadership. Things may look very different to subordinates! Or perhaps there is less pressure to adopt a male model of managerial behaviour in the USA than in Greece. But either way, I think the Greek study should make us wary about generalising – and I find Rosener very prone to generalise.

The trouble with comparisons *between* groups (such as men and women managers) is that they tend to obscure differences *within* the groups. The extent of the differences among women managers is clear from a French study.

Laufer (1982) found that women managers adopted one of four strategies to meet the expectations imposed on them, as women, by their predominantly male senior managers.

1 *Submission to the difference* – these women counted on loyalty and devotion to win them advancement. They did not question the traditional supporting and subordinate position of women in their firms, but tried to excel at the 'female' role. This led to low conflict with male management.
2 *Acknowledgement of the difference* – these female managers recognised that expectations for men and women were different, but tried to bypass conflict by developing functional specialisms. They hoped to gain status based on expertise. Unfortunately this also meant that they tended to bypass senior management careers: functional roles in administration or personnel are less effective springboards to promotion than general management. These women also had to make sacrifices in relation to family, marriage or partnership, and children, but they tended to accept those, too. Throughout their choices they acknowledged that there was a different reality for men and women, and they tried to accommodate themselves to it rather than to change it. This also led to low conflict with male managers.
3 *Assertion of the difference* – these women managers had chosen to enter sectors such as fashion and advertising, where femininity is part of the organisation's image or women are an important target audience. They played up their own feminine 'intuition' as giving them a unique and superior insight into what customers wanted. This strategy did lead to moderate conflict with male management, but these women dealt with

that in acceptably 'feminine' fashion, which defused it somewhat. 'To men whose power is based on figures, charts and formal relationships, they respond by asserting the power of intuition and emotion' (Laufer, 1993, p. 125).

4 *Demanding both equality and difference* – these women challenged the need to choose between career and family, which the 'acknowledgers of the difference' (group 2) had accepted uncritically. They wanted to have both, as male managers could; but there were aspects of 'male' management styles that they consciously rejected. In particular they tried to avoid becoming too obsessed by career goals or taking themselves too seriously. This led to high conflict with male management, since it was often viewed as a failure to take their management role seriously. In fact, one might argue that despite their overt feminism, they were inadvertently and ironically fulfilling a stereotype of women as less serious-minded and more flighty in many male managers' minds.

The word 'difference' recurs in these categories. Even the practitioners of the last strategy, who demand equality with men, also want to be different from them: they do not simply imitate men managers. Earlier feminists were accused – unfairly, in my opinion – of simply aping men, and this generation of feminists can be seen as countering that criticism. They are trying to create positive associations for femininity, in contrast to the negative ones which I identified at the start of this article. Besides, they see enough flaws in the male role model to be wary of it. The author of the French study, Jacqueline Laufer, says:

> It thus seems that far from adopting or rejecting a 'masculine' model of behaviour, the only one considered suitable for success in management, women managers develop different career strategies in accordance with their personality, qualifications, and the sector or type of organization in which they find themselves. These strategies reflect a diversity of models for reconciling feminine and managerial roles.
>
> (Laufer, 1993, p. 125)

'Transformational leadership' is a stirring concept, and Rosener's message of valuing diversity in management styles is very attractive: not only difference between men and women, but, by implication, difference between nationalities and/or ethnic groups. But although she warns against 'linking interactive leadership directly to being female', she also talks about 'women's shared experience'. Is there any such thing – particularly for women of different national, class, ethnic or racial backgrounds?

Within Europe the differences in women's experience are enormous: in Ireland only 25 per cent of women are in paid employment, compared to over 80 per cent in Denmark. So there are great gaps between Irish and Danish women's experience in this very basic area – whether you expect to work outside the home in the first place. All of these examples make me very doubtful about whether there is any such thing as women's shared experience.

If there is a 'shared experience' for many women, I would argue that it lies in not having much power. A survey of 1,000 women managers in local government in England and Wales found that they had little or nothing in common in terms of background and experience. What did unite them was 'their minority status at the management level' (Young and Spencer, 1990). What if women's different way of leading is just a function of comparative formal powerlessness?

It is sometimes asserted that women's different 'style' could be attributed to their differential recruitment into jobs requiring dependence and passivity, and to selective recruitment of particularly conciliatory women for those posts. Rosener admits that her interviewees ascribe their power to personal qualities and contacts, not to 'clout' within their organisations. If and when women do ascend the management ladder in larger numbers, and can wield power and authority by organisational stature, will their style of management still be different? Or is this style merely a temporary, adaptive device rather than any real difference?

Rosener seems to put women into a double bind. She remarks that her successful women managers have learned not to draw attention to themselves, but to praise subordinates and to downplay their own achievements. Yet if a woman doesn't blow her own trumpet, will she get noticed? Throughout Europe women are more likely to be working as functional specialists than as general managers, or in areas such as personnel which are not on fast career tracks (Davidson and Cooper, 1993). Rosener was interviewing women who had already 'got there'; but is self-effacement the right strategy for women who haven't yet cracked the glass ceiling? Doesn't such retiring behaviour just reinforce existing prejudices, and exacerbate the tendency (found in both sexes) to devalue women's competence?

Women have generally been found to attribute their failure to internal causes such as lack of intelligence or competence, but their success to external ones such as luck. (Conversely, men's failure is attributed – by both men and women – to bad luck, and their success to high ability.) The logic of this is that women, and those above them, expect that they should stay at the same level if they succeed, but be sacked or demoted if they fail. After all, the reasoning goes, success was none of their doing but failure was definitely their fault. This attitude may be one reason for the differential ratings given to female general managers for performance-related pay (Alimo-Metcalfe, 1992).

CONCLUSION

Rosener concludes that a 'non-traditional leadership style' works in organisations that accept it. This is a chicken-and-egg situation. Did the success of the women Rosener studied change the managerial culture in their organisations towards a more woman-friendly style? Or did these women managers succeed because they were working in organisations which could afford to adopt something other than a command-and-control model? Rosener tends towards the second answer, I think. But that means that the model of difference is limited in its application, to areas in which there is a great deal of technological change; firms dominated by professionals with valuable skills, who can easily switch organizations; and/or areas in which performance is easy to measure by results. It won't work for all sectors and all organisations.

On the positive side, the organisations in which Rosener's women managers worked may represent the future. Medium-sized, innovative organisations are becoming more and more typical in the aftermath of recession and 'down-sizing'. Hierarchy and 'command-and-control' leadership don't suit such organisations, according to Rosener. Whether or not, 'transformational leadership' is typically female, it may well be the way forward. If women managers can hitch their wagons to this particular star, it could be their way forward, too.

REFERENCES

Alimo-Metcalfe, B. (formerly Alban Metcalfe) (1992) 'Gender and appraisal: findings from a National Survey of Managers in the British Health Service', paper presented at the Global Research Conference on Women in Management, Ottawa, 21–23 October.
Bourantas, D. and Papalexandris, N. (1990) 'Sex differences in leadership styles and subordinate satisfaction', *Journal of Managerial Psychology*, vol. 5, no. 5, pp. 7–10.
Davidson, M. J. and Cooper, C. L. (1993) 'European women in business and management: an overview', in Davidson, J. J. and Cooper, C. L. (1993) *European Women in Business and Management*, Paul Chapman Publishing Ltd, London.
Laufer, J. (1982) *La Féminité Neutralisée: Les Femmes Cadres dans l'Entreprise*, Editions Flammarion, Paris.
Martin, J. (1990) 'Re-reading Weber: searching for feminist alternatives to bureaucracy', paper presented at the Annual Meeting of the Academy of Management, San Francisco, August.
The Open University (1986) *Women into Management. Book 2, A Foot in the Management Door*, Open University Press, Milton Keynes.
Rosener, J. (1990) 'Ways women lead', *Harvard Business Review*, November–December, pp. 119–25.
Schein, V. E. and Mueller, R. (1990) 'Sex-role stereotypes and requisite management characteristics: a cross-cultural look', paper presented at the 22nd International Congress of Applied Psychology, Kyoto, Japan, 22–27 July.
Wolf, N. (1993) *Fire with Fire: The New Female Power and How It Will Change the 21st Century*, Chatto and Windus, London.
Young, K. and Spencer, E. (1990) *Women Managers in Local Government: Removing the Barriers*, INLOGOV, Birmingham.

Chapter 3

Post-modernism and social differentiation

In a society where identities are no longer given but have to be adopted or created, the products we buy make powerful statements about the sort of people we are. Judie Lannon alerts us to the contribution that anthropology can play in understanding the increasingly symbolic and cultural roles played by marketing. She examines the role of brands in today's fragmented and changing societies and considers how brand identity can be managed to appeal to new 'tribes' of consumers who may be searching for shared yet individualistic symbols to express their new identities. This is particularly important in relation to global products and brands which may represent quite different things in different cultures. The scope for misunderstanding, and therefore the risk of a marketing failure, is high.

Mosaics of meaning: anthropology and marketing

Judie Lannon

INTRODUCTION

The social sciences, psychology and sociology in particular, have made considerable contributions to marketing. Yet, with the exception of Levy[1,2] and Barthes,[3] little has been written about the contribution of anthropology to marketing theory. Whereas psychology deals with the individual, and sociology examines social groups, anthropology studies the myths, symbols, rituals and value systems that make up what we know as culture. Yet in contrast to the enthusiasm with which psychologists such as Ernst Dichter explored hidden motivations in consumer behaviour and made these insights eminently accessible to marketers, anthropologists, linked in the popular imagination with the examination of primitive tribes, seem to occupy, quite literally, another world.

However, over the last decade or so, different streams of thought make the contribution of anthropology with its rich understanding of the workings of social systems, institutions and groups particularly relevant in a number of areas.

Symbols and the significance of brands

It is now widely accepted that branding is central to the marketing process. Indeed, marketing and branding could be thought of as synonymous.[4] What the process of branding means to consumers requires an understanding of consumption and exchange rituals. And in this respect, anthropology is the most fundamental of the social sciences to marketing theory. More than other social sciences, it serves as the theoretical underpinning for the significance of branding.

How brands take on symbolic meaning

This perspective leads to a more coherent look at marketing communications: how and why brands take on symbolic meaning and how this can be managed. The approach contrasts the transportation/persuasion model of communication with a more holistic model better suited to planning a brand's total communication.

Social fragmentation: the features of post-modern society

The pursuit of individualism, the fragmentation of traditional social groups, the decline in hierarchy, the acceptance of change, and the questioning of institutional authority are some of the defining features of modern life. The deeper implications for marketing in this have been largely ignored. At the very simplest, authorititative brands and companies serve as signposts through the confusion and clutter of modern life. At a deeper level, an inevitable consequence of this fragmentation in the social fabric is a decline in personal obligations, reciprocities and social links which leaves an emotional gap that companies could exploit through building relationships with their consumers.

Universal tribes

The complexity of global marketing requires a much greater understanding of the nuances of national culture in the marketing of global brands. Anthropology offers approaches that explore the processes by which the themes, myths and symbols that are universal to the human condition are expressed through local milieus.

SYMBOLS AND THE SIGNIFICANCE OF BRANDS

> Modern industrial man needs goods for the same reason as the tribesman: to involve other fellow consumers in his consumption rituals. They need goods to commit other people to their projects. The fact that, in the course of these rituals, foods get consumed, flags get waved and clothes worn is incidental.
>
> (Mary Douglas)[5]

Market research studies aim to discover why people want particular categories or brands and what additional wants and needs could be satisfied. What additional use, ingredient or innovation can we supply that will provide a critical competitive advantage?

However, the anthropologist looks both more broadly and more deeply. The answer Douglas[5] gives in the passage quoted above is deceptively simple. Goods are not merely products with utilitarian values, but symbols of exchange. At at deeper level, the perspective challenges the mental model of the active manufacturer manipulating the passive consumer, the model that, acknowledged or not, underlies much marketing theory.

Some anthropologists[6, 7] go so far as to see the process of exchange as the foundation of both cultural stability and morality. Thus exchange is the basis of social interaction of individuals, groups, institutions and kinship networks. The issues studied by anthropologists in primitive societies and issues requiring study in modern societies may be more closely linked than conventionally acknowledged. Differences may reflect differences in complexity and sophistication rather than differences in kind.

If the 'open-ness' of modern societies in contrast to the 'closed-ness' of primitive societies is a difference in degree rather than in kind, we can see the deeper function of marketing as the central mechanism by which meaning is exchanged. Thus brands, companies and services are the carriers of these meanings, using the definition proposed by Feldwick and Baker[8] of brands as 'entities with which consumers have a relationship based on factors over and above functional performance'. This perspective provides the tools to explore why brands are valuable to people as well as the factors that contribute value and maintain brand and company loyalties.

Modern marketing is then the system whereby consumption myths and consumption rituals involving products and services endowed with symbolic meanings are created and sustained through the mechanism of branding. Since anthropology is the study, inter alia, of the impact of myths and the meanings of rituals on societies the discipline should have much to offer.

Charismatic brands

Cult objects carry a strong emotional charge. They could be described as brands with 'charisma'. Belk, Wallendorf and Sherry[9] suggest that the need for cult objects is related to the blurring of the distinctions between the sacred and the profane in modern life. The thesis is that the distinction between the sacred and profane is a human need; as religion becomes more secular and less satisfying of transcendent, ritualised appetites, people will satisfy the need through different forms of consumption. Macrae's analysis of 'world class' brands[10] describes many brands that seem to have these qualities. The question for the marketer is, how does a brand become charismatic?

If brands can have personalities then it is worth examining the kinds of personalities that exert the strongest influence (Smothers).[11] Charismatic personalities are more compelling, generating extremes of loyalty in their followers. Cult brands do the same thing, as well as commanding larger price premiums.

Using Nike as an illustration, Smothers suggests that one way brands become charismatic is through anchoring the product to a compelling emotional metaphor or something transcendent or sacred. The supposed function of athletic shoes is their use in sports. Yet the vast majority of trainers purchased in the US are not used for sport. In order to increase usage, the brand had to be imbued with new meaning. So advertising for Air Jordan shoes used metaphors of high status and athletic stardom. 'Fly Air Jordan' is translated as 'escape from the inner city'. Thus ownership represents membership in an elite club and generates extremes of loyalty and motivation. So much so, that a teenager was murdered for his shoes. As with all cult brands, this additional buyer loyalty and motivation converts to a higher price (at the end of the 1980s, Air Jordan shoes sold for $115 compared with $30–60 for most other brands).

Typically the term 'cult' refers to a recherché design aesthetic with a suggestion of high price and/or people who are concerned to make statements about their taste or awareness of trends: Zippo lighters, Swatch watches, Mont Blanc pens, Barbours, Range Rovers, Rolex. Yet, it is obvious that the meanings in each of these cases extend beyond design: they are laden with culture and lifestyle associations. Ordinary brands such as the Marlboro cowboy, or more recently, Levi 501s achieved charismatic status with the price premium that this commands.[12]

Charisma in packaged goods?

Package goods may not have the same kind of charisma but 'leadership' is a key characteristic. Bernstein[13] describes a study in which consumers were asked to name the brand leaders in different categories. What consumers were describing were 'leader brands'; brands that led. Consumers ascribed leadership to brands (or companies) who were believed to be constantly innovating, had a heritage of quality and had consistently contemporary imagery. Good examples in the UK are Häagen-Dazs, Nestlé Gold Blend, Mars and Pedigree Chum.

From the marketing standpoint, building equity is to endow a brand with charisma. The process begins with a better understanding of the kinds of meanings a brand is capable of conveying.

Looking for better ways of explaining why people do things

Sidney Levy[2] in one of the rare articles in a marketing journal dealing with the interpretation of consumer mythologies underlines the poverty of much consumer research by quoting the anthropologist, Sanche de Gramont:

> I like to imagine these Three Wise Men of the Occident bent in contemplation over a South American Indian myth about a boy who steals a pet pig from his father and roasts it in the forest. Freud would conclude that the boy is symbolically killing his father because he desires his mother. Marx would say that this youthful member of the proletariat is seizing control of the methods of production in the class struggle against

the landed gentry. Lévi-Strauss would find that, in cooking the pig, the primitive Indian boy had achieved the passage from nature to culture and shown that his thought processes are no different from Einstein's.

Levy[2] observes that a conventional marketing approach would probably accept the boy's explanation that he was hungry, that the pig was convenient, cheap and tasty. Neither of these classes of explanation is wholly helpful; we need a middle way.

A similar experiment required an anthropologist, a psychologist and an exponent of the theory of neurolinguistic programming to interpret the meanings inherent in the advertising for Timotei shampoo. The psychologist concentrated on the equation of the product's natural gentleness with the model's apparently virginal purity, the anthropologist located the universal appeal of the brand in Nordic myths of nature and a lost Arcadia, and the neurolinguistic programmer's interpretation focused on the perfect convergence of cues – colours, soundtrack, visual. The interpretations were indeed different but shared a common symbolic core which contributed to the explanation for the brand's success in countries where hair is predominantly dark. However, the anthropological interpretation was the most successful in discriminating between developed industrial countries, where the nature myth is potent and desirable, and less developed countries where nature is a hard reality to be escaped.

Food rituals and their meanings

Caviar, black pudding, black-eyed peas, haggis, brown rice; in the right context foods such as these can indicate an eater's wealth and social status as well as his or her regional or ethnic loyalty ... The preparation and consumption of food then constitutes one concrete, material form in which abstract meanings of social relationships and cultural beliefs can be expressed.

(Paul Atkinson)[14]

An anthropological perspective on food is particularly necessary now. Health preoccupations, the availability of new and exotic foreign foods, and more individualistic eating patterns are re-defining traditional food rituals. In the past, people were taught by their parents what was appropriate within class and cultural norms. But, as these authorities cease to provide trustworthy answers in the face of conflicting signals from experts, and as the normative cultural boundaries become blurred, the need remains: we still must honour guests, ensure children are fed properly, and distinguish between different occasions.

The significance of the retailer revolution is most dramatically seen in the phenomenon of the Marks & Spencer dinner party. Dinner parties are emotionally loaded affairs and the food and drink served has traditionally been the preserve of the manufacturers of prestige brands. The pride in displaying M & S foods and, perhaps even more significantly, wines, to guests is an important cultural shift and a dangerous development for manufacturers whose brands once played these important status marking roles. Gift status is central to boxed chocolates, traditionally the most difficult market for an own label supplier to penetrate because of the powerful imagery that once surrounded brands like Milk Tray, Dairy Milk, After Eight and Black Magic. Yet these brands seem preserved in amber in the face of M & S Belgian assortments or new foreign entrants such as Ferrero Rocher. There are, no doubt, many causes contributing to the declining fortunes of some of these assortment brands, but one factor may be the failure to recognise shifting signals of status in a more socially mobile society.

The frustrations experienced by the government in trying to change people's diets would at least be understood if the positive, symbolic meanings of the 'bad' foods in maintaining cultural continuity, family links and relationships were more subtly appreciated. Studies describing the social and political meanings of vegetarian foods, foreign foods and other 'unorthodox' foods, through the eyes of working-class Northerners, explain the resistance.[14]

The key for the marketer is: How is this symbolism taken on by brands and how can the process be managed?

HOW BRANDS TAKE ON SYMBOLIC MEANING

The role of communication

Morello[15] contrasts the market research implications of the classical marketing view of brands (bundles of utilities) with a more contemporary view (bundles of meanings). The former perspective concentrated on the itemisation, rating, ranking and trading off of particular product utilities. The latter perspective requires quite a different, more holistic methodology that reflects both function and symbolic meaning.

In order to integrate function and meaning the marketer needs to understand the relationship between the brand (or company) and the consumer, and how all marketing activities are forms of communication orchestrated to interpret the product or service. Central here, is the concept of brand personality and the process by which the identity or truth of a product or company is interpreted and expressed through its packaging, design, colours, shapes, identity and actions, price and distribution, as well as through its functional product features and performance. The functional attributes are overlaid with a kind of patina of symbols and values that contribute to these 'bundles of meanings'.[16, 17, 18]

In addition, each individual brand has its own identity, its own 'personality' and, increasingly, its own more complex 'lifestyle', that helps discriminate it from similar competitors and which includes or excludes the brand from people's repertoires. Biel and Lannon[19] describe them in terms of visual metaphors, examples of which are given below.

Effective visual metaphors in US and European advertising

- Pepperidge Farm's Titus Moody (US) and his bakery wagon and Mr Kipling's (UK) voice and mythical presence both suggest old-fashioned goodness in baked goods.
- The 'Good Hands' of Allstate (US) convey safety, security and (above all) caring and understanding on the part of the company. Because they are human hands, they convey a humanity not usually associated with large impersonal financial corporations.
- Andrex lavatory paper's Labrador puppy (UK) serves as a vehicle for demonstrating the brand's physical properties (long, soft and strong) but also represents the cosy domestic milieu in which the brand is used. Over time, it has succeeded in bringing Andrex out of the lavatory and into the living room.
- The Oxo family milieu (UK) works at many levels to represent the role of the cube (at the emotional heart of family cooking) as well as representing modern family relationships.
- Clearly Esso's tiger in the tank conveys power. The metaphor, however, is evolving in response to current more ecological themes where, in the UK, he is a husband and father, with cubs, concerned about the environment.
- The Wells Fargo Bank stagecoach (US) represents a bank that supports customers by 'coming through no matter what' for them. It also conveys the stability of deep historical roots and suggests that its history is intertwined with the history of the West.

Brand identity is, therefore, not a falsely contrived image, something 'dreamed up by ad men', but a creative transformation and expression of the entity itself.[17] Olins concludes that:

> In an age in which corporate affairs are given so much and such detailed professional consideration, in which virtually every aspect of the industrial and business life is analysed in so much detail, I find it remarkable that the power of symbolism should be so little detailed and so little understood.[20]

Carey[21] observes that 'European and American (communications) work derives from quite different kinds of intellectual puzzles and is grounded in two different metaphors.' The dominant metaphor in American communications study is a transmission or transportation view of communication. Media carry messages as a bus carries passengers. Communications are bought in quantity and measurements related to the strike rate and the extent to which audiences can play back functional product messages or propositions.

Thus repetition and 'hard sell' arise from a model where 'advertising and consumer are on two sides of a counter, and that some kind of confrontation is taking place with one side trying to persuade the other to change attitudes and behaviour and part with money.'[22] The salesman in the living room is a pervasive image. Similarly, propaganda theory explores the mechanisms of influence and control central to the purpose of socialising the waves of immigrants coming to America – hence the concentration on overt persuasion, attitude change and behaviour modification in the work of advertising theorists who drew heavily from this literature.[18]

It is important to identify the mental model in this way because it explains why communication is treated as a downstream activity in marketing companies, and compartmentalised as discrete actions that are unrelated to the company's business strategy.

Carey[21] identifies the transportation and persuasion model as specifically American. He describes the European metaphor as an anthropologically-based model in which communication (of which advertising is merely a special case) becomes the central mechanism in creating myths and rituals, through which a shared culture is created, modified and transformed. This 'shared culture', from a marketing standpoint, could be national culture or tribal. This view of communication lends itself readily to the concept of brand personality.

This begins to provide an explanation of how symbolism and meaning become a part of brands and suggests that brand communications have a greater (and more significant) function than selling or persuasion. If the conventional question is, 'How does advertising persuade people to buy things?' (and this is the question that communications theory has been preoccupied with), a more interesting question, and one more germane to the central question of positioning, is, 'How does communication (in the broadest definition of every action the company takes on behalf of its brands) add values, symbols and meaning to physical products?'

Two features of life, 20 years or so ago, made advertising (particularly television) central to this approach: the stability of cultural archetypes and rituals, and the dominance of television. Neither of these are true today so that a critical question for marketers is how to build and sustain brand values in this very fragmented environment.

The decline of national archetypes and rituals and fragmenting media

In the UK, consciously or unconsciously, creative advertising people drew from the vast pool of cultural meanings available to them from a fairly stable cultural milieu. The metaphors described earlier illustrate the point, as do a number of traditional UK brands developed some 20 to 30 years ago.

After Eight invoked the myth of the upper class, an archetype that served the brand for many years: Hovis used the myth of industrial working-class sentimentality: Mr Kipling cakes appropriated domestic baking skills associated with the country and the calendar art cottage: John Smith bitter invented an eccentric Yorkshire man, and so forth. Beer advertising, in general, draws vividly from both national culture and the tribal-bonding function of beer drinking among English teenage males. Horlicks was 'the food drink of the night' when the nation all retired at 11 o'clock; Kellog's Corn Flakes was 'the sunshine breakfast' when the family ate breakfast together; KitKat appropriated the symbolism of the tea or coffee 'break'.

Many of these cultural rituals and the brands linked to them belong to a bygone age. As the ritual vanished, so might the brand. Thus the success of Lucozade, in dramatically breaking with its sick bed past and reinventing itself as a sports drink through its core values of energy, is particularly impressive.

The personalities of these old brands were built almost entirely on advertising during a period when television advertising was relatively cheap and was socially and ritually more significant. Although the vision of the family clustered round the television set, peering intently at the screen, was always something of an advertiser's fantasy, television had higher status. Today, the screen flickering in the corner is more likely to function as wallpaper than as the centre of attention.

Communications build 'mosaics of meaning'

Consumers receive impressions of brands from a whole range of sources that they do not disentangle: from where it is bought, from people who use it or do not, from its role in cultural activities, from movies, literature, television, editorial, news, fashions, leisure events and activities, and, incidentally, from paid-for media. This process of what Macrae[23] describes as 'designing into a brand its own platform for publicity' together forms 'a mosaic of meaning' and models of marketing communication need to acknowledge this.

Crabtree and Evelyn, an American company of relatively recent origin, through its use of sales literature, packaging and shop layouts that look like apothecary shops, has managed to create a persona of an old English herbalist and parfumier. Similarly, the company manufacturing Aqua Libra, the premium health drink, introduced the brand through the suggestion of a Swiss pedigree and a series of activities suggesting connoisseurship (as described by Macrae, pp. 102–3[10]). Both are illustrations of products for whom brand heritage and presence were invented by skilfully orchestrating a range of marketing activities with only minimal reliance on conventional advertising. Other examples of brands building what could be described as 'lifestyles' for themselves are Häagen-Dazs' launch through careful selection of retail outlets, followed by orchestration of mouth-diffusion and finally mass market media, and Heinz's Weight Watchers frozen meals which are linked with weight control clubs and programmes.[23]

In suggesting companies should build deeper and more committed relationships with their customers, McKenna[24] makes a strong case for the end of the brand as 'a trick'. This is a view that sees advertising as having an essentially fraudulent nature – imagery poured over products like icing on a cake – to achieve a spurious added value. However, as described earlier, skilfully executed advertising interprets and magnifies the brand's meaning, becoming the basis of its charisma. It is in this sense that all marketing communications create value for consumers as well as manufacturers.

To build relations with customers is not an option but a necessity. Marketing communication is part of that process. But there is a deeper issue: from an anthropological standpoint, what does the brand/consumer relationship mean?

POST-MODERNISM

Although the rather more fragmented, diffuse and transitory nature of modern society has led to an erosion of many of the vivid (and stable) cultural archetypes and rituals, the task for the cultural anthropologist examining relationships is no different, merely more complex.

Post-modernism may be no more than a modish piece of jargon, but the phenomena it incorporates may have significance for marketers. It has been described by both social observers[25, 26] and marketing theorists.[27] At its most elementary, the characteristics of contemporary Western society are juxtaposed with features of the early stages of industrial society, as shown in Figure 3.1.

There is an intriguing difference between American and French thinkers on the implications of contemporary social trends for marketing. The differences stem from the two different schools of social anthropological thought in the early part of the century: the individualist tradition of the Americans versus the collectivist tradition (represented by Lévi-Strauss[7]) of the French and Italians.

The individualistic tradition sees the evolution of modern egalitarian society as the ultimate triumph of the individual who has been struggling to free himself from the confining class structures of traditional societies. The increasing 'elective' nature of identity in fluid egalitarian societies, that can transcend age, class, sex, and nationality is described by McCracken[28] as the reason goods are so crucially important to identity.

In contrast, the collectivist tradition sees the preservation of the social

Early Industrial Era	Postmodern Era
Mass production manufacturing	Customised information/services
Expectations of unlimited growth	Recognition of limits
Authority vested in stable institutions	Institutional authority questioned
Hierarchical social order	Egalitarian social order, 'tribes'
Handed down inherited values	'Discovered', individual values

Figure 3.1 Western society characteristics juxtaposed with early stage of industrial society

fabric with its obligations and reciprocities as more important than the needs of the individual. Fabris,[29] for example, describes the evolution of socio-cultural values in Italy over the last 30 years. The direction of social trends through the 1980s was towards modernity of an individualistic, self expressive sort. However, from 1989 to 1991, the trends were reversed with a rise in trends relating to security, family values, stricter moral and ethical values and community values.

This has led Cova[30] to suggest that 'post-modernism can therefore be said to crown not the triumph of individualism but the beginning of its end with the emergence of a reverse movement of a desperate search for the social link'. He locates the implications for marketing precisely in this gap with the notion that service and customisation should not be thought of as ends in themselves. The perfectly customised car or kitchen or piece of jewellery may be satisfying to the individual, but also of value is the relationship, indeed even the dependency on the supplier of that customisation.

> Firms must go beyond the rational satisfaction of demand that character-ised marketing in the 20th century to cope with the postmodern recomposition of communities into ephemeral tribes. The use value of products seems to be taken for granted. What individuals are looking for now are cult objects: aesthetic appeal, emotion, meaning and mainly linking value. This requires the use of ethno-sociological and anthro-pological approaches to understand how to produce these linking objects and services.
>
> (Bernard Cova)[30]

Companies that have structured their organisations around a true service ethos such as Nordstrom, the US department store, or American Express become much more than suppliers to customers. By paying attention and responding through new products and services, companies like these turn their customers into 'partners' and 'advocates'; they engage the people who ultimately pay their salaries in their joint projects. However, the obligations on the part of companies seeking this pseudo-personal relationship are huge and consumers can feel betrayed when these obligations are violated. British Airways' attempts to coerce Virgin's customers is a good example. Consider the customer who wishes to change allegiances but who finds himself locked into thousands of BA air miles. The complex feelings of old loyalties and new resentments is akin to a modern form of feudalism.

The social linking value of objects, brands or services can bind brands closer to their consumers. This linking value is integral to the process of modern tribalism.

Brands and innovation in a tribal world

'Cult objects place the link between those who share the appreciation higher than the thing itself.'[30] Alexander and Valentine[31] quote 14-year-old Josephine talking about her own particular 'style-clan':

> Brosettes signal to each other that they want to be recognised. They don't want to be with anyone who doesn't want to talk about Bros all the time. If I went to a party and saw it was all full of Brosettes in leather jackets with zips and huge Doc Martens with watch straps – or if they were Sharons in their tiny pink skirts over their huge bums and those white high heels and teeny handbags, I would know I wouldn't have a nice time, so I wouldn't go in.

In a similar vein, Wolfe[32] satirised the social bonding power of modern art. The link felt by those supporting the Tate Gallery's purchase of the pile of bricks must have been greater than the appreciation of any one individual of the bricks-as-art.

Innovation, technical or aesthetic, eludes 'scientific' research explanation and tends to be best explained by the style commentators.[33] Yet innovation, and the chain of events that change precipitates, is important to understand from the consumer's standpoint.

The 'Diderot Effect' embodies the dilemma of change and derives from an essay in which Diderot describes being given a new dressing gown.[34] He was very pleased with it and wore it to work in his study. But gradually he began to feel a certain discomfort at the dissonance between his smart new dressing gown and his old rather shabby desk. A new desk was bought to live up to the dressing gown. But the carpet began to look a bit worn and so on to the curtains and chairs and bric-à-brac. Before long, M. Diderot's comfortable, harmonious study was transformed into a place where he felt curiously out of place and ill at ease, all due to the entry into his life of a well intended gift, the new dressing gown.

'Diderot unities' is the anthropologist's term for things that seem to fit together.[28] An obvious example is the constellation of things that coalesced around the rise of the Yuppie. The symbolism of the Filofax announced a new way of working. The other items, the cellular phone, the red braces, the renewed interest in the Rolex, so to speak, 'fell into place' forming a kind of unity, spawning guides, handbooks and articles which identified the 'must have' brands and sped the process on its way. 'Essex Man' is another, if more parochial, example.

This kind of tribalism may seem at odds with the globalising tendencies of multinational companies. Yet 'Yuppie-ism' was a classic example of the global tribe.

BRANDS AND TRIBALISM

Gellner[35] observes that the picture of the world after 1989 is increasingly confused as countries revert to earlier forms of social behaviour – ethnicity, tribalism and territoriality. What holds post-Communist countries together seems not to be the free market economy as predicted, but the chauvinism of individual ethnic groups. The notion that the world is moving in the direction of liberal democracies and free market economies may be illusory, and he looks to sociology and anthropology as more illuminating than either political science or economics.

At the same time, Gellner[35] describes the weaknesses in anthropological thinking as the over-emphasis on meaning, that ignores structure completely, and the pre-occupation with cultural determinism, which ignores the fluidity and adaptability of modern Western societies in the face of increased global communications. These two characteristics dominate the popular view of the anthropologist and no doubt contribute to the exclusion of genuinely valuable ideas and approaches or, at best, relegate them to the exploration of the unique and peculiar nature of an individual culture.

Global marketers face a similar dilemma. Cultural factors can play an overwhelming role in the acceptance of a brand, but this role varies. Hofstede[36] calls culture the 'software of the mind', a computer analogy representing the patterns of thinking, feeling, and potential action learned throughout a lifetime. McCracken[28] describes culture as both a 'lens through which all phenomena are seen' and 'a blueprint' which 'determines how the world will be fashioned by human effort'. In the world of marketing management, Hofstede,[36] Trompenaars[37] and others provide valuable insight into how cultural values affect business organisations by identifying the factors that differentiate cultures – tolerance of inequality, individualism versus collectivism, masculinity versus femininity, the avoidance of

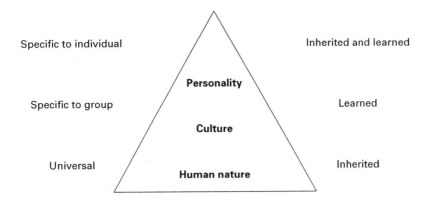

Figure 3.2 Programming on three levels

uncertainty, virtue versus truth, the management of time. This framework makes it possible to think of countries as groups or clusters.

Global brand marketing in mature economies require concepts and frameworks that allow for exploration of the similarities of cultures and peoples rather than concentration exclusively on their differences. Hofstede,[36] for example, argues that people are programmed in not one but three levels, as shown in Figure 3.2.

If one takes the visual representation of Hofstede's model literally, much the largest part of the human condition is universal human nature, the base of the triangle. In some product categories – fields where goods are consumed for what they express to others about the individual personality or aspirations – brands appear to work in different cultures because they appeal to dreams and archetypes that are buried deep in the human psyche.

These brands transcend specific cultural definition by evoking apparently universal myths, archetypes, heroes, stereotypes. Country mythologies such as the Marlboro cowboy or the various American myths evoked by Levi's are likely to be common across cultures. However, others may need more subtle interpretation, such as work with the pantheon of male and female archetypes developed by Degrese and Amory.[38] As shown by Wolfe,[39] these archetypes seem to be universal in structure but can vary in emphasis according to culture. The development of the radical perfume concept 'Poison' from Christian Dior took a less dramatic, less 'sorceress-like' direction in America, compared with Europe.

Similarly, Body Shop's ecological philosophy, the mind/body holism represented by Evian and other mineral waters, the multiculturalism of Benetton, the empowerment theme of Apple computers are examples of meanings that transcend geographical boundaries, linking people in what could be thought of as 'virtual tribes'.

The success of a global brand does not necessarily imply that the brand carries identical meanings worldwide. McDonald's is pointed to as the quintessential global brand. But, looked at from the consumer's standpoint, it is not a global brand, it is a global product. The consumer's experience of the McDonald's brand is entirely different in Moscow (a status symbol), from what it is in Milan (a chic sort of slumming), or in Milwaukee (cheap, good-value American fast food).

The distinction is useful for companies struggling with the tension between global product strategies and apparently different local brand requirements. Some of this tension could be resolved by looking for the deeper structure of meaning and exploring how individual cultures express it. The concept underlying Guinness advertising in the UK (the mysterious, eccentric and individualistic male conspicuously set apart from the male bonding role of mass lagers), was re-interpreted for the Hong Kong market in a way that reflected Chinese culture.

IMPLICATIONS

• Many consumer markets are maturing; products are becoming similar to each other and thus brands are differentiated more by symbolic meanings.
• Diffusion and fragmentation of consumer groups makes it more difficult to identify coherent target groups; fashion and aesthetics play an increasing role in providing satisfactions.
• Intangibles of service and information are intimately and integrally bound up with the functional product.
• The relationships consumers have with the company itself are as important as relationships with the company's brands.
• Globalism and tribalism are growing simultaneously.

In this environment, an anthropological perspective has a number of far reaching implications:

1 Creating brand equity could be thought of as the process of endowing a brand with charisma. Marketers need to understand the social processes in which their brands feature, and the meanings their brands carry in these social processes.
2 However, this will be more difficult to achieve as conventional communications media fragment, and many different communications vehicles are required. The issue is how to integrate the much wider range of communications available into a 'mosaic of meaning' where all pieces add up to a coherent whole.
3 The paradox of individualism – its opportunity for self-expression on

the one hand and its isolating consequences on the other – means that the provision of customised goods and services is providing value that goes beyond function. Cases of failed 'relationship marketing' can be traced to an inadequate understanding of the relationship itself, its reciprocities and obligations.

4 Finally, marketers operating across cultures need a range of concepts, methodologies and frameworks that explore deeper levels of myth and meaning with the aim of understanding how unifying universal themes are interpreted and expressed by different cultures. This approach helps reconcile the need for global positionings with the need for local expressions.

NOTE REFERENCES

1 Levy, S. (1978) 'Hunger and Work in a Civilised Tribe', *American Behavioural Scientist*, Volume 21, Number 4, March.
2 Levy, S. (1981) 'Interpreting Consumer Mythology: A Structural Approach to Consumer Behaviour', *Journal of Marketing*, Volume 45, Summer.
3 Barthes, R. (1972) *Mythologies*, trans. Annette Lavers, London, Jonathan Cape.
4 Ambler, T. (1993) 'Are Branding and Marketing Synonymous?', *The Journal of Brand Management*, Volume 1, Number 1.
5 Douglas, M. (1982) *In The Active Voice*, Routledge and Kegan Paul Ltd, London.
6 Mauss, M. (1954) *The Gift*, trans. Ian Cunnison, The Free Press, New York.
7 Lévi-Strauss, C. (1969) *The Elementary Structures of Kinship*, Beacon Press, Boston.
8 Feldwick, P. and Baker, C. (1991) 'The Longer and Broader Effects of Advertising; Some Observations and Recent Evidence', ESOMAR Seminar – How Advertising Works and How Promotions Work, April.
9 Belk, R. W., Wallendorf, M. and Sherry, J. F. Jr. (1989) 'The Sacred and Profane in Consumer Behaviour: Theodicy on the Odyssey,' *Journal of Consumer Research*, Volume 16.
10 Macrae, C. (1991) *World Class Brands*, Addison-Wesley, Wokingham.
11 Smothers, N. (1993) Can Products and Brands Have Charisma? in *Brand Equity and Advertising*, Aaker and Biel (Eds). Lawrence Erlbaum Associates, Hove, New Jersey.
12 Restall, C. and Croll, I. (1987) 'The Dream Machine: Developing a Cross Cultural Framework for Understanding Advertising', proceedings of MRS Conference.
13 Bernstein, H. (1992) The Power of Leadership Brands, address given to Advertising Research Foundation Seminar: Measuring Brand Equity, February, New York City.
14 Atkinson, P. (1979) 'The Symbolic Significance of Health Foods in Nutrition and Lifestyles', Turner, M. (Ed), Applied Science Publishers Ltd, Essex, England.
15 Morello, G. (1993) 'The Hidden Dimensions of Marketing' *Journal of the Market Research Society*, Volume 35, Number 4, October.
16 King, S. (1971) What is a Brand?, Booklet published by J. Walter Thompson, London.
17 King, S. (1991) 'Brand Building in the 90s', *Journal of Marketing Management*, Volume 7, Number 1, January.

18 Lannon, J. and Cooper, P. (1983) 'Humanistic Advertising: A Holistic Cultural Perspective', *International Journal of Advertising*, Volume 2, July-September, pp. 195–213.
19 Biel, A. and Lannon, J. A. (1993) 'Steel Bullet in a Velvet Glove: The Use of Metaphor in Advertising' *Admap*, issue 328, April, pp. 15–18.
20 Olins, W. (1989) *Corporate Identity*, Thames and Hudson, London.
21 Carey, J. (1975) 'Communication and Culture', *Communication Research*, April.
22 Goodyear, M. (1991) 'Brands and Culture', *Survey Magazine (MRS)*, Volume 8, Number 3, Winter.
23 Macrae, C. (1993) 'Brand Benchmarking Applied to Global Branding Processes', *The Journal of Brand Management*, Volume 1, Number 5.
24 McKenna, R. (1991) *Relationship Marketing*, Addison Wesley. USA.
25 Anderson, W. T. (1990) *Reality Isn't What It Used To Be*, Harper Row, New York.
26 Ogilvy, J. (1990) 'This Postmodern Business', *Marketing and Research Today*, Volume 18, Number 1, February, pp. 4–22.
27 Cova, B. and Badot, O. (1994) *Marketing Theory and Practice in a Postmodern Era*, Marketing Theory and Practice, 3rd ed.
28 McCracken, G. (1988) *Culture and Consumption. New Approaches to the Symbolic Character of Consumer Goods and Activities*, Indiana University Press, Bloomington and Indianapolis.
29 Fabvis, G. (1991) 'Consumer Studies: New Perspectives', in *Consumer Behaviour and Strategic Marketing: Anything New?*, ISIDA, Palermo.
30 Cova, B. (1993) 'Beyond Marketing: From Marketing to Societing?', Conference Proceedings: Re-thinking Marketing: New Perspectives on the Discipline and Profession, Brownlie, Saren, Wensley and Whittington, (Eds), Warwick Press, Coventry.
31 Alexander, M. and Valentine, V. (1989) 'Cultural Class – Researching the Parts that Social Class Cannot Reach', MRS Conference Proceedings.
32 Wolfe, T. (1989) *The Painted Word*, Black Swan (Transworld), London.
33 Sudjic, D. (1985) *Cult Objects*, London, Paladin Books.
34 Diderot, D. (1964) Regrets on Parting with My Old Dressing Gown, in *Rameau's Nephew and Other Works*, by Denis Diderot, trans. Barzun, J. and Bowen, R. H., Bobbs-Merrill, New York, pp. 309–317.
35 Gellner, E. (1993) *The Times Literary Supplement*, 16th July, pp. 3–4.
36 Hofstede, G. (1991) *Culture and Organisations*, McGraw-Hill Book Company Europe, Maidenhead, England.
37 Trompenaars, F. (1993) *Riding the Waves of Culture*, The Economist Books, London.
38 Degrese, C. and Amory, P. (1986) *Le Grand Jeu de la Seduction*, Robert Laffont, S. A., Paris.
39 Wolfe, O. H. (1989) 'High Touch Research Applied to Fine Fragrances Development: The Poison Case History' ESOMAR Seminar: Research for Flavours and Fragrances, Lyon, 7–9th June.

Chapter 4

Green and ethical issues

The phenomenon of the green consumer seemed to burst on the marketing scene in the late 1980s. Concerns like holes in the ozone layer or the destruction of tropical rain forests seized the public imagination and led to them seeking ways in which they could have an influence on these issues. Some producers of environmentally friendly products went from being small scale 'fringe' organizations to becoming multi-nationals almost overnight. Many existing large firms, such as supermarkets, were quick to emphasise the eco-friendliness of *their* offerings and activities. Yet the very ability of marketers to capitalise on this demand and make green claims for products which didn't really justify them led to a cooling of enthusiasm for green marketing – although the bottle banks and ban on CFCs remain.

In this article, Bodo Schlegelmilch highlights the change in consumer values and behaviour, argues that they really *have* become more 'green, ethical and charitable' and gives some examples of how these attitudes are affecting marketing and business policy.

Green, ethical and charitable: another marketing ploy or a new marketing era?

Bodo B. Schlegelmilch

INTRODUCTION

Marketing has a bad reputation! Indeed, it is often held responsible for a whole variety of sins, including ruining the environment (Peattie, 1992), spreading unethical business behaviour (Smith and Quelch, 1993) and being uncharitable (Rundle, 1989). Typical complaints about marketing are directed towards annoying, deceptive and wasteful advertising (Kangun, Carson and Grove, 1991); products that are not safe or are of poor quality (Kotler and Mantrala, 1985); price discrimination (Stern and Eovaldi, 1984); style changes and planned product obsolescence which waste resources (Siebert, 1973); as well as confusing and deceptive packaging and labelling (de Truck and Goldhaber, 1989). This list, of course, could easily be extended.

However, the concerns are not new. The first Consumers' League was formed in New York as early as 1891; a second strong consumer movement could be observed in the 1930s, when consumer prices were raised in the midst of the depression and drug scandals emerged (Hermann, 1970). The 1960s witnessed another flaring up of consumer discontent. Influential writings by the economist John Kenneth Galbraith (1958, 1967), the journalist Vance Packard (1957) and the lawyer Ralph Nader (1968) vociferously criticised the marketing profession and defended consumer rights.

So, if the concerns are not new, what is? Has the focus of the criticism shifted? Are marketers more responsive to criticism? Below, it will be argued that both are in fact the case. It will be demonstrated that the *scope of consumer concerns has widened* and that *companies are responding better* to these concerns than ever before. It will become apparent that marketing has started to move into a new green, ethical and charitable era and that these new issues are now *extending the scope of research* conducted in marketing.

THE NEW CONSUMER

Consumers are becoming wiser. Their concern has widened from traditional consumerism issues like product safety, fair pricing and more informative advertising to include green concerns, ethical considerations and charitable effects of consumption. As *The Times* (12 June 1991) eloquently puts it:

> Consumption is no longer viewed as primarily an individual economic act; like production, it is seen as a social process with social consequences.

The green consumer

In July 1989, a Mori poll showed that the proportion of consumers choosing products on the basis of 'environmental performance' had increased from 19% to 42% in less than one year (Prothero, 1990). The facts speak for themselves (Schlegelmilch and Diamantopoulos, 1990):

- In a series of different surveys 80–90% of respondents claim to put environmental issues high on their list of concerns.
- A series of polls has shown that 2 out of 3 people are willing to pay higher taxes to secure a better environment.
- Green support is particularly strong among social groups ABC1s; aged 25–44.
- Penetration of green products is about 20% and repeat purchase is currently running at over 50%; 27% of people are prepared to pay up to 25% more for environmentally friendly products.
- Different degrees of 'greenness' can be observed.

As to the latter, a distinction can be made between four segments (Murphy, 1989):

i the *'green activists'*, who are members or supporters of environmental organisations (5–15%);
ii the *'green thinkers'*, who actively seek out green products and may engage in time-consuming support activities such as having multiple bins at home (25–30%);
iii the *'green consumer base'*, who feel that they have taken special action to express their environmental concern be it, a little arduously, the purchase of non-CFC aerosols (45–60%) and; finally,
iv the *'generally concerned'*, which includes everyone who voices concern for the environment (80–90%) whether it is followed by action or not.

To date, there are no signs that the green concern is beginning to slow down. In fact, many observers have predicted that the 1990s will be the 'environment decade' (Fisher, 1990; Gross, 1990). In a recent poll drawn from the marketing directors and managers of the UK's top 300 advertisers, 92% expressed the view that consumers are now more interested in green issues than a year ago (*Marketing*, 14.6.1990). And as far as these managers are concerned, 43% would even be willing to accept a smaller company car for environmental reasons (*Marketing*, 21.6.1990).

Although concern for the environment is likely to remain at a high level, *consumers are also becoming more sceptical about 'environmentally friendly' claims* made by companies (*Management Consultancy*, September 1989; *Marketing*, 21.2.1991). Based on 1200 face-to-face interviews conducted throughout the UK, Green Monitor concluded that 56% of all consumers are suspicious about such claims (*Marketing*, 17.5.1990). Indeed, some green claims are so spurious that ITV companies and the Advertising Standards Authority (ASA) have expressed their concern and plan to establish guidelines for 'Green TV Advertisements' (Kavanagh, 1990). In this context, Friends of the Earth have established a 'Green Con of the Year' award which is given to companies making inaccurate/misleading claims regarding their environmental friendliness; the 1990 'winner' was Eastern Electricity. British Rail's Intercity service was also highlighted for misleading recycling logos.

The ethical consumer

In recent years, consumers have become increasingly *disillusioned with unethical and sometimes straightforward illegal business practices.* The press reported at length about the allegations surrounding the Distillers takeover by Guinness, the practices of companies like Rockwell International, which defrauded the US Air Force, the car hire company Hertz, which overcharged customers and insurers $13 million for repairs of damaged rental cars, and the Chrysler Corp., which used to spin back odometers on cars used by executives and later sold to consumers (Schlegelmilch, 1989). News like this depresses the confidence consumers have in business executives. This is reflected in a study by the Institute of Business Ethics (1988), which found that only 17% of the British public rated the honesty of top businessmen as 'high'.

Moreover, a recent BARB/Mintel (1991) study showed that two-thirds of the shoppers say that ethical issues influence their buying habits. And what is the biggest ethical issue identified? Irresponsible marketing!

However, while neither the concern of consumers nor the unethical or illegal behaviour of businessmen is new (Vogel, 1987), *consumers are now much more willing and able to exert pressure on companies to behave more ethically.* Numerous avenues are open, including complaints to consumer watchdogs, lobbying via special interest groups (e.g. the American Association of Retired Persons, AARP) and, as a final measure, the organisation of consumer boycotts. In this context, a particularly interesting development is the emergence of ethical investors (Cooper and Schlegel-milch, 1993). These are people who are only willing to invest in companies that are not engaged in activities of which they disapprove. While this typically means no investment in companies connected with products such as arms, tobacco, alcohol and nuclear energy (Button 1988), it also extends to issues like unacceptably low wages paid to black South Africans, political donations and water pollution. Of course, all this makes it necessary to watch the ethical behaviour of companies very closely. To this end, a whole new industry is developing, set up to provide exactly such monitoring services. The principal organisation providing such a service in the UK is the Ethical Investment Research Service (EIRIS). Established in 1983, the organisation aims to:

i provide information on a wide range of issues which will help concerned investors apply positive or negative ethical and social criteria to social investment;
ii identify forms of investment which meet certain non-financial require-ments on the part of the investor; and
iii promote a wider understanding of and debate on corporate responsi-bility issues (The *Ethical Investor*, 1990, p. 5).

The charitable consumer

Consumers are also becoming more charitable. The 1980s have seen a large *increase in the number of charities* in the USA, Canada and the UK (Saxon-Harrold, 1990; Knapp, 1991). Estimates suggest that there are now more than 55,000 registered charities in Canada, 907,000 in the US and 175,000 in Britain (Schlegelmilch, Diamantopoulos and Love, 1992). A new charity registers with the Charity Commission every thirty minutes (Sambrook, 1991).

Recent figures by the British Charities Aid Foundation (1991) further suggest that donations to charities by individuals alone totalled between £3.4 billion and £5 billion during the July 1989 to June 1990 period. The same survey reveals that 74% of the interviewees claimed to have given money to charity in the month prior to being interviewed.

But a charitable orientation is not only reflected in the donation of money. *Donation of time is often equally important.* To this end, the British Charity Household Survey (Charities Aid Foundation, 1991) revealed that 29% of the interviewees reported to have undertaken at least one voluntary activity (out of 39 they were asked about) in the month prior to being interviewed. While the typical time given was only 40 minutes per person, it is estimated that the volunteering by all adults in Britain adds up to about 2 to 3 billion hours during the last annual reporting period.

Having demonstrated that large proportions of today's consumers are indeed green, ethical and charitable, the focus now shifts to ways in which companies are responding to these changes. Maintaining the pattern set above, firstly responses to green concerns are addressed, secondly some reactions to ethical issues are reviewed, and lastly examples of company strategies aimed at benefiting from the consumers' charitable orientation are provided.

THE COMPANY RESPONSES

The green response

There are numerous ways in which companies have responded to various forms of green pressure (Simintiras, Schlegelmilch and Diamantopoulos, 1993). Below, three of these are highlighted. Firstly, the greening of product offerings, secondly, the increasing use of specialised environmental consultancy agencies, and thirdly high-level organisational changes. Prior to this, however, it is worth pointing out that firms do not only *react* but can, of course, also be proactive. Companies such as Body Shop, founded during the 1970s by the far-sighted Anita Roddick, clearly took a lead when the environmental pressure from consumers was nowhere near as strong as it is today. Still, such companies tend to be exceptions.

Turning to the first issue, that is the *greening of product offerings*, it appears that most companies have responded to the new wave of environmentalism by at least attempting to eliminate or reduce the harmful components in the products they manufacture. Among the first to react were manufacturers of toiletries, detergents, paper products and petroleum (Prothero, 1990). There have also been numerous new product introductions which attempted to capitalise on the environmental concern. But while some companies have been doing this very profitably, there are also several firms which got their response to the growth of environmentalism badly wrong. On the successful side are the legendary stories of shoppers who bought biodegradable washing powder, organically grown food and low-mercury batteries by the ton. The UK sales of the Belgium Ecover cleaner and detergent company, for example, have increased in one year from £1 million to £10 million (*Management Consultancy*, 1989).

Among the green casualties, on the other hand, are Bradford and Bingley, which launched a Green Personal Equity Plan in July 1989 and had to withdraw it two months later due to lack of interest (Prestridge, 1989). Criticised also were BP's 'Supergreen' petrol, which was shown to contain several toxic chemicals despite its 'pollution free' tag (Peattie, 1990), and Proctor & Gamble's 'green' nappies on the grounds that disposables still destroy trees (*Management Consultancy*, September 1989).

To get their new 'green' image right, companies are increasingly turning to *environmental consultancies*. Between 1988 and 1990, the number of

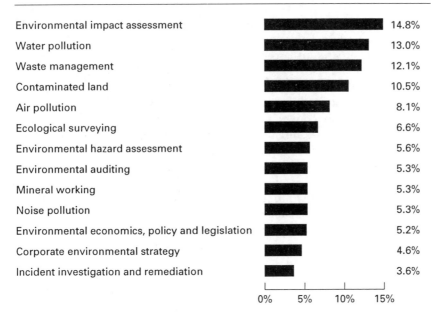

Environmental impact assessment	14.8%
Water pollution	13.0%
Waste management	12.1%
Contaminated land	10.5%
Air pollution	8.1%
Ecological surveying	6.6%
Environmental hazard assessment	5.6%
Environmental auditing	5.3%
Mineral working	5.3%
Noise pollution	5.3%
Environmental economics, policy and legislation	5.2%
Corporate environmental strategy	4.6%
Incident investigation and remediation	3.6%

Figure 4.1 Main work areas of environmental consultancies

firms in the UK that specialise in such services has increased from 120 to 225 and their turnover has increased by 75% to £200 million (*Financial Times*, 18.10.1990). Figure 4.1 shows the main work areas of environmental consultancies. Another interesting facet of industries' response to environmentalism was pointed out by Touche Ross Management Consultants, who found that an increasing number of British companies – 30% of their sample – appointed *board members responsible for environmental management*. However, the consultants also noted the fact that British companies appear to move less quickly than some of their European counterparts. All of the Dutch companies surveyed, 80% of the Danish companies and 75% of the German companies had already appointed board members with a specific environmental remit (Market Research Society, 1990).

The ethical response

Faced with increasing concern about their ethical behaviour, many companies, in particular in the US, are now taking *steps to incorporate ethics into their organisation*. Allied, Chase Manhattan, Boeing and General Electric conduct in-house training in business ethics. General Motors has sponsored conferences in the field of business ethics. General Mills has issued guidelines for dealing with suppliers, competitors and customers and seeks recruits who share its values. Johnson & Johnson has developed a 'credo' of corporate values, holds company-wide meetings to challenge the Credo's tenets and surveys to ascertain compliance (*Business Week*, 1988; De George, 1987). A survey among British companies (Schlegelmilch and Houston, 1989) revealed that 42% had introduced codes of ethics, among them British Gas and British Rail, and organised seminars in business ethics for senior executives. Countless other examples of attempts to incorporate ethics into organisations are examined in casebooks on the subject (e.g. Beauchamp, 1989; Hoffman and Moore, 1990; Molander, 1980).

Of interest also is the establishment of *ethical investment funds*. The first to be established in the UK was the Friends Provident Stewardship Fund in 1984 (*Financial Times* Supplement, 21.4.1989). This was followed by the Ethical Investment fund in 1986 as well as the NM Unit Trust Conscience Fund and an ethical investment fund offered by Scottish Equitable, both in 1989. A very recent phenomenon is also the emergence of particular 'environmental investment funds'. The Merlin Ecology Fund, introduced in 1988, was the first one in the UK to specialise exclusively in environmentally friendly investment (*The Times*, 5.6.1989); an indication that green issues and ethical issues are clearly overlapping.

A rather different facet of corporate ethics is the *display of ethical concern*. Examples are a series of 30–second advertisements by Fuji Film, intended to challenge prejudice about race and social disability (*Today*, 4.7.1991; *Sunday Times*, 24.6.1990; *Observer*, 22.7.1990). While the commercial impact of these advertisements is unquestioned, resulting in a 50% increase in brand share in the test area, the wisdom of promoting products with a social message has been widely questioned. On the one hand, Fuji Film received praising letters from organisations such as MENCAP (Royal Society for Mentally Handicapped Children and Adults), the Commission for Racial Equality, and the United Kingdom Sports Association For People with Mental Handicap. On the other hand is the Independent Television Commission (ITC), which received no less than 115 complaints. While the ITC did not uphold the complaints, it urged advertisers to take greater care on the grounds of taste (*Daily Telegraph*, 19.7.1991). The verdict on this issue in terms of consumer acceptance is still outstanding.

The charitable response

Turning to the charitable response of companies, an event springs to mind which happened on a recent transatlantic flight with Virgin Atlantic. During the flight, as on most Virgin Atlantic flights, a film was shown explaining the charitable involvement of the company. Following this, a collection was held for a children's charity. In keeping with this image, the in-flight magazine *Hot Air* also pointed out that Virgin uses biodegradable bags, plants a tree in the California countryside for every passenger who flies with them to Los Angeles, and is involved in a waste recycling programme. Again, this indicates that green, ethical and charitable behaviour appear to go hand-in-hand.

Some may still be sceptical and view this as the idiosyncratic behaviour of the flamboyant founder of Virgin Atlantic, Richard Branson. However, there are numerous examples of hard-nosed, well-established companies which use contributions to charities to foster their goals. And clearly, this is not referring to corporate philanthropy, but to so called 'cause-related marketing' (Varadarajan and Menon, 1988), that is contributions to a cause on behalf of customers who engage in revenue-producing transactions (*Business Week*, 1982; Wall, 1984). Here are three examples:

- Heinz Baby Food pledged to contribute 6 cents to a hospital for each Heinz baby food label sent in by consumers.
- Coca-Cola gave 10 cents for every proof-of-purchase from one of their coffee brands to the Texas Department of Highways to help clean up highways and plant wild flowers.
- American Express promised to donate a cent to the renovation of the Statue of Liberty for each use of its charge card.

Some of these campaigns have achieved staggering results. American Express reported an increase in card usage of 28% during the promotion period. Overall, the $6 million national promotion campaign resulted in a $1.7 million contribution (Varadarajan and Menon, 1988).

Some charities have now gathered a considerable expertise in cooperating with companies in cause-related marketing activities. The World Wide Fund for Nature (WWF), for example, boasts past licensing agreements of their cuddly Panda logo with Ariel Ultra, Pampers and Cadbury. Recently, they got involved in a cooperation with Tipp-Ex: the Panda logo will appear on the product together with the caption, 'purchase of this product enables Tipp-Ex to make a donation to the World Wide Fund for Nature UK' (*Marketing*, 1991, p. 14).

Interesting variants of cause-related marketing are also the so-called '*affinity cards*' (Yang, 1986). The general idea is to promote credit cards to a specific group of people with the promise that a certain proportion of the amount charged to the card will be donated to some cause. Here are some examples:

• Midland	National Trust	Visa
	Artscard (87 organisations)	MasterCard
	Care Card (18 charities)	MasterCard
• Co-Operative	Help the Aged	Visa
	RSPB	Visa
• Leeds Permanent	Imperial Cancer Research	Visa

	British Heart Foundation	Visa
	Mencap	Visa
• TSB	Save the Children	Visa
• NatWest	World Wide Fund for Nature	Visa

RESEARCH IN THE NEW MARKETING ERA

Having demonstrated from the consumer and the company point of view that a new green ethical and charitable marketing era has indeed arrived, one pertinent question arises: How do these developments affect the marketing discipline? For a start, marketers are now placing more emphasis on the environmental movement, the ethical concerns and the potential behind charitable cooperation and their impact on purchase behaviour. Mainstream marketing journals have started publishing a variety of papers on these three issues. On a more fundamental level, however, *the marketing discipline is changing its orientation.* It is going away from viewing itself solely as a representative of company interests concerned with what to produce and how to sell. Now, a more even-handed approach is called for, concerned with the welfare of producers, consumers and society as a whole.

Below some examples are provided of how this development is shaping research in marketing.

Research on green issues

Two projects fall under this heading. The first one is concerned with the *perceived environmental impact of rail and road freight transport* (Schlegelmilch and Diamantopoulos, 1990). This is a qualitative study primarily attempting to establish attitudes with regard to the relative environmental friendliness of freight transported by road and rail. To this end, some 70 in-depth interviews with key informants/experts were conducted, some of which lasted over an hour. These interviewees included MPs, members of the House of Lords, as well as the environmental correspondents of nearly all the major national newspapers. The main groups of informants are shown in Figure 4.2.

Given that, overall, British Rail was clearly perceived to be more environmentally friendly than road transport, it is not surprising that Sir Bob Reid, the Chairman of British Rail, commented positively on this work in the press: 'It is a significant and exciting project and will provide an important input into Railfreight's developing strategy for the next decade' (Reid, 1991). The project is currently extended through a large-scale (10 000 questionnaires) quantitatively based tracking study which aims to gauge the opinions of the general public on the ecological impact of freight transport.

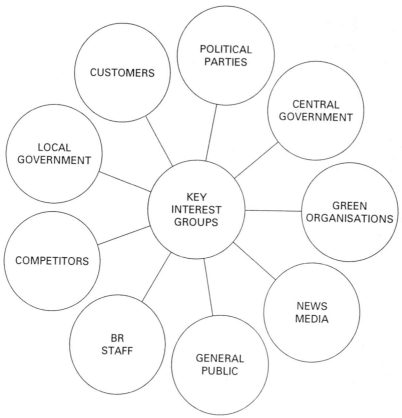

Figure 4.2 Groups of key informants

The second piece of 'green' research (Schlegelmilch, Diamantopoulos and DuPreez, 1992) aims to determine the *importance of green product attributes*, such as the fact that a car can be recycled, in relation to other product attributes, such as speed. The work has been designed to enable comparisons between students and 'ordinary' consumers along four different product groups and across five different countries. The key statistical technique applied to the data has been conjoint analysis. However, for the present purpose, the simple importance rankings included in Table 4.1, which compares British and German car buyers, provide a taste for the kind of managerially relevant information which can be distilled from the data.

For each product attribute two important measures are given: firstly, the proportion of respondents in each country who consider the particular attribute to be important, secondly, below the first value, the proportion of respondents who included the attribute among their top five considerations when purchasing a car. Among others, the results show greater German preferences for the green product attributes '3-way catalytic converter' and 'reusable chassis'. In contrast, there is a greater British preference for 'performance' and 'acceleration'. Of course, this makes one wonder why British motorways have a speed restriction and the German Autobahnen have none.

Research on ethical issues

Turning to research on ethical issues, there are again two examples that illustrate the work conducted in this area. The first focuses on a series of surveys (Langlois and Schlegelmilch, 1990; Schlegelmilch and Langlois, 1989, 1990; Schlegelmilch, 1989, 1990; Schlegelmilch and Houston, 1989, 1990) aiming to investigate the spread and usage of so called *corporate codes of ethics*, that is statements setting down corporate principles, ethics, rules of conduct, and so on. In one of these surveys, a questionnaire was sent to the largest 600 French, German and British companies, requesting information on whether they had codes of ethics and, if so, what topics they addressed. While this was undoubtedly an easy exercise, the fact that this kind of research had never been conducted in Europe before resulted in considerable press coverage, including an interview with BBC Radio Four and a report in the *Financial Times*. Table 4.2 provides some results, indicating that only 41% of the sampled European companies introduced corporate codes of ethics. This is in sharp contrast to US findings, where 75% of the respondents to a survey of Fortune 500 companies (Centre for Business Ethics, 1986) stated that they had formed (written) codes of ethics. A comparison of subjects addressed in such codes (Table 4.3) also reveals a number of significant differences between the European sample and equivalent US results.

The second example of work on ethics is a project conducted in cooperation with the US Ethics Resource Centre and the Wharton Business School of the University of Pennsylvania (Schlegelmilch and Robertson, 1993; Robertson and Schlegelmilch, 1993). Here, the previous work is taken a step further through exploring *whether ethical issues are universally perceived* and to what extent corporate ethics initiatives have been formalised. Using a sample of US, UK, German, and Austrian firms, the findings indicate that managerial perceptions of what constitutes an ethical issue vary by country and by type of industry. The managers' base country and the type of industry also influence the comprehensiveness of their written ethics policies and training. Company size, in contrast, has little bearing on both manager's perception of ethical issues and the comprehensiveness of ethics policies and training.

Table 4.1 Attribute preferences in Britain and Germany

Attribute	Britian (n=197) (%)	(Rank)	Germany (n=213) (%)	(Rank)	Significance (2-tailed) Z-Test
Fuel consumption	85.3	(1)	89.2	(1)	NS[a]
	81.2	(1)	82.2	(1)	NS
Motor performance	68.5	(2)	58.2	(3)	0.05
	64.5	(2)	43.7	(3)	0.001
Anti-lock brake	57.4	(3)	52.1	(5)	NS
system	47.2	(3)	40.8	(4)	NS
3-way catalytic	51.3	(4)	85.0	(2)	0.001
converter	39.1	(4)	76.1	(2)	0.001
Acceleration	47.2	(5)	34.7	(14)	0.01
	36.0	(5)	13.6	(13)	0.001
Number of doors	44.7	(6)	54.9	(4)	0.05
	25.4	(7)	21.1	(10)	NS
Power-assisted	39.1	(7)	44.1	(9)	NS
steering	25.9	(6)	23.0	(9)	NS
Fully galvanised	38.6	(8)	43.7	(10)	NS
chassis	20.8	(10)	30.5	(5)	0.05
Gearbox (manual/	36.5	(9)	47.4	(6)	0.05
automatic)	21.3	(9)	17.4	(12)	NS
Central locking	35.0	(10)	41.8	(12)	NS
	9.6	(14)	11.7	(15)	NS
Country-of-origin	33.0	(11)	45.5	(8)	0.01
	24.4	(8)	27.7	(6)	NS
Luggage space	32.5	(12)	37.6	(13)	NS
	16.2	(11)	23.5	(8)	0.05
Air-conditioning	29.9	(13)	19.7	(17)	0.01
	12.2	(12)	7.5	(16)	NS
Sunroof	27.4	(14)	46.0	(7)	0.001
	9.1	(15)	13.1	(14)	NS
Height-adjustable	19.3	(15)	27.2	(16)	0.05
seats	7.1	(16)	1.9	(18)	0.01
Shape of chassis	16.2	(16)	42.3	(11)	0.001
	11.2	(13)	24.9	(7)	0.001
Reusable chassis	8.1	(17)	30.0	(15)	0.001
	5.6	(17)	19.7	(11)	0.001
Sport seats	6.6	(18)	12.7	(18)	0.05
	2.0	(18)	3.8	(17)	NS

Note: [a]NS=not significant.

Research on charitable issues

In the area of charity marketing, the Charities Aid Foundation, the umbrella organisation and research arm of all UK charities, is sponsoring a research assistant and, perhaps even more important, permitting access to their large annual household survey data bank. This success builds on previous work in the area, which investigated questions like the *targeting*

Table 4.2 Adoption of codes of ethics

	UK No. of firms	(%)	France No. of firms	(%)	W. Germany No. of firms	(%)	Total No. of firms	(%)
Complete Sample								
With codes	33	41	15	30	30	51	78	41
Without codes	47	59	35	70	29	49	111	59
Total	80	100	50	100	59	100	189	100
Reduced Sample (excluding foreign affiliates)								
With codes	20	31	7	18	24	47	51	33
Without codes	45	69	31	82	27	53	103	67
Total	65	100	38	100	51	100	154	100

Table 4.3 Subjects addressed in corporate codes of ethics

Subjects	Total European countries No.	(%)	United States[a] n=118 No.	(%)	Chi-square significance Europe vs US
Employee conduct	78	100	47	55	p<0.01
Community & environment	51	65	50	42	NS[b]
Customers	52	67	96	81	p<0.05
Shareholders	42	54	NA	NA	NA[c]
Suppliers & contractors	15	19	101	86	p<0.01
Political interests	12	15	113	96	p<0.01
Innovation and technology	26	33	18	15	p<0.01

Notes:
[a] US comparison is based on a survey of the Foundation of the Southwestern Graduate School of Banking (1980).
[b] NS=not significant.
[c] NA=no comparable data available.

of fund-raising appeals (Schlegelmilch, 1988), the *scope for market segmentation in the charity market* (Schlegelmilch and Tynan, 1989) and the *characteristics of charity volunteers* (Schlegelmilch and Tynan, 1989). The key findings from this work demonstrate that it is relatively easy to distinguish donors and non-donors a priori on the basis of socio-demographic, geographic and psychographic variables. Moreover, it was found that generous donors (and volunteers) can also be identified, based on these segmentation variables. Surprisingly, no links were revealed between the type of charity (e.g. children's charity versus animal protection) and the characteristics of donors contributing to such charities. Finally, it was demonstrated that donors with preferences for particular types of appeals, for example door-to-door collections versus television appeals, have different socio-demographic and psychographic characteristics. It is apparent that these insights contribute to the efficiency and effectiveness of fund-raising efforts.

As far as the new Charities Aid Foundation funded work is concerned, a first paper has been developed which provides *an inter-disciplinary review of the determinants of charity giving* (Schlegelmilch, Diamantopoulos and Love, 1992). Subsequently, a number of analyses have been conducted focusing, among others, on factors affecting the *amount of money and time donated to charity* (Diamantopoulos, Schlegelmilch and Love, 1993) and on modelling donor and volunteer behaviour by means of path analyses (Love, Schlegelmilch and Diamantopoulos, 1993).

CONCLUSION

This chapter has attempted to illustrate some changes in consumer values and behaviour, reviewed a range of company responses to these changes and provided examples of how the research agenda in marketing has been shaped by these developments. What then are the main issues to be remembered? Three key points emerge:

1 Consumers have changed and are now much more interested in green, ethical and charitable issues.
2 Companies are well aware of these changes and are in the process of adapting not only their product offerings but also their ethical positions.
3 The new era has also begun for the discipline itself, which is now increasingly concerned with non-traditional marketing issues.

Taking these collectively, it has hopefully been demonstrated that marketing is indeed facing a new era and that the *green, ethical and charitable developments are not just another marketing ploy.*

REFERENCES

BARB/Mintel (1991) *The Green and Ethical Shopper*, London.
Beauchamp, T. L. (1989) *Case Studies in Business, Society and Ethics*, Englewood Cliffs, NJ: Prentice-Hall.
Broadbent, Simon and Jacobs, Brian (1984) *Spending Advertising Money*, 4th edn. London: Business Books.
—— *Business Week* (1982) 'AmEx shows the way to benefit from giving'. 18 October, pp. 44–45.
—— *Business Week* (1988) 'Businesses are signing up for Ethics 101'. 15 February, pp. 56–57.
Button, J. (1988) A *Directory of Green Ideas*, London: Routledge.
Centre for Business Ethics (1986) Are corporations institutionalizing ethics? *Journal of Business Ethics*, 5, No. 2, 85–91.
Charities Aid Foundation (1991) *Charity Household Survey 1989/90*. Tonbridge: CAF.
Cooper, M. and Schlegelmilch, B. B. (1993) 'Ethical investment: A review of

key issues and a call for future research'. Working Paper: European Business Management School, University of Wales, UK.

Daily Telegraph (1991) TV ads 'Too Short for Social Messages', 19 July, p. 5.

De George, R. T. (1987) 'The status of business ethics: Past and future'. *Journal of Business Ethics*, 6, No. 3, 201–211.

de Truck, M. A. and Goldhaber, G. M. (1989) 'Effectiveness of product warning labels: effects of consumer's information processing objectives'. *Journal of Consumer Affairs*, 23, No. 1, 111–126.

Diamantopoulos, A., Schlegelmilch, B. B. and Love, A. (1993) 'Giving to charity: Determinants of cash donations through prompted giving'. In R. Varadarajan and B. Jaworski (eds), *Marketing Theory and Applications*, Vol. 4, Proceedings of the American Marketing Association 1993 Winter Educators' Conference, Newport Beach, CA, 20–23 February.

Financial Times (1990) 'Intangible cost of the environment'. 18 October, p. 13.

Financial Times Supplement (1989) 'Environmental trusts an unlikely alliance'. 21 April, p. 27.

Fisher, A. B. (1990) 'What consumers want in the 1990s'. *Fortune*, 121, 16 January, pp. 108–112.

Galbraith, J. K. (1958) *The Affluent Society*. Boston, Houghton Mifflin.

—— (1967) *The New Industrial State*. Boston: Houghton Mifflin.

Gross, F. B. (1990) 'The weaning of the green: Environmentalism comes of age in the 1990s'. *Business Horizons*, 33, September-October, 40–46.

Hermann, R. O. (1970) *The Consumer Movement in Historical Perspective*. Department of Agricultural Economics and Rural Sociology, Pennsylvania State University, February.

Hoffman W. M. and Moore, J. M. (1990) *Business Ethics: Readings and Cases in Corporate Morality*, 2nd edn. New York: McGraw-Hill.

Institute of Business Ethics (1988) *Company Philosophies and Codes of Business Ethics*. London.

Kangun, N., Carson, L. and Grove, S. J. (1991) 'Environmental advertising claims: A preliminary investigation'. *Journal of Public Policy & Marketing*, 10, No. 2, 47–58.

Kavanagh, M. (1990) 'TV fights fake green ads'. *Marketing*, 15 March, p. 1.

Knapp, M. (1991) 'Commentary'. In J. McQuillan (ed.), *Charity Trends*, 12th edn. Tonbridge: Charities Aid Foundation.

Kotler, P. and Mantrala, M. K. (1985) 'Flawed products: Consumer responses and marketing strategies'. *Journal of Consumer Marketing*, 2, No. 3, 27–36.

Langlois, C. and Schlegelmilch B. B. (1990) 'Do corporate codes of ethics reflect national character? Evidence from Europe and the United States'. *Journal of International Business Studies*, 21, No. 4, 519–539.

Love, A., Schlegelmilch, B. B. and Diamantopoulos, A. (1993) 'Charity marketing: An empirical analysis of donor and volunteering behaviour in the UK'. Research Report submitted to the Charities Aid Foundation, London.

Management Consultancy (1989) 'Keep your head in the green revolution'. September, 56–57.

Marketing (1990a) Marketing forum. 17 May, 14 June and 21 June.

—— (1990b) 'WWF pandas to push green Tipp-Ex', 10 January, p. 14.

—— (1991) Consumers grow skeptical of advertisers' green campaigns. 21 February, p. 7.

Market Research Society (1990) 'Attitudes to environmental issues'. *Newsletter of the Market Research Society*, October.

Molander, E. A. (1980) *Responsive Capitalism: Case Studies in Corporate Social Conduct.* New York: McGraw-Hill.

Murphy, O. (1989) 'Green is the colour'. *Survey,* Winter 9–11.

Nader, R. (1968) *The Great American Gyp.* The New York Review of Books, Nyrev Inc.

Observer (1990) 'Fuji: Every picture tells a story'. 22 July, p. 37.

Packard, V. (1957) *The Hidden Persuaders,* New York: Pocket Books.

Peattie, K. J. (1990) Painting marketing education, *Journal of Marketing Management,* 6, No. 2, 105–125.

—— (1992) *Green Marketing,* London: Business Handbooks, Pitman.

Prestridge, J. (1989) 'Green and ethics sprout forth'. *Money Management,* November, 63–71.

Prothero, A. (1990) 'Green consumerism and the social marketing concept: Marketing strategies for the 1990s.' *Journal of Marketing Management,* 6, No. 2 (Autumn), 87–103.

Reid, Sir Bob (1991) British Rail Press Release following the Railfreight Conference at Wansford, 22–23 October.

Robertson, D. C. and Schlegelmilch, B. B., (1993) 'Corporate Institutionalization of ethics in the United States and Great Britain'. *Journal of Business Ethics,* 12, 133–144.

Rundle, R. (1989) 'A crackdown on "Charity" sweepstakes'. *Wall Street Journal,* 6 March.

Sambrook C. (1991) 'Charities need cash not drive'. *Marketing,* editorial.

Saxon-Harrold, S. (1990) 'The voluntary sector: A selection of international statistics'. In J. McQuillan (ed.), *Charity Trends,* 12th edn. Tonbridge: Charities Aid Foundation.

Schlegelmilch, B. B. (1988) 'Targeting of fund-raising appeals – How to identify donors'. *European Journal of Marketing,* 22, No. 1, 33–41.

—— (1989) 'The ethics gap between Britain and the United States: A comparison of the state of business ethics in both countries'. *European Management Journal,* 7, No. 1, 57–64.

—— (1990) 'Die Kodifizierung ethischer Grundsätze in europäischen Unternehmen: Eine empirische Untersuchung'. *Die Betriebswirtschaft,* 3, 365–374.

Schlegelmilch, B. B. and Diamantopoulos, A. (1990) 'The perceived environmental impact of rail and road freight transport: A qualitative analysis'. Report submitted to the British Railways Board, University of Wales, Swansea, European Business Management School.

Schlegelmilch, B. B., Diamantopoulos, A. and DuPreez, J. P. (1992) 'Consumer preferences as barriers to standardising marketing programmes in the single European market: The role of country-of-origin and ecological product attributes'. In V. L. Crittenden (ed.), *Developments in Marketing Science,* vol. XV. Proceedings of the Annual Conference of the Academy of Marketing Science, San Diego, California. 21–26 April, 1992, pp. 189–194.

Schlegelmilch, B. B., Diamantopoulos, A. and Love, A. (1992) 'Determinants of charity giving: An interdisciplinary review of the literature and suggestions for future research'. In C. T. Allen *et al.* (eds), *Marketing Theory and Applications,* vol. 3, Proceedings of the American Marketing Association 1992 Winter Educators' Conference, San Antonio, Texas, 15–18 February, pp. 507–516.

Schlegelmilch, B. B. and Houston, J. E. (1989) 'Corporate codes of ethics in large UK companies: An empirical investigation of use, content and attitudes'. *European Journal of Marketing,* 23, No. 6, 7–24.

—— (1990) 'Does British business need a corporate code of ethics?' *Management*

Decision: A Selection of the Best Articles Published by MCB University Press Journals During 1989, 28, No. 7, 38–43.

Schlegelmilch, B. B. and Langlois, C. (1989) 'Do corporate codes of ethics reflect national character? Evidence from Europe and the United States'. Second European Conference on Business Ethics, Barcelona, Spain, 27–29 September.

—— (1990) 'New US corporate culture and old Japanese corporate values: Two not-too-distant relatives'. Third European Conference on Business Ethics, Milan, Italy, 3–5 October.

Schlegelmilch, B. B. and Robertson, D. C. (1993) 'Ethical polymorphism: A comparative study of US and European managers'. Working Paper, European Business Management School, University of Wales, Swansea.

Schlegelmilch, B. B. and Tynan, C. (1989) 'The scope for market segmentation within the charity market: An empirical analysis'. *Managerial and Decision Economics*, 10, 127–134.

—— (1989) 'Who volunteers – An investigation into the characteristics of charity workers'. *Journal of Marketing Management*, 5, No. 2, 133–151.

Siebert, H. (1973) *Das produzierte Chaos*, Stuttgart.

Simintiras, A., Schlegelmilch, B. B. and Diamantopoulos, A. (1993) 'Greening the marketing mix: A review of the literature and an agenda for future research'. Proceedings of the 22nd Annual Conference of the European Marketing Academy, Barcelona, Spain.

Smith, N. C. and Quelch, J. A. (1993) *Ethics in Marketing*, Homewood, Il.: Irwin.

Stern, L. W. and Eovaldi, T. L. (1984) *Legal Aspects of Marketing Strategy: Antitrust and Consumer Protection Issues*, Englewood Cliffs, NJ: Prentice-Hall.

Sunday Times (1990) 'TV ads turn to social realism'. 24 June, p. 7.

The Ethical Investor (1990a) Friends provident in top twenty. Spring, p. 2.

——(1990b) 'Areas of research offered by EIRIS'. Spring, p. 5.

The Times (1989) 'Moral lure of green portfolio'. 5 June, p. 36.

——(1991) 'Customers should always have rights'. 12 June, p. 12.

Today 1991 'Is this offensive or just ageist?' 4 July, p. 6.

Varadarajan, P. R. and Menon, A. (1988) 'Cause-related marketing: A coalignment of marketing strategy and corporate philanthropy'. *Journal of Marketing*, 52, July, 58–74.

Vogel, D. (1987) 'Could an ethics course have kept Ivan from going bad?' *Wall Street Journal*, 27 April.

Wall, W. L. (1984) 'Companies change the ways they make charitable donations'. *Wall Street Journal*, 21 June, pp. 1, 19.

Yang, J. E. (1986) 'Group affinity is used to sell credit cards'. *Wall Street Journal*, 23 September, p.33.

Chapter 5

Information and communication technologies

This chapter, and the book from which it is taken, are the result of an international research programme sponsored by ten major corporations, including General Motors, British Petroleum and Eastman Kodak, and two US government organizations. The research programme – Management in the 1990s – was charged with the task of developing a joint perspective on the challenges of the turbulent business environment and the role of information and communication technologies as tools and catalysts for change. The chapter explains the central importance of information and communication technologies in all organizations, and points towards some of the opportunities and challenges for management that information and communication technologies represent.

Information technology and organizational transformation

Michael S. Scott Morton

The Management in the 1990s Research Program was created in 1984 to examine the profound impact that information technology (IT) is having on organizations of all kinds. Its mission was to explore how IT will affect the way organizations will be able to survive and prosper in the competitive environment of the 1990s and beyond. The program began with two basic premises:

1 The business environment is and will remain turbulent.
2 IT will continue its rapid evolution over at least the next decade.

A closer look at these premises and at the way the program was organized will help in understanding [management in the 1990s].

TURBULENT BUSINESS ENVIRONMENT

Turbulence in the business environment puts pressure on organizations to be sure they can effectively meet the fundamental changes that are occurring. The program identified four kinds of changes with which organizations must contend.

Social

The heightened expectations of people in Western Europe and North America are giving rise to pressures to improve the quality of working life and the quality of the environment. This is resulting in a changing concept of what constitutes *value*. This is particularly true of the prices people are willing to pay for products and services and the amount of damage to the environment that they will tolerate.

Political

The changing regulatory and governmental roles of the Western governments have resulted in a new competitive climate and a new set of rules for competition. This is also happening in other parts of the world. [. . .]

Technical

There is obviously technical change in the IT area, [. . .] but there are significant changes in other areas such as materials, with advances in super-conductivity, ceramics, and advanced composites, to name just three. There are also major changes in the biosciences and bioengineering, where major technical breakthroughs are likely to continue to evolve rapidly.

Economic

The twin deficits in the United States, in the budget and in trade, will continue to cause economic turbulence for some years. The fact of considerable global trade, particularly among the 'Triad' (EEC, North America, and Japan), will merely exacerbate the uncertainty surrounding firms. This trade results in shifting benchmarks for acceptable product quality, and it places new demands on corporations and nations.

THE RAPID EVOLUTION OF INFORMATION TECHNOLOGY

The second premise behind the management in the 1990s Research Program is that information technology now consists of a powerful collection of elements that are undergoing change and have wide and significant applicability. These elements go well beyond what has been available during the last thirty years, in what might be termed the data processing era. In the 1990s we expect organizations to experience the effects of the integration and evolution of a set of elements collectively termed *information technology*. The research program considers these elements to consist of the following:

1 *Hardware*. This ranges from large-scale mainframe computers to small-scale microcomputers.
2 *Software*. This ranges from traditional languages such as COBOL and their fourth-generation equivalents to expert systems that have emerged from developments in artificial intelligence.
3 *Networks*. These telecommunications networks range from public to private, broadband to narrowband.
4 *Workstations*. These range from those designed for engineers' with large computational capabilities and the ability to display dynamic, three-dimensional color graphics, to professional workstations used by bank lending officers or a market analyst in a consumer goods company. The

latter rely on models, heuristics, and simple graphics and often have very large databases included in the system.

5 *Robotics.* These range from robots with 'vision' and 'hands' used on the factory floor to a variety of devices familiar to the average person on the street, such as automatic teller machines.

6 *Smart chips.* 'Intelligent' chips are used in products to enhance functionality or reliability. For example, they are used in automobile braking systems to prevent skidding and in elevators to improve response time and to detect impending failures. In simpler forms they now appear in products such as the 'active card' used to track via satellite the movement of shipping containers.

The continuing evolution and integration of these six elements of IT have now reached a threshold of cost and ease of use that is having widespread organizational impact.

CHANGE

Both premises – business turbulence and technological change – imply potential organizational change. The external forces associated with environmental turbulence must be reacted to for survival. IT offers the opportunity for organizations to react constructively. Because of the combined effect, there is no reason why organizations will necessarily continue in their present form.

These challenges suggest that it will not be possible to survive as a company just by working harder within existing organizational structures and using conventional practices and tools. Given what IT now allows an alert organization to do, an organization that merely works faster and harder will become uncompetitive in the global marketplace of the 1990s and beyond.

THE MANAGEMENT IN THE 1990s RESEARCH PROGRAM

A group of faculty at the MIT Sloan School of Management came together in 1984 to address the consequences of this turbulent and changing environment. These faculty members approached a number of organizations with the request to fund a multiyear cooperative research program. The researchers wanted a reality-based business perspective on framing the problems to study and on the interpretation and responses to the research findings. Thus, the sponsors were asked to contribute more than money; they were asked to support the program with time and effort.

The initial ten sponsors that agreed to participate were American Express Company; Arthur Young and Company; British Petroleum; BellSouth Corporation; Digital Equipment Corporation; Eastman Kodak Company;

General Motors Corporation; International Computers Ltd.; MCI Communications Corporation; and the U.S. Internal Revenue Service. This group of faculty and sponsors became the Management in the 1990s Research Program. During the course of the study, the original ten sponsors were joined by two additional supporting organizations: CIGNA Corporation and the U.S. Army.

Program objectives

The faculty and sponsors agreed that the effort would have two principal objectives:

1 To help the managers throughout the world understand the kinds of impact IT will have on business missions, organizational structures, and operating practices.
2 To provide contributions to the theories of management that grow from our understanding of the impacts of IT, and to develop new curricula for the MIT Sloan School of Management.

[. . .]

IT IN PERSPECTIVE

Information technology has important general-purpose power to manipulate symbols used in all classes of work, and therefore, as an 'information engine,' it can do for business what the steam engine did in the days of the Industrial Revolution. It goes beyond this, however, as a technology that permits one to manipulate models of reality, to step back one pace from the physical reality. Such an ability lies at the heart of IT's capacity to alter work fundamentally.

The telegraph and telephone were the forebears of IT and were central to the rise of the modern industrial corporation. The application of those technologies resulted in the mass-production, vertically integrated hierarchical organization. But there is nothing sacred about such an organizational form. At a particular moment in time, around the turn of the century, the conditions in the marketplace of the newly industrializing Western world were conducive to the emergence of this form. The pressures of global competition and the enabling coordinative capabilities of IT have led to experimentation, and an evolution away from the traditional hierarchical organization can be expected.

Information is the lifeblood of any organization. Little can be done successfully without it. Hence, the cost of handling and processing information is important. In the data processing era this was also true, but it was less critical to organizational success, as data processing principally dealt with back-office clerical functions and the technology was

Table 5.1 Computing cost-performance trends

Constant Functionality*	1980 4.5 MIPS	1990 4.5 MIPS	2000 4.5 MIPS
Cost			
Original projection (1981)	$4.5 million	$300,000	—
Modified projection (1988)	—	$100,000	$10,000
Number of people of equivalent cost			
Original projection (1981)	210	6	—
Modified projection (1988)	—	2	0.125

Note: * Metaphor for constant functionality is millions of instructions per second (MIPS)

still expensive. Technology costs have dropped, and one can go beyond numerical data for algorithmic processing and move to qualitative information and heuristic manipulation. This, in turn, can be combined with the ability to work with pictures and drawings, and then one can connect all this to virtually any location in the world. Such power is new in kind; it represents a step-function change from what was available before.

The economics of IT have changed both absolutely and relatively. At an absolute level, we are expecting to see IT cost-performance ratios continue to change in the range of 20 to 30 percent a year. Such change can lead to very considerable differences over relatively short intervals of time. Table 5.1, based on results of an earlier MIT study, illustrates the profound consequences of such a compounding change. In 1980 the cost of a computer with a processing power of 4.5 MIPS was $4.5 million, the cost equivalent of 210 employees of a certain skill level. The cost of a machine of this power was projected to decline to $300,000 in 1990, the cost equivalent of 6 workers of the same skill level. The actual 1990 cost will be closer to $100,000. The cost of such a machine in the year 2000 is likely to be no more than $10,000, the cost equivalent of only a fraction of a worker. Thus, organizations are faced with radically different trade-offs over time among processing power, human effort, and dollars with which to best meet the organization's objectives. [. . .]

IT is different

Information technology exerts such a strong influence because it can affect both production and coordination. Production refers to the task of producing any good or service that the organization is in business to sell. It is not limited to physical production but includes the intellectual production of things such as loans or other 'soft' products. The production jobs that are most affected by IT are those in which information and/or knowledge makes a difference. We call such production workers 'information workers' or 'knowledge workers'. The fraction of the work force that falls into this category has grown to be very large. In manufacturing industries it averages around 40 percent, and in service industries more than 80 percent. The information worker processes information without significant modification, a task that is typically classified as clerical, such as order entry. The knowledge worker category covers those who add value to the original information. This would include engineers and designers required to design new products, those who trade in the securities market, those in financial institutions who lend money to companies or individuals, and all those who produce budgets, market research analyses, legal briefs, and so on. The use of IT to change the nature of both such categories of production work is widely recognized.

Just as important is the use of IT to change the ways in which coordination activities are carried out. Coordination tasks make up a large part of what organizations do. With IT the effects of both distance and time can shrink to near zero. For example, it is possible today to make financial trades in global markets anywhere in the world from any city. A similar activity is placing orders to a supplier's plant or accepting orders directly from a customer's site to one's own organization. The airline reservation systems are among the most visible and oldest examples of such coordination.

Organizational memory is another feature of coordination affected by IT. Corporate databases now provide an enormous reservoir of information that can be used for constructive management of the organization. Personnel records indicating who has had what job, at what salary, and with what training form the basis for understanding the skill mix in a company and help identify possible candidates for certain jobs. Thus, IT can be thought of as affecting coordination by increasing the organization's memory, thereby establishing a record that allows for the detection of patterns. Although this has been true for some time, the added power of heuristics and artificial intelligence provides important additional tools for using information.

In summary, the traditional organizational structures and practices do not have to stay the same as we move into the 1990s. All dimensions of the organization will have to be reexamined in light of the power of the new IT. The economics are so powerful and apply to so much of the organization that one has to question everything before accepting the status quo.

MAJOR FINDINGS OF THE RESEARCH

We see six major implications from the research. The first and most basic is that the nature of work is changing.

Finding 1. IT is enabling fundamental changes in the way work is done

The degree to which a person can be affected by the rapid evolution of information technology is determined by how much of the work is based on information – that is, information on what product to make or what service to deliver and how to do it (the production task), as well as when to do it and in conjunction with whom (the coordination task). In many organizations the people in these two categories account for a large proportion of the work force.

IT is available to radically alter the basic cost structure of a wide variety of jobs, jobs affecting at least half the members of the organization. IT is only an enabler, however; to actually change jobs takes a combination of management leadership and employee participation that is, thus far, extremely rare.

We saw change in three kinds of work being enabled by IT in ways that portend the kind of patterns we expect throughout the 1990s.

Production work

The potential impact of IT on production work is considerable. This is most apparent when the nature of production work is broken up into three constituent elements:

1 Physical production affected by robotics (increasingly with 'vision'), process control instrumentation, and intelligent sensors.
2 Information production affected by data processing computers for the standard clerical tasks such as accounts receivable, billing, and payables.
3 Knowledge production affected by CAD/CAM tools for designers; workstations for those building qualitative products such as loans or letters of credit; and workstations for those building 'soft' products such as new legislation or new software. [. . .]

These forms of change are readily understood in the case of physical products and standard information processing but do not seem to be easily grasped and exploited when it comes to knowledge work. As a result, organizations appear to be very slow in exploiting and utilizing technology to increase the effectiveness of knowledge production.

Coordinative work

IT, as it has been defined in this research program, includes six elements, one of which is communications networks. These are currently being installed at a rapid rate by nations and organizations, and we expect this to continue throughout the 1990s. Such networks are being utilized within a building, within an organization, between organizations, and between countries. However, their use has been less than it might be, there is a lack of standards that permit easy connectivity. This situation has begun to improve, and we can expect this improvement to accelerate through the 1990s as the enormous economic benefits to industries and societies become more obvious.

The new IT is permitting a change in the economics and functionality of the coordination process. As a result we can see changes in three areas:

1 Distance can be shrunk toward zero, becoming increasingly irrelevant as far as information flow is concerned. Thus, the location of work can be reexamined, as can potential partners. Even in 1989 leading companies had design teams in different countries working together on a single product.
2 Time can shrink toward zero or shift to a more convenient point. Airline reservation systems are a leading example of IT in a time-critical setting. Organizations located in different time zones yet required to work together are utilizing store-and-forward and common databases as a way to shift time.
3 Organizational memory, as exemplified by a common database, can be maintained over time, contributed to from all parts of the organization, and made available to a wide variety of authorized users.

Beyond memory is the organization's ability to share skills. In a sense, such 'group work', or the utilization of teams, combines the three aspects of coordination: distance, time, and memory. This combined effect has more impact than the three elements by themselves.

This change in the economics and functionality of coordination fundamentally alters all the tasks in an organization that have to do with coordinating the delivery of products and services to customers and the actual production of such goods and services. To the extent that an organization's structure is determined by its coordinative needs, it too is subject to potential change.

Management work

The third IT-enabled change in work is the work done by managers. The principal dimensions of management work that can be most affected are those of direction and control. *Direction*, as used here, is concerned with sensing changes in the external environment and also with staying in close touch with the organization, its members' ideas and reactions to their views of the environment. Relevant, timely information from these two sources can be crucial input to the organization's direction-setting process. This is as true for a sophisticated strategic planning system as for an informal executive support system or customer feedback system.

The *control* dimension of management work has two key aspects for our purposes here. The first is the measurement task, that is, measuring the organization's performance along whatever set of critical success factors has been defined as relevant. The second aspect is to interpret such measures against the plan and determine what actions to take. Effective control is a critical dimension of organizational learning as it feeds back to future direction setting, and both of these can be fundamentally changed by the increasing availability of IT.

Finding 2. IT is enabling the integration of business functions at all levels within and between organizations

The continuing expansion of public and private telecom networks means that the concept of 'any information, at any time, anywhere, and any way I want to look at it, is increasingly economically feasible. The infrastructure to permit this is being put in place by different companies at different rates. Those organizations that have created a significant enterprise-level infrastructure will be able to compete effectively in the 1990s. Additionally, the ability to electronically connect people and tasks within and between firms will be increasingly available and affordable. Boundaries of organizations are becoming more permeable; where work gets done, when, and with whom is changing. This can be a difficult, often revolutionary, move whose impact is blunted by people's unwillingness to exploit the new opportunities. However, in a few situations components are being designed with suppliers in weeks, not months; parts are ordered from suppliers in hours, not weeks; and questions are answered in seconds, not days. This enormous speed-up in the flow of work is made possible by the electronic network. [. . .]

Finding 3. IT is causing shifts in the competitive climate in many industries

At the level of the industry, information technology has a unique impact on the competitive climate and on the degree of interrelatedness of products or services with rivals. This can lead to unprecedented degrees of simultaneous competition and collaboration between firms. This effect of IT is spreading rapidly. For example, parts suppliers that are linked electronically with purchasers for design and manufacturing are not uncommon.

Another illustration is the creation of an electronic linkage between the U.S. Internal Revenue Service (IRS) and tax preparation firms. The linkage was created to enable the electronic filing of individual income tax returns prepared by those firms. This has opened up opportunities for lending or borrowing what is, in aggregate, some $70 billion. This is causing the creation of new arrangements between multiple financial services firms.

The second unique impact of IT on competitiveness concerns the importance of standards. It is now important to know when to support standards and when to try to preempt competitors by establishing a proprietary de facto standard. Every industry has an example. For illustration here, we cite the attempt by the major insurance companies to tie agents to their systems. The general agents retaliated by using the industry association to grow their own network with its open standards to protect themselves.

Understanding the changed nature of one's competitive climate is important in an era of growing IT pervasiveness. [. . .]

It is possible for an organization in the decade of the 1990s to capture benefits. This appears to come from being an early (or different) mover with a business benefit enabled by IT and then investing actively in innovations that continue to increase the benefits to the user of the innovation. In other words, the benefits do not flow from the mere use of IT but arise from the human, organizational, and system innovations that are added on to the original business benefit. IT is merely an enabler that offers an organization the opportunity to vigorously invest in added innovations if it wishes to stay ahead of its competitors.

The empirical fact that existing organizations constantly move – or are moved – to different points in the competitive matrix and that new organizations appear on the competitive horizon adds considerable importance to the functions of scanning and environmental monitoring. Effective scanning of the business environment to understand what is changing is critical if an organization is to proactively manage its way through an environment made additionally turbulent with changes in technology.

Finding 4. IT presents new strategic opportunities for organizations that reassess their missions and operations

A turbulent environment, the changing nature of work, the possibilities of electronic integration, and the changing competitive climate are all compelling reasons for the third stage in the evolution of the organization of the 1990s. In short, *automate* and *informate* set the stage for transformation.

Research during the 1990s program suggests that the three findings just discussed – new ways of doing work, electronic integration, and the shifting competitive climate – present an organization with an opportunity, if not a pressing need, to step back and rethink its mission and the way it is going to conduct its operations.

There appear to be three distinct stages that organizations are going through as they attempt to respond to their changing environments: automate, informate, and transformation.

Automate

IT applications in this stage are designed to take the cost out of 'production'. Savings are usually achieved by reducing the number of workers. For information handlers such as order entry clerks, this can result in effectively being eliminated from the work force. For other production workers, manual operations are replaced by machine actions under computer control. For example, an operator no longer has to change valve settings by hand but instead watches a computer screen and types instructions.

This requires fewer operators with consequent direct cost savings. Beyond process control and automation of traditional paper processing (for example, bank check clearing), IT is being used for automation with the scanner and bar code, the universal product code (UPC). This is now used not only for packaged goods but also for inventory in warehouses and a host of other tracking applications. These kinds of IT tools can give rise to enormous cost reductions.

The new IT tools, used by the 'production' workers who are left after automation, often generate information as a by-product. This is clearly seen in the case of process control where the operators have information from multiple sensors and watch screens and type in instructions. In the automate stage, however, little or no use is made of this new information beyond direct control of the existing process.

Informate

Informate is a term (first coined by Shoshana Zuboff) that describes what happens when automated processes yield information as a by-product.

The informate stage as we saw it in the 1990s program has three distinguishing characteristics. The first is that production work involves new tools that provide information that must be used to get the job done; for example, the operator must read the screen to see if the process is within tolerance. This work can be fairly 'simple', as in monitoring machines, or it can involve complex new skills, such as using a 3–D dynamic color workstation for engineering design. Similarly, the foreign exchange trader working in several markets on a real-time basis has to use a set of computer-based tools that are quite different from the telephone and voice with which the job used to be done. At a more mundane level, a salesperson making a presentation to a potential customer uses financial models to demonstrate the savings on this month's 'deal'. All these knowledge workers are having to develop new skills to work with new information tools. These often involve new ways of thinking.

The second distinguishing characteristic of the informate state is that the new IT tools often generate new sorts of information as a by-product of the basic task. For example, the process control operator might notice that one limit is always exceeded when the weather is hot; the foreign exchange trader may notice that certain accounts are building a position in certain currencies; or the salesperson, by analyzing twelve months of sales data, notices buying patterns in some of the customers. Thus, the process of using the new IT tools develops some by-product information that in turn can require a different kind of conceptual grasp by the person concerned. Thus, 'invisible' work is going on in the worker's mind. This kind of work may require changes in skills and management practices if it is to be used successfully to improve the organization's performance. It requires an ability to see patterns and understand the overall process rather than just looking at controlling the information on the screen. In this situation the production worker becomes an 'analyzer', a role involving a different level of conceptual skill from what was needed before as a 'doer', or machine minder.

The third distinguishing characteristic of the informate stage is that the new skills and information are developed to the point where new market opportunities can be opened up. This may require a broader view of one's job and an identification with the whole organization rather than one's narrow piece of it. For example, American Hospital Supply (AHS) was able to sell the patterns of their customers' buying behavior, detected by the AHS sales force, back to the producer of the original product. The salespeople concerned had noticed that there were patterns with certain kinds of customers. They alerted the management to these patterns and in turn came up with the idea that this would be a valuable by-product that could be sold and thus form the basis for a new business.

Transformation

The changing nature of work does not stop with the informate stage but goes on to the transformation stage. The term *transformation* has been chosen deliberately to reflect the fundamental difference in character exhibited by organizations (or parts of organizations) that have been through the first two stages and have begun on the third.

All successful organizations in the 1990s will have to pass through this stage, a stage characterized by leadership, vision, and a sustained process of organization empowerment so basic as to be exceptionally hard to accomplish. In a way, it can be thought of as the necessary follow-on to 'total quality'. The total quality programs are a uniquely American phenomenon of the late 1980s. They have served as a very useful rallying cry to energize organizations so that they could fix the woefully inadequate practices that had crept into their operations and management procedures. The concept of transformation includes the broad view of quality but goes beyond this to address the unique opportunities presented by the environment and enabled by IT. [...]

Finding 5. Successful application of IT will require changes in management and organizational structure

The 1990s program has shown that information technology is a critical enabler of the re-creation (redefinition) of the organization. This is true in part because it permits the distribution of power, function, and control to wherever they are most effective, given the mission and objectives of the organization and the culture it enjoys.

Organizations have always managed some form of matrix structure, a matrix involving functions, products, markets, and geography in some combination. With the new IT, unit costs of coordination are declining significantly. This means that over the next decade we can afford more coordination for the same dollar cost. In addition, IT is causing changing economies of scale. For example, flexible manufacturing permits smaller organizations to also be low-cost producers. Thus, IT is enabling a breakup, a dis-integration, of traditional organizational forms. [...] IT's ability to affect coordination by shrinking time and distance permits an organization to respond more quickly and accurately to the marketplace. This not only reduces the assets the organization has tied up but improves quality as seen by the customer. [...]

Management has the challenging task of changing the organizational structure and methods of operation to keep it competitive in a dynamically changing world. Research has shown that IT provides one set of tools that can enable such change. However, to think through the new systems and processes so that they can be exploited effectively is a major challenge for line management.

Finding 6. A major challenge for management in the 1990s will be to lead their organizations through the transformation necessary to prosper in the globally competitive environment

Before looking at the findings about organizational transformation, it is useful to provide some context. An organization can be thought of as comprised of five sets of forces in dynamic equilibrium among themselves even as the organization is subjected to influences from an external environment. This is represented in Figure 5.1. In this view, a central task of general management is to ensure that the organization, that is, all five 'forces' (represented by the boxes), moves through time to accomplish the organization's objectives. [...]

The 1990s research has pinpointed some characteristics of the organizations that will be able to successfully go through the transformation

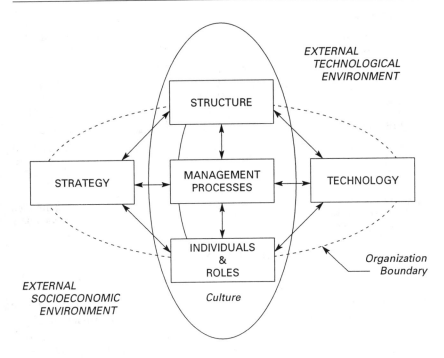

Figure 5.1 The MIT 90s framework

process. The first, and obvious, fact is that none of the potentially beneficial enabling aspects of IT can take place without clarity of business purpose and a vision of what the organization should become. A clear mission visible to, and understood by, the organization is a well-known prerequisite for any major organization change. However, when the issue at hand is organizational transformation, enabled by technology, it appears particularly important to invest a large amount of time and effort in getting the organization to understand where it is going and why. This effort is further complicated by the lack of knowledge and skills, not to say fear, of new technology. There appear to be two other important preconditions of successful transformation. One is that the organization has been through a process of aligning its corporate strategy (business and IT), information technology, and organizational dimensions. The second precondition is that the organization have a robust information technology infrastructure in place, including an electronic network, and understood standards.

Given that there is a vision and an understood view of the business purpose, the challenge in the management of transformation can be summed up in Figure 5.2.

Research suggests that the 'gray ellipse' in Figure 5.1 and the three

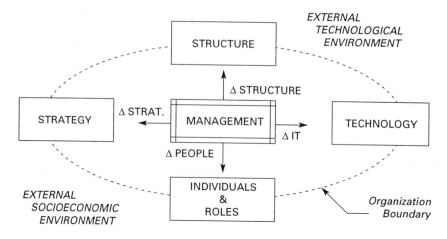

Figure 5.2 The role of management in the change process

forces included, which represent the 'people issues', are critical in the transformation process. One root cause for the lack of impact of IT on the improved economic performance of organizations is an organization's unwillingness to invest heavily and early enough in human resources. Changing the way people work can be extremely threatening and therefore takes a great deal of investment. There must be investment in new skills, in psychological ownership of the change process, and in a safety net under the employee so that there is no fear of taking prudent risks. These investments are required throughout the organization as management itself is part of the required change.

The ultimate goal of this change is to give all employees a sense of empowerment. They need to feel that they can make a difference, that their efforts directly affect the organization's performance, and that they are able to take on as much responsibility and commensurate reward as they are willing to work for. [. . .]

SUMMARY CONCLUSIONS

This introduction has discussed the six major impacts of IT that have emerged from the research carried out by the 1990s program. These can be focused and regrouped to correspond to the five forces in an organization (shown in Figure 5.1) that can be influenced.

Technology

IT will continue to change over the next decade at an annual rate of at least 20 to 30 percent. This will lead to greater shrinkage of time and distance effects, greater interconnectedness, and better organizational memory with greater capture of organization 'rules' (heuristics).

Individuals and roles

People will have new tools with which to work and increasing connectivity to information and other people. Much additional training will be needed to ensure effective use of the tools, and more education will be required to allow individuals to cope with the blurring of boundaries between job categories and tasks.

Structure

As the way work is performed changes, and as coordination costs drop enormously, new organizational structures become possible, as do new ways of working. Ad hoc teams will become more attractive as a way to get jobs done. IT will be a critical enabler of organizational restructuring.

Management processes

Changes induced by IT will cause a redistribution of power and control. In addition, the shrinkage of distance and time effects can cause a speed-up in information flow. Thus, new methods of planning and control will be required, as organizations design ways to cope with a different kind of 'management of interdependence'.

Strategy

IT changes the nature and degree of interrelatedness within an industry and organization. As a result, boundaries blur and new collaborations are possible. However, IT by itself does not provide any sustainable competitive advantage. Such advantage comes from a sustained effort by line management to use IT to get closer to the customer's real needs. This constant flow of innovation and improvement requires vision and implementation skills if it is to be effective.

THE CHALLENGE OF THE 1990s

No impact from information technology is yet visible in the macro-economic data available. A very few individual firms are demonstrably better off, and there is a larger group of isolated examples of successful exploitation in particular individual functions or business units. However, on average the expected benefits are not yet visible.

One major explanation of this lack of impact lies in the enormous strength of historical precedence. The Western economies have had more than half a century of doing business in a certain way. These ways are very hard to discard, and it appears to be harder yet to learn new ones.

Understanding one's organizational culture, and knowing what it means to have an innovative culture, is a key first step in a move toward an adaptive organization. This in turn seems to require innovative human resource policies that support the organization's members as they learn to cope with a changing and more competitive world. To accomplish this successfully is one of the major challenges for an organization in the decade of the 1990s.

REFERENCE

Zuboff, S. 1988. *In the Age of the Smart Machine: The Future of Work and Power.* New York: Basic Books.

Chapter 6

A shrinking world

The growth of transnational corporations and world trade, the scale of international investment, the globalization of industries, the ever more immediate communication links, international migration, the continuing trend towards European integration – all these changes mean more managers (and public officials) than ever before are encountering and working with counterparts brought up in a different culture. Once, and it is embarrassingly recently, Anglo-American managers and management theorists confidently assumed that the management practices they encountered abroad would either be essentially the same as those at home – or they would be inferior. The French (or Germans, Spaniards or Japanese . . .) would doubtless be quaintly Gallic (or Germanic, Mediterranean, Oriental . . .) but underneath it all management was management. It is now clear that this is not the case. Writing for an American audience, Geert Hofstede provides a quick tour of the world, highlighting the extent to which management is embedded in and reflects very different ways of life.

Cultural constraints in management theories

Geert Hofstede

Management as the word is presently used is an American invention. In other parts of the world not only the practices, but the entire concept of management may differ, and the theories needed to understand it, may deviate considerably from what is considered normal and desirable in the USA. [...] In this article we take a trip around the world to demonstrate that there are no such things as universal management theories.

Diversity in management *practices* as we go around the world has been recognized in US management literature for more than thirty years. The term 'comparative management' has been used since the 1960s. However, it has taken much longer for the US academic community to accept that not only practices but also the validity of *theories* may stop at national borders, and I wonder whether even today everybody would agree with this statement. [...]

MANAGEMENT THEORISTS ARE HUMAN

Employees and managers are human. Employees as humans was 'discovered' in the 1930s, with the Human Relations school. Managers as humans, was introduced in the late 1940s by Herbert Simon's 'bounded rationality' and elaborated in Richard Cyert and James March's *Behavioral Theory of the Firm* (1963, and recently re-published in a second edition). My argument is that management scientists, theorists, and writers are human too: they grew up in a particular society in a particular period, and their ideas cannot help but reflect the constraints of their environment.

The idea that the validity of a theory is constrained by national borders is more obvious in Europe, with all its borders, than in a huge borderless country like the US. Already in the sixteenth century Michel de Montaigne, a Frenchman, wrote a statement which was made famous by Blaise Pascal about a century later: '*Vérite en-deça des Pyrenées, erreur au-delà*' – There are truths on this side of the Pyrenées which are falsehoods on the other. [...]

The linguistic origin of the word 'management' is from Latin *manus*, hand, via the Italian *maneggiare*, which is the training of horses in the *manege*; subsequently its meaning was extended to skillful handling in general, like of arms and musical instruments. However, the word also became associated with the French *menage*, household, as an equivalent of 'husbandry' in its sense of the art of running a household. The theatre of present-day management contains elements of both *manege* and *menage* and different managers and cultures may use different accents.

The founder of the science of economics, the Scot Adam Smith, in his 1776 book *The Wealth of Nations*, used 'manage', 'management' (even 'bad management') and 'manager' when dealing with the process and the persons involved in operating joint stock companies (Smith, V.i.e.). British economist John Stuart Mill (1806–1873) followed Smith in this use and clearly expressed his distrust of such hired people who were not driven by ownership. Since the 1880s the word 'management' appeared occasionally in writings by American engineers, until it was canonized as a modern science by Frederick W. Taylor in *Shop Management* in 1903 and in *The Principles of Scientific Management* in 1911.

While Smith and Mill used 'management' to describe a process and 'managers' for the persons involved, 'management' in the American sense – which has since been taken back by the British – refers not only to the process but also to the managers as a class of people. This class

1 does not own a business but sells its skills to act on behalf of the owners and
2 does not produce personally but is indispensable for making others produce, through motivation.

Members of this class carry a high status and many American boys and girls aspire to the role. In the US, the manager is a cultural hero.

Let us now turn to other parts of the world. We will look at management in its context in other successful modern economies: Germany, Japan, France, Holland, and among the Overseas Chinese. Then we will examine management in the much larger part of the world that is still poor, especially South-East Asia and Africa, and in the new political configurations of Eastern Europe, and Russia in particular. We will then return to the U.S. via mainland China.

Germany

The manager is not a cultural hero in Germany. If anybody, it is the engineer who fills the hero role. Frederick Taylor's *Scientific Management* was conceived in a society of immigrants – where large number of workers with diverse backgrounds and skills had to work together. In Germany this heterogeneity never existed.

Elements of the mediaeval guild system have survived in historical continuity in Germany until the present day. In particular, a very effective apprenticeship system exists both on the shop floor and in the office, which alternates practical work and classroom courses. At the end of the apprenticeship the worker receives a certificate, the *Facharbeiterbrief*, which is recognized throughout the country. About two thirds of the German worker population holds such a certificate and a corresponding occupational pride. In fact, quite a few German company presidents have worked their way up from the ranks through an apprenticeship. In comparison, two thirds of the worker population in Britain have no occupational qualification at all.

The highly skilled and responsible German workers do not necessarily need a manager, American-style, to 'motivate' them. They expect their boss or *Meister* to assign their tasks and to be the expert in resolving technical problems. Comparisons of similar German, British, and French organizations show the Germans as having the greatest proportion of personnel in productive roles and the lowest both in leadership and staff roles.

Business schools are virtually unknown in Germany. Native German management theories concentrate on formal systems. The inapplicability of American concepts of management was quite apparent in 1973 when the US consulting firm of Booz, Allen and Hamilton, commissioned by the German Ministry of Economic Affairs, wrote a study of German management from an American view point. The report is highly critical and writes among other things that 'Germans simply do not have a very strong concept of management.' Since 1973, from my personal experience, the situation has not changed much. However, during this period the German economy has performed in a superior fashion to the US in virtually all respects, so a strong concept of management might have been a liability rather than an asset.

Japan

The American type of manager is also missing in Japan. In the United States, the core of the enterprise is the managerial class. The core of the Japanese enterprise is the permanent worker group; workers who for all practical purposes are tenured and who aspire at life-long employment. They are distinct from the non-permanent employees – most women and subcontracted teams led by gang bosses, to be laid off in slack periods. University graduates in Japan first join the permanent worker group and subsequently fill various positions, moving from line to staff as the need occurs while paid according to seniority rather than position. They take part in Japanese-style group consultation sessions for important decisions, which extend the decision-making period but guarantee fast implementation afterwards. Japanese are to a large extent controlled by their peer group rather than by their manager.

Three researchers from the East-West Center of the University of Hawaii, Joseph Tobin, David Wu, and Dana Danielson, did an observation study of typical preschools in three countries: China, Japan, and the United States. Their results have been published both as a book and as a video. In the Japanese preschool, one teacher handled twenty-eight four-year olds. The video shows one particularly obnoxious boy, Hiroki, who fights with other children and throws teaching materials down from the balcony. When a little girl tries to alarm the teacher, the latter answers 'what are you calling me for? Do something about it!' In the US preschool, there is one adult for every nine children. This class has its problem child too, Glen, who refuses to clear away his toys. One of the teachers has a long talk with him and isolates him in a corner, until he changes his mind. It doesn't take much imagination to realize that managing Hiroki thirty years later will be a different process from managing Glen.

American theories of leadership are ill-suited for the Japanese group-controlled situation. During the past two decades, the Japanese have developed their own 'PM' theory of leadership, in which P stands for performance and M for maintenance. The latter is less a concern for individual employees than for maintaining social stability. In view of the amazing success of the Japanese economy in the past thirty years, many Americans have sought for the secrets of Japanese management hoping to copy them.

There are no secrets of Japanese management, however; it is even doubtful whether there is such a thing as management, in the American sense, in Japan at all. The secret is in Japanese society; and if any group in society should be singled out as carriers of the secret, it is the workers, not the managers.

France

The manager, US style, does not exist in France either. In a very enlightening book, unfortunately not yet translated into English, the French researcher Philippe d'Iribarne (1989) describes the results of in-depth observation and interview studies of management methods in three subsidiary plants of the same French multinational: in France, the United States, and Holland. He relates what he finds to information about the three societies in general. Where necessary, he goes back in history to trace the roots of the strikingly different behaviors in the completion of the same tasks. He identifies three kinds of basic principles (*logiques*) of management. In the USA, the principle is the fair *contract* between employer and employee, which gives the manager considerable prerogatives, but within its limits. This is really a labor *market* in which the worker sells his or her labor for a price. In France, the principle is the *honor* of each class in a society which has always been and remains extremely stratified, in which superiors behave as superior beings and subordinates accept and expect this, conscious of their own lower level in the national hierarchy but also of the honor of their own class. The French do not think in terms of managers versus nonmanagers but in terms of *cadres* versus *non-cadres*; one becomes cadre by attending the proper schools and one remains it forever; regardless of their actual task, cadres have the privileges of a higher social class, and it is very rare for a non-cadre to cross the ranks.

The conflict between French and American theories of management became apparent in the beginning of the twentieth century, in a criticism by the great French management pioneer Henri Fayol (1841–1925) of his U.S. colleague and contemporary Frederick W. Taylor (1856–1915). The difference in career paths of the two men is striking. Fayol was a French engineer whose career as a *cadre supérieur* culminated in the position of Président-Directeur-Général of a mining company. After his retirement he formulated his experiences in a pathbreaking text on organization: *Administration industrielle et générale*, in which he focussed on the sources of authority. Taylor was an American engineer who started his career in industry as a worker and attained his academic qualifications through evening studies. From chief engineer in a steel company, he became one of the first management consultants. Taylor was not really concerned with the issue of authority at all; his focus was on efficiency. He proposed to split the task of the first-line boss into eight specialisms, each exercised by a different person; an idea which eventually led to the idea of a matrix organization.

Taylor's work appeared in a French translation in 1913, and Fayol read it and showed himself generally impressed but shocked by Taylor's 'denial of the principle of the Unity of Command' in the case of the eight-boss-system.

Seventy years later André Laurent, another of Fayol's compatriots, found that French managers in a survey reacted very strongly against a suggestion that one employee could report to two different bosses, while U.S. managers in the same survey showed fewer misgivings. Matrix organization has never become popular in France as it has in the United States.

Holland

In my own country, Holland or as it is officially called, the Netherlands, the study by Philippe d'Iribarne found the management principle to be a need for *consensus* among all parties, neither predetermined by a contractual relationship nor by class distinctions, but based on an open-ended exchange of views and a balancing of interests. In terms of the different origins of the word 'manager', the organization in Holland is more *menage* (household) while in the United States it is more *manege* (horse drill).

At my university, the University of Limburg at Maastricht, every semester we receive a class of American business students who take a program in European Studies. We asked both the Americans and a matched group of Dutch students to describe their ideal job after graduation, using a list of twenty-two job characteristics. The Americans attached significantly more importance than the Dutch to earnings, advancement, benefits, a good working relationship with their boss, and security of employment. The Dutch attached more importance to freedom to adopt their own approach to the job, being consulted by their boss in his or her decisions, training opportunities, contributing to the success of their organization, fully using their skills and abilities, and helping others. This list confirms d'Iribarne's findings of a contractual employment relationship in the United States, based on earnings and career opportunities, against a consensual relationship in Holland. The latter has centuries-old roots; the Netherlands were the first republic in Western Europe (1609–1810), and a model for the American republic. The country has been and still is governed by a careful balancing of interests in a multi-party system.

In terms of management theories, both motivation and leadership in Holland are different from what they are in the United States. Leadership in Holland presupposes modesty, as opposed to assertiveness in the United States. No US leadership theory has room for that. Working in Holland is not a constant feast, however. There is a built-in premium on mediocrity and jealousy, as well as time-consuming ritual consultations to maintain the apparence of consensus and the pretence of modesty. There is unfortunately another side to every coin.

The overseas Chinese

Among the champions of economic development in the past thirty years we find three countries mainly populated by Chinese living outside the Chinese mainland: Taiwan, Hong Kong and Singapore. Moreover, overseas Chinese play a very important role in the economies of Indonesia, Malaysia, the Philippines and Thailand, where they form an ethnic minority. If anything, the little dragons – Taiwan, Hong Kong and Singapore – have been more economically successful than Japan, moving from rags to riches and now counted among the world's wealthy industrial countries. Yet very little attention has been paid to the way in which their enterprises have been managed. *The Spirit of Chinese Capitalism* by Gordon Redding (1990), the British dean of the Hong Kong Business School, is an excellent book about Chinese business. He bases his insights on personal acquaintance and in-depth discussions with a large number of overseas Chinese businesspeople.

Overseas Chinese American enterprises lack almost all characteristics of modern management. They tend to be small, cooperating for essential functions with other small organizations through networks based on personal relations. They are family-owned, without the separation between ownership and management typical in the West, or even in Japan and Korea. They normally focus on one product or market, with growth by opportunistic diversification; in this, they are extremely flexible. Decision making is centralized in the hands of one dominant family member, but other family members may be given new ventures to try their skills on. They are low-profile and extremely cost-conscious, applying Confucian virtues of thrift and persistence. Their size is kept small by the assumed lack of loyalty of non-family employees, who, if they are any good, will just wait and save until they can start their own family business.

Overseas Chinese prefer economic activities in which great gains can be made with little manpower, like commodity trading and real estate. They employ few professional managers, except their sons and sometimes daughters who have been sent to prestigious business schools abroad, but who upon return continue to run the family business the Chinese way.

The origin of this system, or – in the Western view – this lack of system, is found in the history of Chinese society, in which there were no formal laws, only formal networks of powerful people guided by general principles of Confucian virtue. The favors of the authorities could change daily, so nobody could be trusted except one's kinfolk – of whom, fortunately, there used to be many, in an extended family structure. The overseas Chinese way of doing business is also very well adapted to their position in the countries in which they form ethnic minorities, often envied and threatened by ethnic violence.

Overseas Chinese businesses following this unprofessional approach command a collective gross national product of some 200 to 300 billion US dollars, exceeding the GNP of Australia. There is no denying that it works.

MANAGEMENT TRANSFER TO POOR COUNTRIES

Four-fifths of the world population live in countries that are not rich but poor. After World War II and decolonization, the stated purpose of the United Nations and the World Bank has been to promote the development of all the world's countries in a war on poverty. After forty years it looks very much like we are losing this war. If one thing has become clear, it is that the export of Western – mostly American – management practices *and* theories to poor countries has contributed little to nothing to their development. There has been no lack of effort and money spent for this purpose: students from poor countries have been trained in America, and teachers and Peace Corps workers have been sent to the poor countries. If nothing else, the general lack of success in economic development of other countries should be sufficient argument to doubt the validity of Western management theories in non-Western environments.

If we examine different parts of the world, the development picture is not equally bleak, and history is often a better predictor than economic factors for what happens today. There is a broad regional pecking order with East Asia leading. The little dragons have passed into the camp of the wealthy; then follow South-East Asia (with its overseas Chinese minorities), Latin America (in spite of the debt crisis), South Asia, and Africa always trails behind. Several African countries have only become poorer since decolonization.

Regions of the world with a history of large-scale political integration and civilization generally have done better than regions in which no large-scale political and cultural infrastructure existed, even if the old civilizations had decayed or been suppressed by colonizers. It has become painfully clear that development cannot be pressure-cooked; it presumes a cultural infrastructure that takes time to grow. Local management is part of this infrastructure; it cannot be imported in package form. Assuming that with so-called modern management techniques and theories outsiders can develop a country has proven a deplorable arrogance. At best, one can hope for a dialogue between equals with the locals, in which the Western partner acts as the expert in Western technology and the local partner as the expert in local culture, habits, and feelings.

Russia and China

The crumbling of the former Eastern bloc has left us with a scattering of states and would-be states of which the political and economic future is extremely uncertain. The best predictions are those based on a knowledge of history, because historical trends have taken revenge on the arrogance of the Soviet rulers who believed they could turn them around by brute power. One obvious fact is that the former bloc is extremely heterogeneous, including countries traditionally closely linked with the West by trade and travel, like the Czech Republic, Hungary, Slovenia, and the Baltic states, as well as others with a Byzantine or Turkish past; some having been prosperous, others always extremely poor.

The industrialized Western world and the World Bank seem committed to helping the ex-Eastern bloc countries develop, but with the same technocratic neglect for local cultural factors that proved so unsuccessful in the development assistance to other poor countries. Free market capitalism, introduced by Western-style management, is supposed to be the answer from Albania to Russia.

Let me limit myself to the Russian republic, a huge territory with some 140 million inhabitants, mainly Russians. We know quite a bit about the Russians as their country was a world power for several hundreds of years before communism, and in the nineteenth century it has produced some of the greatest writers in world literature. If I want to understand the

Russians – including how they could so long support the Soviet regime – I tend to re-read Lev Nikolayevich Tolstoy. In his most famous novel *Anna Karenina* (1876), one of the main characters is a landowner, Levin, whom Tolstoy uses to express his own views and convictions about his people. Russian peasants used to be serfs; serfdom had been abolished in 1861, but the peasants, now tenants, remained as passive as before. Levin wanted to break this passivity by dividing the land among his peasants in exchange for a share of the crops; but the peasants only let the land deteriorate further. Here follows a quote:

> (Levin) read political economy and socialistic works ... but, as he had expected, found nothing in them related to his undertaking. In the political economy books – in (John Stuart) Mill, for instance, whom he studied first and with great ardour, hoping every minute to find an answer to the questions that were engrossing him – he found only certain laws deduced from the state of agriculture in Europe; but he could not for the life of him see why these laws, which did not apply to Russia, should be considered universal. ... Political economy told him that the laws by which Europe had developed and was developing her wealth were universal and absolute. Socialist teaching told him that development along those lines leads to ruin. And neither of them offered the smallest enlightenment as to what he, Levin, and all the Russian peasants and landowners were to do with their millions of hands and millions of acres, to make them as productive as possible for the common good.

In the summer of 1991, the Russian lands yielded a record harvest, but a large share of it rotted in the fields because no people were to be found for harvesting. The passivity is still there, and not only among the peasants. And the heirs of John Stuart Mill (whom we met before as one of the early analysts of 'management') again present their universal recipes which simply do not apply.

Citing Tolstoy, I implicitly suggest that management theorists cannot neglect the great literature of the countries they want their ideas to apply to. The greatest novel in the Chinese literature is considered Cao Xuequin's *The Story of the Stone*, also known as *The Dream of the Red Chamber* which appeared around 1760. It describes the rise and fall of two branches of an aristocratic family in Beijing, who live in adjacent plots in the capital. Their plots are joined by a magnificent garden with several pavillions in it, and the young, mostly female members of both families are allowed to live in them. One day the management of the garden is taken over by a young woman, Tan-Chun, who states:

> I think we ought to pick out a few experienced trust-worthy old women from among the ones who work in the Garden – women who know

something about gardening already – and put the upkeep of the Garden into their hands. We needn't ask them to pay us rent; all we need ask them for is an annual share of the produce. There would be four advantages in this arrangement. In the first place, if we have people whose sole occupation is to look after trees and flowers and so on, the condition of the Garden will improve gradually year after year and there will be no more of those long periods of neglect followed by bursts of feverish activity when things have been allowed to get out of hand. Secondly there won't be the spoiling and wastage we get at present. Thirdly the women themselves will gain a little extra to add to their incomes which will compensate them for the hard work they put in throughout the year. And fourthly, there's no reason why we shouldn't use the money we should otherwise have spent on nurserymen, rockery specialists, horticultural cleaners and so on for other purposes.

As the story goes on, the capitalist privatization – because that is what it is – of the Garden is carried through, and it works. When in the 1980s Deng Xiaoping allowed privatization in the Chinese villages, it also worked. It worked so well that its effects started to be felt in politics and threatened the existing political order; hence the knockdown at Tienanmen Square of June 1989. But it seems that the forces of privatization are getting the upper hand again in China. If we remember what Chinese entrepreneurs are able to do once they have become Overseas Chinese, we shouldn't be too surprised. But what works in China – and worked two centuries ago – does not have to work in Russia, not in Tolstoy's days and not today. I am not offering a solution; I only protest against a naive universalism that knows only one recipe for development, the one supposed to have worked in the United States.

A THEORY OF CULTURE IN MANAGEMENT

Our trip around the world is over and we are back in the United States. What have we learned? There is something in all countries called 'management', but its meaning differs to a larger or smaller extent from one country to the other, and it takes considerable historical and cultural insight into local conditions to understand its processes, philosophies, and problems. If already the word may mean so many different things, how can we expect one country's theories of management to apply abroad? One should be extremely careful in making this assumption, and test it before considering it proven. Management is not a phenomenon that can be isolated from other processes taking place in a society. During our trip around the world we saw that it interacts with what happens in the family, at school, in politics, and government. It is obviously also related to religion and to beliefs about science. Theories of management always had to be interdisciplinary, but if we cross national borders they should become more interdisciplinary than ever. [. . .]

The American culture profile is reflected in American management theories. I will just mention three elements not necessarily present in other countries: the stress on market processes, the stress on the individual, and the focus on managers rather than on workers.

The stress on market processes

During the 1970s and 80s it has become fashionable in the United States to look at organizations from a 'transaction costs' viewpoint. The economist Oliver Williamson has opposed 'hierarchies' to 'markets'. The reasoning is that human social life consists of economic transactions between individuals. We found the same in d'Iribarne's description of the US principle of the contract between employer and employee, the labor market in which the worker sells his or her labor for a price. These individuals will form hierarchical organizations when the cost of the economic transactions (such as getting information, finding out whom to trust etc.) is lower in a hierarchy than when all transactions would take place on a free market.

From a cultural perspective the important point is that *the 'market' is the point of *departure* or *base model*, and the organization is explained from market failure. A culture that produces such a theory is likely to prefer organizations that internally resemble markets to organizations that internally resemble more structured models, like those in Germany or France. The ideal principle of control in organizations in the market philosophy is *competition* between individuals. [. . .]

The stress on the individual

I find this constantly in the design of research projects and hypotheses; also in the fact that in the US psychology is clearly a more respectable discipline in management circles than sociology. Culture, however, is a collective phenomenon. Although we may get our information about culture from individuals, we have to interpret it at the level of collectivities.
[. . .]
Culture can be compared to a forest, while individuals are trees. A forest is not just a bunch of trees: it is a symbiosis of different trees, bushes, plants, insects, animals and micro-organisms, and we miss the essence of the forest if we only describe its most typical trees. In the same way, a culture cannot be satisfactorily described in terms of the characteristics of a typical individual. There is a tendency in the US management literature

to overlook the forest for the trees and to ascribe cultural differences to interactions among individuals.

A striking example is found in the otherwise excellent book *Organizational Culture and Leadership* by Edgar H. Schein (1985). On the basis of his consulting experience he compares two large companies, nicknamed 'Action' and 'Multi'. He explains the differences in culture between these companies by the group dynamics in their respective boardrooms. Nowhere in the book are any conclusions drawn from the fact that the first company is an American-based computer firm, and the second a Swiss-based pharmaceutical firm. This information is not even mentioned. A stress on interactions among individuals obviously fits a culture identified as the most individualistic in the world, but it will not be so well understood by the four-fifths of the world population for whom the group prevails over the individual.

One of the conclusions of my own multilevel research has been that culture at the national level and culture at the organizational level – corporate culture – are two very different phenomena and that the use of a common term for both is confusing. If we do use the common term, we should also pay attention to the occupational and the gender level of culture. National cultures differ primarily in the fundamental, invisible values held by a majority of their members, acquired in early childhood, whereas organizational cultures are a much more superficial phenomenon residing mainly in the visible practices of the organization, acquired by socialization of the new members who join as young adults. National cultures change only very slowly if at all; organizational cultures may be consciously changed, although this isn't necessarily easy. This difference between the two types of culture is the secret of the existence of multinational corporations that employ, as I showed in the IBM case, employees with extremely different national cultural values. What keeps them together is a corporate culture based on common practices.

The stress on managers rather than workers

The core element of a work organization around the world is the people who do the work. All the rest is superstructure, and I hope to have demonstrated to you that it may take many different shapes. In the US literature on work organization, however, the core element, if not explicitly then implicitly, is considered to be the manager. This may well be the result of the combination of extreme individualism with fairly strong masculinity, which has turned the manager into a culture hero of almost mythical proportions. For example, he – not really she – is supposed to make decisions all the time. Those of you who are or have been managers must know that this is a fable. Very few management decisions are just 'made' as the myth suggests it. Managers are much more involved in maintaining networks; if anything, it is the rank-and-file worker who can really make decisions on his or her own, albeit on a relatively simple level.

An amusing effect of the US focus on managers is that in at least ten American books and articles on management I have been misquoted as having studied IBM *managers* in my research, whereas the book clearly describes that the answers were from IBM *employees*. My observation may be biased, but I get the impression that compared to twenty or thirty years ago less research in this country is done among employees and more on managers. But managers derive their *raison d'être* from the people managed: culturally, they are the followers of the people they lead, and their effectiveness depends on the latter. In other parts of the world, this exclusive focus on the manager is less strong, with Japan as the supreme example.

CONCLUSION

[. . .]

The management theorist who ventures outside his or her own country into other parts of the world is like Alice in Wonderland. He or she will meet strange beings, customs, ways of organizing or disorganizing and theories that are clearly stupid, old-fashioned or even immoral – yet they may work, or at least they may not fail more frequently than corresponding theories do at home. Then, after the first culture shock, the traveller to Wonderland will feel enlightened, and may be able to take his or her experiences home and use them advantageously. All great ideas in science, politics and management have travelled from one country to another, and been enriched by foreign influences.

Part II

Emergent concepts and issues

Chapter 7

High involvement organizations

As organizations changed, shaped by new ideas and new environmental pressures, some writers pointed to the emergence of a particular class of organization known as *High Involvement Organisations* (e.g. Walton, 1985; Lawler, 1986). Such organizations set out to secure very high levels of employee involvement by giving individuals unusual degrees of self-management designed to achieve very demanding business objectives. Even if relatively few organizations possess all the characteristics of High Involvement Organizations as strictly defined, many others now have areas and units with heightened individual responsibility. More is expected, and with broader, shifting and more loosely defined roles, staff at all levels have to join in, often making work central to their lives. The expression 'it's not so much a job, more a way of life' is becoming less of a quip, and more a description of people's work.

Managing in such contexts presents new challenges, two of which are considered in the following articles. First Bowen *et al.* argue that recruitment for high-involvement work cannot be conducted in the conventional way – as if staff were being recruited for traditional, well defined jobs. They suggest that high involvement organizations have evolved a fundamentally different approach to recruitment, one with far-reaching implications.

Staff and managers in high involvement organizations are liable to experience higher levels of stress though obviously stress, can and does arise in other contexts too. In the second article in this chapter, Daniels asks whether managers should care about stress, and reviews recent thinking on the ways of managing occupational stress.

References

Walton, R. E. (1985) 'From control to commitment in the workplace' *Harvard Business Review* March–April, pp. 76–84.
Lawler, E. E. (1986) *High Involvement Management*. San Francisco: Josey Bass.

Hiring for the organization, not the job

David E. Bowen, Gerald E. Ledford, Jr. and Barry R. Nathan

Conventional selection practices are geared toward hiring employees whose knowledge, skills, and abilities (KSAs) provide the greatest fit with clearly defined requirements of specific jobs. Traditional selection techniques rarely consider characteristics of the organization in which the jobs reside. Traditional techniques also ignore characteristics of the person that are irrelevant to immediate job requirements. In common management parlance, the organization hires new 'hands' or new 'heads' – that is, parts of people.

A new model of selection is emerging, however, that is geared toward hiring a 'whole' person who will fit well into the specific organization's culture. It reflects a fundamental reorientation of the selection process toward hiring 'people', not just KSAs, for 'organizations', not just jobs. This leads to hiring practices that seem peculiar, and needlessly extravagant, from a traditional human resource standpoint. Consider the hiring practices of three different organizations.

- AFG Industries builds two new float glass plants. The plants use practices such as work teams, extensive training, and skill-based pay that create a high level of employee involvement. The hiring process for factory workers includes screening formal CVs (not job applications), personality testing, pre-employment training that simulates some plant jobs, interviews with panels of managers and/or employees, and a medical exam.

- Sun Microsystems is the fastest-growing US company in the past five years, with annual growth averaging more than 100 percent. Filling open jobs is critical to Sun's effectiveness, phenomenal growth, and profitability. Yet, the hiring process is extremely time-consuming and labor-intensive. Potential hires at all levels are brought into the organization from four to seven times for interviews with up to twenty interviewers. The process is full of ambiguity, lacks formal rules, and demands that all employees engage in problem solving to get themselves hired.

- Toyota (USA) screens 50,000 applications for 3,000 factory jobs in the initial staffing of its plant in Georgetown, Kentucky. Each employee hired invests at least eighteen hours in a selection process that includes a general knowledge exam, a test of attitudes toward work, an interpersonal skills assessment center, a manufacturing exercise designed to provide a realistic job preview of assembly work, an extensive personal interview, and a physical exam.

As we shall see, these organizations adopt unusual hiring practices to find employees who fit the *organization* and to encourage those who do not fit to seek employment elsewhere. Although potential hires with skills that meet the demands of specific jobs are not ignored, these companies maintain that the person-job fit needs to be supported and enriched by person-organization fit. These companies are willing to invest substantial resources in rigorously assessing this fit. Why and how organizations approach hiring in this way are explored in this article.

[. . .]

THE NEW SELECTION MODEL: HIRING FOR PERSON-ORGANIZATION FIT

Figure 7.1 presents in the new selection model for hiring for person-organization fit. As we shall see, it differs from the traditional selection model in several important ways. Our model represents a synthesis of the steps taken by the organizations mentioned in our opening case examples as well as by other progressive firms. Although any one firm may not fully implement every step, all of these steps together offer the best guarantee of person-organization fit.

We will describe the steps in the model and then present a case description of a firm where hiring practices are a close match to the ideal. First, however, we clarify the meaning of 'person-organization fit'.

Person-organization fit

The model in Figure 7.1 places the selection process in the context of a rich interaction between the person and the organization, both of which are more broadly defined and assessed than in the traditional selection model.

Person-organization fit requires that two types of fit be achieved in the hiring process:

1 between the KSAs of the individual and the task demands or critical requirements for the job; and
2 between the overall personality of the individual (e.g. needs, interests, and values) and the climate or culture of the organization.

1	ASSESS THE OVERALL WORK ENVIRONMENT
	– Job analysis
	– Organizational analysis

$\downarrow$

2	INFER THE TYPE OF PERSON REQUIRED
	– Technical knowledge, skills and abilities
	– Social skills
	– Personal needs, values, and interests
	– Personality traits

$\downarrow$

3	DESIGN "RITES OF PASSAGE" FOR ORGANIZATION ENTRY THAT ALLOW BOTH THE ORGANIZATION AND THE APPLICANT TO ASSESS THEIR FIT
	– Tests of cognitive, motor, and interpersonal abilities
	– Interviews by potential co-workers and others
	– Personality tests
	– Realistic job previews, including work samples

$\downarrow$

4	REINFORCE PERSON–ORGANIZATION FIT AT WORK
	– Reinforce skills and knowledge through task design and training
	– Reinforce personal orientation through organization design

Figure 7.1 A hiring process for person–organization fit

The traditional selection model focuses almost exclusively on the first type of fit (KSAs – job) while tending to ignore, or assessing far less rigorously, the second type (personality – climate/culture).[1] The narrow focus of the traditional selection model reflects several factors. One is that managers tend to think of individual job performance as the key outcome of the hiring process and they believe that job performance is a function of the fit between KSAs and task demands. Additionally, the traditional selection model is more concerned with finding new employees than with retaining them. There is less attention to whether the whole person finds the organization's culture satisfying enough to stay. Organizations have also been constrained by the unavailability of proven selection technologies for producing the fit between personality and climate/culture. This situation can be improved, we believe, by following the steps for hiring that are described next.

Step one: assess the work environment

The job analysis of the traditional model of selection is also conducted in the new model. It remains instrumental in achieving the fit between individual KSAs and task demands. Alternative job analysis techniques include the position analysis questionnaire, task inventories, and critical incident techniques.

The purpose of an organizational analysis is to define and assess the work environment in terms of the characteristics of the organization, rather than just in terms of the characteristics of a specific job. It identifies the behaviors and responsibilities that lead to organizational effectiveness, and implies the personal characteristics most likely to be associated with such behaviors and responsibilities. Organizational analysis also is important because job analysis data may quickly become outdated as rapidly changing products and technologies reshape employees' jobs. The organization's overall philosophy and values are likely to be more stable and consequently, the more important long-term focus for fit.

Techniques for organizational analysis are not well-established, largely because there is little research that systematically associates the characteristics of organizations and individual behavior patterns. Managers need to identify the important dimensions of the organization and their implications for the kinds of employees who would best fit those situations. Although organizational analysis techniques are not nearly as well-developed as job analysis techniques, a variety of methods are available. For example, the training field offers guidelines for conducting an organizational analysis as one component of a training needs analysis. Organization characteristics assessed include short- and long-term goals, staffing needs, properties of the environment (for example, stability), and employee perceptions of organization climate. Organizational culture audits have emerged in the last decade that offer both qualitative and quantitative methods for describing an organization's norms and values.[2]
[. . .]

Organization analysis does not replace job analysis. Rather it ensures that important components of the work *context* as well as its content are identified and evaluated for their importance to job success. While many job analyses include evaluations of the work context, the person-organization fit model explicitly recognizes that successful employees have knowledge, skills, abilities, and other personal characteristics that match both the *content* and the *context* of the job.

Step two: infer the type of person required

In step two, managers deal with applicants in terms of who they are, not just what they can do. It is still necessary to infer from the job analysis the KSAs that employees need to be technically competent. However, step two also requires inferring, from the organizational analysis, the needs, values and interests – that is, the personality – an employee must possess to be an effective member of the organization. For example, if the organizational analysis reveals that teamwork is a key norm or value in the setting, then selection tools must be used to find people who are team players. Furthermore, social and interpersonal skills will be necessary, in addition to the cognitive and motor abilities that are the dominant skills-focus of the traditional selection model. [. . .]

Organizations also must pay attention to technical skills needed by the organization. Often applicants with the most appropriate personalities and social skills are not those with the right technical skills. If the organization faces the need to upgrade technical skills quickly, it may be forced to make tradeoffs. Organizations in this situation often place greater weight on personality and social skills, on the grounds that it is easier to train technical skills than change personalities or develop social skills. This can lead to increased short-term training costs and temporary overstaffing. However, if the work technology is complex and training times are long, management may be forced to hire some employees who better fit the organization's technical requirements than its cultural requirements. [. . .]

Step three: design 'rites of passage' that allow the organization and the individual to assess fit

The battery of screens used in the new approach to hiring may seem designed to discourage individuals from taking the job. Yet, these screens have several purposes. First, the use of multiple screening methods, raters, and criteria has long been recommended by researchers as the best approach to hiring. Yet most organizations still hire employees using a single interview with a single interviewer. More sophisticated techniques, if used, typically are reserved for executives and sometimes sales people. Second, multiple screenings not only allow the organization to select employees, but also provide applicants with sufficient realistic information about the work environment so that they can make an informed choice about whether they even want the job. Third, the people who join the organization feel special. They have survived the elaborate rites of passage necessary to join the organization. They experience the sense of accomplishment associated with completing boot camp when entering military service. [. . .]

Sun Microsystems offers a good example of the use of rites of passage to allow mutual assessment of fit. This fast-growing Silicon Valley firm, like many high-technology companies, is constantly changing in response to rapidly developing markets, evolving technologies, and the pace of internal growth. Employees who prefer clear job descriptions, stability, a leisurely pace, and predictability would be unhappy at Sun. The hiring process is such a challenge, and so full of ambiguity, that unsuitable applicants tend to give up before the process is completed. Those hired have survived multiple interviews with many different possible co-workers. A joke at Sun is, 'after seven sets of interviews, we put applicants on the payroll whether they've been hired or not'. The hiring process thus introduces prospective employees to the culture of the organization.

Realistic job previews (RJPs) provide applicants with information about organizations. Examples of RJPs are the Toyota USA job simulations/work sample tests that show applicants the repetitive nature of manufacturing work and the requirements for teamwork. Applicants can then make informed choices about whether they would be satisfied there. 'Turned-off' applicants may drop out of the hiring process. Those hired are more likely to join the organization with a sense of commitment and realistic expectations. Fundamentally, an RJP helps individuals decide if they want to join an organization, based on their own assessment of their personality and how it might fit with a particular type of organization.

Step four: reinforce person-organization fit at work

Selection is clearly the first and, arguably, the most important step in implementing a fragile system philosophy. However, the hiring process must be integrated with, and supported by, the firm's other human resource management practices. Japanese-owned plants in the U.S. and high involvement organizations illustrate this point.

Japanese automobile manufacturers operating in the United States provide examples of how to accomplish this. The Japanese 'Auto Alley' in the U.S. provided more than 6,000 assembly jobs in 1989. Key operations include Nissan in Smyrna, Tennessee; Toyota in Georgetown, Kentucky; Honda in Marysville, Ohio; Mazda in Flat Rock, Michigan; and Diamond-Star Motors Corporation in Normal, Illinois. The Japanese have attempted to create a certain type of organization, characterized by now-familiar values of teamwork, consensual decision-making, peer control, egalitarianism, and non-specialized career paths. Broad job classifications encourage employee flexibility, rather than identification with specific jobs. Extensive on-the-job training and job rotation further increase flexibility. Group activities encourage employees to contribute ideas for organizational improvement and promote teamwork. Employment stability helps the organization realize a return on its training and other investments in human resources, and increases employee loyalty to the organization. Thus, a selection system in such organizations typically screens for interest in work variety, social needs and skills, and organization commitment. [. . .]

```
┌─────────────────────────────────────────────────────────────────┐
│ POTENTIAL BENEFITS                                                │
│ 1  MORE FAVORABLE EMPLOYEE ATTITUDES (SUCH AS GREATER JOB         │
│    SATISFACTION, ORGANIZATION COMMITMENT, AND TEAM SPIRIT)        │
│ 2  MORE DESIRABLE INDIVIDUAL BEHAVIORS (SUCH AS BETTER JOB        │
│    PERFORMANCE AND LOWER ABSENTEEISM AND TURNOVER)                │
│ 3  REINFORCEMENT OF ORGANIZATIONAL DESIGN (SUCH AS SUPPORT FOR    │
│    WORK DESIGN AND DESIRED ORGANIZATIONAL CULTURE)                │
│                                                                   │
│ POTENTIAL PROBLEMS                                                │
│ 1  GREATER INVESTMENT OF RESOURCES IN THE HIRING PROCESS          │
│ 2  RELATIVELY UNDEVELOPED AND UNPROVEN SUPPORTING SELECTION       │
│    TECHNOLOGY                                                     │
│ 3  INDIVIDUAL STRESS                                              │
│ 4  MAY BE DIFFICULT TO USE THE FULL MODEL WHERE PAYOFFS ARE GREATEST│
│ 5  LACK OF ORGANIZATIONAL ADAPTATION                              │
└─────────────────────────────────────────────────────────────────┘
```

Figure 7.2 Potential benefits and problems with hiring for person–organization fit

BENEFITS AND PROBLEMS FROM HIRING FOR PERSON-ORGANIZATION FIT

Clearly, the new approach to hiring for person-organization fit requires more resources than the traditional selection model. Is it worth the cost? Consider the potential benefits (see Figure 7.2).

1 *Employee attitudes.* Researchers have long proposed that a fit between individual needs and organizational climates and cultures would result in greater job satisfaction and organization commitment. There is ample data documenting that the realistic job previews typically used in the new selection model are associated with higher on-the-job satisfaction.[3] Greater team spirit also is likely when new employees have shared the experience of moving successfully through the demanding rites of passage that lead to organizational entry. [. . .]

2 *Employee behaviors.* Studies indicate that high involvement organizations, which typically use the new selection model, have low rates of absenteeism, turnover, and grievances. The data are even clearer that using realistic job previews in Step 3 is associated with lower turnover. We also have presented a strong case that person-organization fit will result in employees displaying more of what have been labelled 'organizational citizenship behaviors.' These are behaviors that employees perform above and beyond explicit job requirements. The thinking here is that fitted employees see themselves as really belonging to the organization and willing to invest their own resources in its on-going maintenance.

3 *Reinforcement of organization design.* [...] Researchers often argue that the power of such an organization derives from the mutual reinforcement of its parts, including the selection process. The hiring process helps select employees who are interested in challenging, responsible, varied jobs and pay systems that reward needed behaviors and performance.

Potential problems

Hiring for person-organization fit may also have its disadvantages (see Figure 7.2):

1 *Greater investment in hiring.* This model requires a much greater investment of resources in the hiring process. For example, Mazda in Flat Rock, Michigan, spends about $13,000 per employee to staff its plant. It appears that organizations hiring within this model are spending the same time and money on hiring an assembly worker as they do in conducting an executive search.

  The costs of making revisions in the hiring process are also different in the new model. A traditional hiring process needs to be revised whenever the requirements of the job change significantly. A hiring process for person-organization fit needs to be changed whenever the business, technological, or cultural requirements of the organization change significantly. This means that changes in hiring practices for person-organization fit are likely to be less frequent but much greater in scope than changes in traditional hiring processes. A change in hiring practices for person-organization fit may well involve a change in how every new employee is hired.

2 *Undeveloped selection technology.* The supporting selection technology is still relatively undeveloped and unproven. One problem is the still-thin track record of successfully validating personality tests against job performance. However, the present authors' study in which measures of growth needs and social needs predicted candidates' performance in a pre-employment simulation of high-involvement work demonstrates that personality measures, carefully chosen and developed, can be validated. Yet until personality tests acquire a deeper inventory of successful validation studies, organizations will doubt their usefulness.

  In the context of person-organization fit, techniques for assessing people are more developed than those for assessing work environments. Even on the people side, though, the field is not nearly as sophisticated in measuring work-related personality facets as it is in assessing KSAs. Moreover, there is a great need for techniques of organizational analysis that are as sophisticated as those for job analysis (e.g., the Position Analysis Questionnaire). Overall, the challenge in organizational analysis is to: (a) identify relevant underlying dimensions of settings and how they can be measured, (b) determine the major impact on individual attitudes and behaviors, and organizational effectiveness, and (c) determine how such impacts differ depending upon individuals' personality. [. . .]

3 *Employee stress.* Individuals fitted to 'fragile systems' may find their organizational lives to be more stressful. The firms in the Japanese Auto Alley, high-involvement organizations, firms in Silicon Valley, and so on, which rely on carefully selected people for system effectiveness are also laying substantial claims to those people's lives. This higher level of involvement at work may be associated with experiencing more stress on the job. These workers have reported that they now take work problems home with them and feel the strains more typically associated with managerial roles.[4]

4 *Difficult to use the full model where the benefits are greatest.* A new hiring model may offer the greatest potential benefits to new organizations, such as new plants and startup companies. This is because hiring the right kinds of employees can help establish the desired culture of the organization from the very beginning. In existing organizations that are attempting to change their culture, there may be a long period in which the proportion of employees with unwanted attributes drops through attrition, while the proportion of employees with desired attributes gradually increases due to an improved hiring process.

Most of the hiring models we have described can be used in new organizations. However, one component of the model, specifically formal selection testing, often cannot be used appropriately or legally early in the life of the organization because the tests have not yet been validated. By the time the validation studies have been conducted, most of the workforce will have been hired. In some circumstances, it may be possible to avoid this problem by validating the tests before hiring in the new organization. For example, many companies that develop one high involvement organization (or other unusual culture) go on to develop others. [. . .]

5 *Lack of organizational adaptation.* A problem could arise in hiring for the organization if it led to a workforce in which everyone had the same personality profile. The organization might become stagnant because everyone would share the same values, strengths, weaknesses, and blindspots. (Obviously, the issue is the same whether employees all tend to have the same point of view because of the selection system or because of training and socialization.) There has been considerable debate about whether a powerful organizational culture, whatever its source, leads to success or leads to dry rot and lack of innovativeness. There is some evidence, for example, indicating that organizations with little internal variability in employee perspectives perform better in the short run but worse in the long run, presumably as a result of inferior adaptation.[5]

However, we expect that significant internal variability will co-exist with person-organization fit. Even the best selection system is still imperfect; we do not succeed in hiring only the 'right types'. More fundamentally, the hiring process still results in variability on the desired characteristics. Even though all those hired may meet minimum standards, some will be higher than others on the desired characteristics. Finally, employees are not clones of one another just because they are similar on some personality dimensions. We would expect considerable variation on demographic, cultural, and personality dimensions that were not the basis for selection.

THE FUTURE OF HIRING FOR PERSON-ORGANIZATION FIT

What does the future hold for this more sophisticated and elaborate approach to employee selection? Will it be adopted by an increasingly large share of corporations?

We believe that hiring for the organization, not the job, will become the only effective selection model for the typical business environment. The defining attributes of this business environment – such as shortened product life cycles, increasingly sophisticated technologies, growing globalization of markets, shifting customer demands – make for very transitory requirements in specific employee jobs. Organizational success in this environment requires hiring employees who fit the overall organization, not those who fit a fixed set of task demands. Employee personalities must fit the management philosophy and values that help define the organization's uniqueness and its fitness for the future.

We also believe that senior managers must become more 'person-oriented' in their own implicit resolution of the person-situation controversy if hiring for person-organization fit is to become a more common approach to selection. Again, generally speaking, managers tend to believe that tightly controlled situations are more effective in shaping employee performance than less-structured situations that allow the expression of individual differences. Managers who believe this are more inclined to spend resources on creating strong situations via job descriptions, close supervision, and so on than on sophisticated selection procedures.

Finally, we offer an important caveat to 'person-oriented' managers who are committed to hiring for person-organization fit. They must manage a paradox. They must build strong organizational cultures yet, at the same time, design work situations that are weak enough to allow the unique qualities of individual employees to impact work performance. The key ingredient in balancing this paradox is to create a strong organizational culture with values that empower employees to apply their individual potentials to the conduct of their work. In this way, fragile systems release the employee energy necessary to compete in today's business environment.

NOTES

1 See John P. Wanous, *Organizational Entry: Recruitment Selection, and Socializ-ation of Newcomers*, (Reading, Mass: Addison-Wesley Publishing Company, 1980) for a more complete discussion of these two types of fit and how both the organization and individual approach them.
2 Caren Siehl and Joanne Martin, 'Measuring Organizational Culture: Mixing Qualitative and Quantitative Methods', in M. O. Jones et al. (Eds) *Inside Organ-izations* (Beverly Hills: Sage, 1988).
3 For a review of the research findings, see S. C. Premack and J. P. Wanous, 'A Meta-Analysis of Realistic Job Preview Experiments', *Journal of Applied Psy-chology*, 1985, 70, 706–719.
4 E. E. Lawler III, 'Achieving Competitiveness by Creating New Organizational Cultures and Structures' in D. B. Fishman and C. Cherniss (Eds), *The Human Side of Corporate Competitiveness* (Newbury Park: Sage Publications), 69–101.
5 D. R. Denison, *Corporate Culture and Organizational Effectiveness* (New York: Wiley, 1990).

Understanding stress and stress management

Kevin Daniels

An employer owes a duty to his employees not to cause them psychiatric damage by the volume or the character of the work they are required to perform. . . . there is no logical reason why risk of injury to an employee's mental health should be excluded from the scope of the employer's duty.

(Mr Justice Coleman, November, 1994)

As organizations begin to recognize the importance of people as a source of competitive advantage, as the pace of technological and industrial change quickens and competitive pressures increase, many organizations are beginning to realise the importance of understanding stress and how to manage stress. This chapter offers a simple framework for thinking about work-related stress, how it arises and how it can be managed. It is derived from the dominant psychological theory of stress, the transactional model. The transactional model views stress as a process that involves a close interaction between people and their working environments: a stressful environment for one person may not necessarily be stressful for another. Therefore, the transactional model suggests that there are at least two strategies for managing stress at work. The first of these is to help the individual directly; either by providing counselling for individuals with severe stress related problems or involving people in preventative interventions that help to promote psychologically and physically healthy attitudes and behaviours. The second stress management strategy is to change the organizational environment, for example by redesigning jobs to minimize the number and severity of stressful events that people may experience. Finally, this chapter will describe the political reality of implementing stress management interventions and consider some solutions to these political problems.

THE TRANSACTIONAL MODEL OF STRESS

The common-sense view of stress portrayed in the popular media is that stress is a part of modern life, too much stress is bad for our health but a little stress is actually good for us. Many people say they 'work best under stress'. To state that a little stress is good for us is unhelpful because it confuses stress with stimulation. We all need a bit of excitement and interest in our lives, but too much stimulation, such as very loud noise at work, is unhealthy. This illustrates the problems of defining stress and the many ways in which the term is commonly used. Some people think stress is the same as stimulation or work load; others thing that stress is the same as anxiety or anger. For stress to be a useful concept, we need a much clearer definition.

One commonly agreed definition is that stress is a psychological process which occurs when an individual's perception of the environment of him/herself is noticeably different from what the individual desires (Daniels, 1992). Stress arising from perceptions of the environment may occur when an individual isn't given the resources she or he believes necessary to do an important piece of work. Stress arising from self-perceptions may occur when a manager agrees to take on responsibilities and duties that are not consistent with longer term career goals. This difference between perception and desire leads to some psychological discomfort; usually experienced, at least initially, as anxiety, anger or sadness, each associated with a specific physiological response.

The transactional model tries to detail the stages in the process through which people came to experience stress and the consequences of that experience. The transactional model emphasises the *perceptual* aspects of the process, in which an event must be appraised as stressful before it can influence psychological and physical health (Lazarus, DeLongis, Folkman and Gruen, 1985). Appraising events as stressful does not necessarily have to be conscious, as anyone will testify that has felt a little bit anxious a few weeks before an important job interview, even before they have begun to consciously think about preparing for the interview. Stress theorists recognise that different events have different characteristics and individuals have different ways of coping with these stimuli, different perceptions of the demands of the stimuli and different perceptions of the importance of meeting those demands (Beehr and Bhagat, 1985). Hence, what one person finds stressful, another may not. As such, the transactional model indicates that daily on-going events such as working late or arguments with colleagues may or may not be stressful, as well as major life events such as redundancy.

Figure 7.3 shows a simple, idealised version of the transactional model. It provides a framework for understanding how stress arises and how different factors interact.[1] The five major stages in the model are the occurrence of an event, appraisal of that event, coping choices, immediate impact upon well-being and re-appraisal and longer-term consequences. Individual characteristics influence all five stages and characteristics of the organizational and social environment influence three stages.

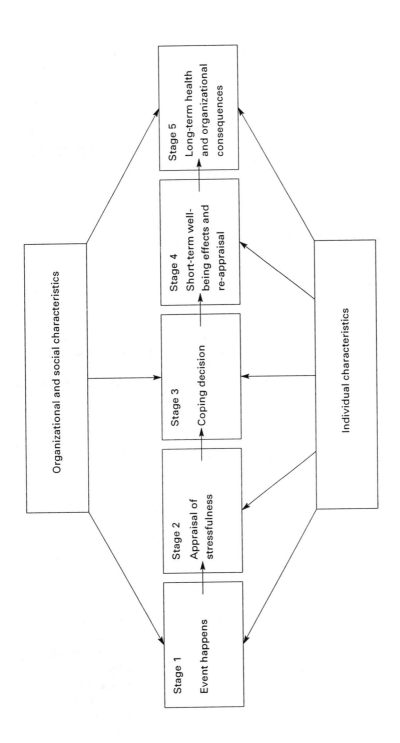

Figure 7.3 A transactional model of stress

In the first stage, a potentially stressful event happens. Organizational characteristics may influence this event; for instance organizations may require employees to work very long hours to create or sustain competitive advantage, managerial communications may seem unreasonable or may be conflicting and ambiguous. Individual characteristics also influence the event; for instance where two people have incompatible working styles, arguments may occur. However, it is possible that other factors may also cause the event; government legislation, the moves of competitors, the internationalization of markets and chance events can all influence the occurrence of potentially stressful events.

At the second stage, the individual appraises the event as benign, neutral or stressful. The stress process will end after benign or neutral appraisals. Where there is a noticeable difference between how the event affects the individual and what the individual desires, then the event is appraised as stressful. As an example of the three types of appraisal, consider having to work a few extra hours every day for a few months. Ambitious managers may think of this as an opportunity to show their determination and commitment to senior management and thus enhance their career prospects. Consultants working on a short project in a strange city may view working the extra hours as just something that needs to be done before they can go back home. Managers with young families may view the extra hours as taking the time they should and must spend with their children. However, even a seemingly benign event can be stressful if the benefits are less than expected; how would an ambitious manager feel if working extra hours did not lead to an expected promotion? Stressful appraisals can vary along many dimensions; severity, duration, frequency and relevance to the individual. An event that is severe, on-going, frequent and relevant to the individual has a greater potential to adversely affect an individual's immediate and long term physical and psychological well-being (Dewe, 1991). Individual characteristics also influence this stage of appraisal; for instance, typically anxious individuals are more likely to appraise events as stressful (Burke, Brief and George, 1993).

At the next stage, the individual decides how he or she will cope with the event. Broadly, there are two forms of coping; *problem focused coping* directed as changing the event, and *emotion focused coping* directed at regulating individual responses to the event (Lazarus and Folkman, 1984). Typically, people use a mixture of both approaches. Emotion focused coping can be useful for coping with stressful events that are not very severe, not relevant to the individual, infrequent and of short duration. Some forms of emotion focused coping (eg. having an alcoholic drink, smoking, denying a problem exists) are harmful in themselves if extended over a period, although other forms such as taking regular exercise can provide other health benefits and promote psychological well-being directly. Nevertheless, exclusive long term reliance on emotion focused coping can be harmful, since the stressful event is not changed into something more benign. In this respect, problem focused coping is generally more successful. Two factors influence how the individual decides to cope; the coping resources available in the social and organizational environment and individual characteristics. The most useful social and organizational resources are:

1 *Control over the job.* This can allow the individual to change those aspects of the working environment that he or she finds stressful. For instance, rescheduling work to allow more time on important or difficult work.

2 *Support obtained from colleagues at work and from outside work.* Support can take many forms; helping the individual to re-appraise the event as less stressful than originally thought, supplying tangible help with the problem or simply conveying feelings of care and esteem to the individual.

If there is sufficient job control and/or social support, then the individual may have the necessary resources to use problem focused coping. If these resources are scarce, then the individual may have to use emotion focused coping exclusively, which typically uses less coping resources. However, individual characteristics also influence the coping resources available. For instance, people who are usually in a good mood are more likely to receive social support, since such people are more likeable (Staw, Sutton, and Pelled, 1994).

Importantly, individual characteristics ultimately influence the coping decision; people who are confident in their ability to change the environment are more likely to make effective use of job control and social support when they are available than those who are less confident (Daniels and Guppy, 1994); and prior experience of similar events can help people to learn effective coping behaviours (Terry, 1994).

The immediate reaction to the event occurs at the next stage. As noted above, both emotion focused and problem focused coping can be successful, although problem focused coping is typically more useful. If coping is successful, then psychological well-being remains constant at least, although successful coping may even enhance well-being through feelings of competence (Bandura, 1977). Coping will be unsuccessful when the event is too stressful for emotion focused coping to work, or the necessary resources are not available for problem focused coping. When coping is unsuccessful, then psychological well-being becomes poorer and the individual is likely to feel emotions such as anger, anxiety, short-term depression and perhaps even lose some confidence. More stressful events, especially very severe or long lasting events, are probably more likely to cause anxiety and depression. At this stage, the event will be re-appraised. The event may have ended, but if it is on-going then the individual must decide whether it is still stressful and if so, how to cope with the event again. The individual's mood will influence these decisions, as noted earlier.

The first four stages of the stress process are likely to happen relatively quickly. However, if the event is especially severe, on-going, or there is a long-term sequence of stressful events and coping continues to be unsuccessful, then the individual may enter the fifth stage. The fifth stage involves long-term health and organisational outcomes of the stress process (Schuler, 1982). Such outcomes can happen after a few hours of exposure to a stressful event or may take several years to appear. Long-term individual outcomes can include coronary heart disease, cancer, hypertension, susceptibility to infectious diseases, psychosomatic complaints such as back pains, the onset of diabetic attacks amongst sufferers, drug/alcohol dependence, anxiety, depression and suicidal behaviour. Organizational outcomes can include job dissatisfaction, low commitment, absenteeism, staff turnover, occupational accidents and poor performance. Individual characteristics can influence this stage. Life style and hereditary factors can predispose individuals to certain diseases, whilst ability and general attitudes towards work may influence organizational outcomes.

THE THEORY OF STRESS MANAGEMENT

Table 7.1 shows some of the symptoms of stress and groups them into four categories, depending on whether they are organizational or individual and whether they are psychological or behavioural/physical. In isolation, each symptom is unlikely to be caused by stress, but if even a few symptoms are noticed, there could be stress problems, which left alone may become critical. In this case, a more thorough investigation by human resource or occupational health professionals, by means of interviews, questionnaires, observations and staff records, can help identify the most likely causes and suggest the best course of action. The transactional model suggests that both individual and organizational characteristics can be usefully changed both to limit stressful events at work and to help improve coping methods. Murphy (1988) has grouped stress management strategies under three headings; primary interventions targeted at the organization, secondary interventions and tertiary interventions, both targeted at the individual.

Primary stress management interventions are based on the premise that certain environments and certain events are stressful for most people (e.g. Warr, 1987) or that similar coping resources are useful to most people. Accordingly, primary interventions involve job and organization re-design to eliminate events that could be stressful or to provide necessary coping resources. Instituting autonomous self-managing work teams may be especially effective for increasing job performance and reducing other symptoms of stressful work environments (cf. Cotton, 1993), although

Table 7.1 Some of the symptoms of stress

	Individual	Organizational

Psychological	Irritability, anger
	Anxiety,
	  problems relaxing
	  feeling bored,
	  tired
	Loss of concentration,
	  memory
		Low job satisfaction
		Low commitment,
		Poor motivation

Behavioural/physical	Changes in appetite
	Problems sleeping
	Frequent headaches
	Muscle spasms,
	  palpitations
	Backpain
	Increased smoking,
	  caffeine,
	  alcohol & drug intake
	Stomach pains,
	  heartburn,
	  frequent diarrhoea
	  or constipation
		Increased absenteeism
		Lower productivity
		Greater staff turnover
		Lower quality output
		More accidents

other primary interventions that attempt to increase the amount of autonomy and participation available to individuals are usually successful
(Murphy, 1988). Other primary stress management interventions can
include limiting the amount of work to be done, limiting the hours of
stressful work, expanding employee training opportunities, improving
work conditions, recruiting and selecting of individuals that can cope with
the demands of the job, restructuring job tasks, changing job roles and
changing communication styles.

Secondary interventions seek to enhance individuals' ability to cope with
the cause of stress, to cope with the emotional/physiological symptoms of
stress, or to improve health directly. Secondary interventions are targeted
at individuals who have not yet displayed extreme symptoms of stress.
Examples of secondary interventions are relaxation training, employee
fitness programmes, meditation, problem-solving skills training, time
management and combinations of these methods. Although there are inconsistencies, there is some evidence that the benefits of secondary stress
management interventions can endure (Murphy, 1984). It seems that
problem-solving skills training may have the longest-lasting effects
(Tunnecliffe, Leach and Tunnecliffe, 1986), but programmes that consist
of several different methods are the most successful (Bruning and
Frew, 1987).

Tertiary stress management interventions are implemented when an individual is suffering from extreme symptoms of stress. They are concerned

with counselling the employee, either to change his/her perception of work, change destructive behaviours, manage emotions or to provide him/her with a more effective coping repertoire. Most of these programmes concern non-clinical counselling, and these are referred to as employee assistance programmes (EAPs). EAPs usually have the prime aim of rehabilitating the individual into the work place and line managers often make initial diagnoses (Marsden and Guppy, 1987). Although EAPs are becoming popular, it is unclear just how effective they are (Murphy, 1988). Psychotherapy, conducted by a clinical psychologist, is another form of tertiary intervention. The little evidence that is available indicates that psychotherapy may be very useful for helping people under extreme work stress (Firth and Shapiro, 1986, Firth-Cozens and Hardy, 1992).

Primary stress management interventions are potentially the most effective form of stress management, since they have the widest coverage of all the interventions, they are preventative and job/organization re-design is more enduring than secondary and tertiary interventions. Nevertheless, they are not appropriate in every circumstance: primary interventions are likely to be most successful when both

1 most of the recipients of the intervention experience common sources of stress or need similar coping resources, and
2 the sources of stress are easily removed or the coping resources easily provided.

In jobs that are inherently stressful (e.g. emergency services), secondary interventions are more likely to provide useful prevention. Tertiary stress management interventions are most likely to be appropriate where either

1 a very small fraction of the work force show extreme stress symptoms, or
2 a major stressful event has already affected health, and the event is unlikely to reoccur.

An example of the former situation would be where certain vulnerable individuals receive counselling for rehabilitative purposes. Counselling for post traumatic stress disorder after a major disaster, such as an aeroplane crash, is an example of the latter.

It is clear that prior assessment of stress related problems is useful for identifying the most appropriate form of intervention. In many instances, the results of an assessment of stress in an organization will indicate that a combination of interventions can be effective. For example, Steffy, Jones, Murphy and Kunz (1986) report a comprehensive approach to stress management that includes all three levels of intervention. Their approach involves job re-design, health education programmes and EAPs being introduced together for the whole organization. It is equally important to monitor the progress of interventions: stress management interventions can be both costly and sometimes unsuccessful, so it is important to ensure that they are effective. Figure 7.4 summarizes the various stages we have discussed in implementing a stress management intervention: assessment, evaluation, implementation and monitoring.

THE POLITICAL REALITY OF STRESS MANAGEMENT

Figure 7.4 shows an ideal process. It is rare for organizations to assess stress-related problems, even rarer for organizations to implement stress management interventions and rarer still for organizations to monitor the success of interventions. Moreover, where stress management interventions do occur, they are likely to be tertiary interventions, regardless of the requirements of the situation. These observations present an interesting paradox – it appears important for organizations to manage stress, yet the majority of organizations appear either

1 not to manage stress at all, or
2 to manage stress incorrectly.

Some of these problems may result from confusion about the nature and consequences of stress, but stress management, like any other aspect of management, has political dimensions.

Research, talking to other stress researchers and my own experience both as a stress researcher and conducting stress management seminars with managers indicate that there are two common problems in introducing stress management initiatives:

1 the denial of stress as a problem, and
2 a tendency to blame individuals.

In the face of either response, it helps to be as specific as possible about causes and consequences – rather than just attributing the problems generally to 'stress'. In addition, practical experience does suggest other strategies that can help to overcome these responses – these are discussed below. However, these strategies are themselves difficult to implement and they may not always be successful. Intelligent stress management requires a very thorough grasp of the political context of an organization.

Individuals and organizations may deny the existence of stress-related problems for a number of reasons. One reason is impression management. This is most likely to occur in organizations dominated by a 'macho' approach to work and/or in jobs that reward long hours, individual performance and competitive behaviour (e.g. management consultancy). In such organizations, being seen to have stress-related difficulties can be seen as a weakness, but coping successfully with excessive job demands can be seen as a sign of strength which may lead eventually to some form of reward or recognition (e.g. promotion). One consequence is that the majority of members of such organizations deny the existence of

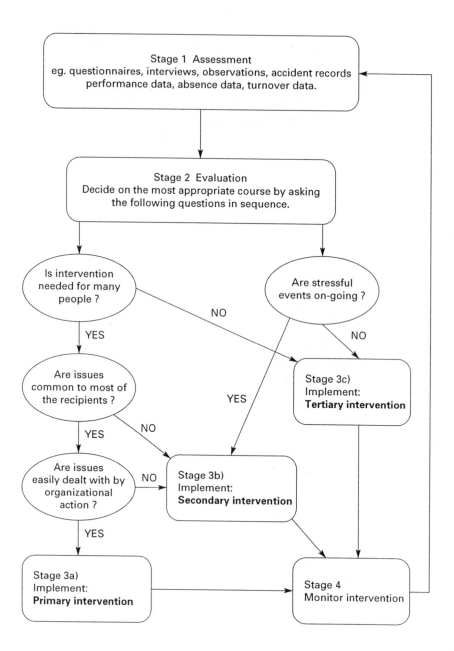

Figure 7.4 Stages in implementing stress management

stress-related problems, and therefore there is no evidence to support the case for implementing any form of stress management. One way round this problem is to assess stress-related problems in a way that guarantees the anonymity of staff. This requires regular formal surveys, often conducted by external stress researchers, rather than informal interviews and observations.

Another consequence of this form of denial is that any stress management initiatives are resisted or not used. Being seen to take part in psychologically healthy organizational practices, using stress management techniques or counselling may all be seen as signs of weakness. Ways round this problem can include

1 informing organizational members that the same, or more, rewards will be available to those that use psychologically healthy practices or stress management techniques,
2 persuading senior managers to set a 'good example' and
3 providing a confidential counselling service.

Another reason for denial is that the existence of stress-related problems across an organization implies dysfunctional organizational practices for which senior managers can be blamed or held responsible. For example, a large organization asked me to perform an assessment of stress and psychological health. One of the key findings of the survey was that nearly 40% of the workforce were exhibiting stress symptoms that fell within the psychiatric range. Unable to accept the results of the survey without acknowledging shortcomings in current organizational practices, my final report was suppressed by the personnel department and no organizational action was taken. Although this may appear to be an extreme example, I know of other stress researchers with similar experiences.

While denial may allow organizations to escape some of the blame for stress-related problems, another strategy that organizations adopt is to blame the individuals that suffer from stress-related problems. One symptom of this is the relative frequency of tertiary interventions relative to secondary and primary interventions. Since tertiary interventions are focused upon specific individuals, implementing them implies that stress is an individual problem, not the result of psychologically unhealthy organizational practices that affect everyone to a greater or lesser extent. One way to allow organizations to acknowledge that stress-related problems can be caused by dysfunctional organisational practices, is to pass the 'ownership' of stress management to senior managers. This allows senior managers a chance to avoid embarrassment by becoming powerful advocates of the benefits of stress management.

CONCLUSIONS: STRESS AND STRESS MANAGEMENT INTO THE 21ST CENTURY

This chapter has provided a view of current theory in the field of work-related stress and some of the technical and political issues of stress management interventions. Where do we go from here? As it is becoming more common to 'pursue competitive advantage through people', the number of organizations attempting formal stress management may increase as organizations seek to limit turnover and absenteeism and to increase commitment. However, changes in society and industry will affect the types of stressful events that people experience. Research into work-related stress and stress management practices will have to develop to keep pace with these changes and to address unsolved problems in our current understanding of stress. Moves away from lifetime employment to short-term contracts, the need for commercial organizations to change more quickly to gain and sustain competitive advantage, advances in information technology and the rise of the tele-worker may not only place more and novel demands on managers and workers, but may also increase uncertainty. Increasing training opportunities may be one strategy to provide people with the resources to cope with new demands and change, and help with further career development at the same time.

The increase in the number of global industries is likely to continue, with a corresponding increase in the number of organizations that will operate across nations. Also, it seems likely that more organizations will form alliances to gain access to local knowledge and resources. In both instances, the effects of organizational and national culture may have strong effects on the stress process. We know that both organizational and national cultures influence attitudes and beliefs about what can be done and what should be done at work, and we also know that attitudes and beliefs influence people's appraisals of stressful events and their decisions on how to cope with stress. It would be an important step forward for the practice of stress management to uncover the links between collective culture and the stress process. Knowledge of these effects may be crucial for understanding how to tailor stress management interventions to different social contexts.

NOTES

1 This model is based on more specific and more rigorously formulated models (eg. Schuler, 1982, Lazarus and Folkman, 1984, Cox, 1987, Schonpflug and Battman, 1988, Edwards, 1992).
2 Anyone spotting similar symptoms in themselves may have some form of stress-related problem – although it may also be a medical problem. If the problem is stress-related, it is important to make the best use of available coping resources to remove possible sources of stress. Seeking social support, maximizing

opportunities to control the working environment (e.g. by restructuring sched-ules and time management techniques), engaging in exercise and even changing attitudes (e.g. realizing the importance of rest) or lifestyle (e.g. by refusing to work weekends) can all be useful in minimizing the experience of stress.

REFERENCES

Bandura, A. (1977) 'Self-efficacy: towards a unifying theory of behavioral change', *Psychological Review*, 84, 191–215.

Beehr, T. A., Bhagat, R. S. (1985) 'Introduction to human stress and cognition in organizations'. In T. A. Beehr and R. S. Bhagat, *Human Stress and Cognition in Organizations*. Chichester: Wiley.

Bruning, N. S., Frew, D. R. (1987). 'Effects of exercise, relaxation, and management skills training on physiological stress indicators: a field experiment'. *Journal of Applied Psychology*, 72, 515–521.

Burke, M. J., Brief, A. P., George, J. M. (1993). 'The role of negative affectivity in understanding relations between self-reports of stressors and strains: a comment on the applied psychology literature'. *Journal of Applied Psychology*, 78, 402–412.

Cotton, J. L. (1993). *Employee Involvement: Methods for Improving Performance and Work Attitudes*. Newbury Park, California: Sage.

Cox, T. (1987). 'Stress, coping and problem solving'. *Work and Stress*, 1, 5–14.

Daniels, K. (1992). 'Occupational stress and control: Implications for employee well-being'. Unpublished PhD thesis, Cranfield University.

Daniels, K., Guppy, A. (1994) 'Occupational stress, social support, job control and psychological well-being'. *Human Relations*, 47, 1523–1544.

Dewe, P. (1991). 'Measuring work stressors: the role of frequency, duration and demand'. *Work and Stress*, 5, 77–91.

Edwards, J. R. (1992). 'A cybernetic theory of stress, coping, and well-being in organizations'. *Academy of Management Review*, 17, 238–274.

Firth, J., Shapiro, D. A. (1986). 'An evaluation of psychotherapy for job-related distress'. *Journal of Occupational Psychology*, 59, 111–119.

Firth-Cozens, J., Hardy, G. E. (1992). 'Occupational stress, clinical treatment and changes in job perceptions'. *Journal of Occupational and Organizational Psychology*, 65, 81–88.

Lazarus, R. S., DeLongis, A., Folkman, S., Gruen, R. (1985). 'Stress and adaptational outcomes: the problem of confounded measures'. *American Psychologist*, 40, 770–779.

Lazarus, R. S., Folkman, S. (1984). *Stress, Appraisal and Coping*. Springer, New York.

Marsden, J., Guppy, A. (1987). 'Developing an occupational response to alcohol problems: lessons from the American experience'. *The Occupational Psychologist*, 2, August, 20–24.

Murphy, L. R. (1988). 'Workplace interventions for stress reduction and preven-tion'. In C. L. Cooper and R. Payne (eds.), *Causes, Coping and Consequences of Stress at Work*. Chichester: Wiley.

Schonpflug, W., Battman W. (1988). 'The costs and benefits of coping'. In S. Fisher and J. Reason (Eds), *Handbook of Life Stress*. Wiley, Chichester.

Schuler, R. S. (1982). 'An integrative transactional process model of stress in organ-izations'. *Journal of Occupational Behavior*, 5, 5–19.

Staw, B. M., Sutton, R. I., Pelled, L. H. (1994). 'Employee positive emotion and favourable outcomes at the workplace'. *Organization Science*, 5, 51–71.

Steffy, B. D., Jones, J. W., Murphy, L. R., Kunz, L. (1986). 'A demonstration of the impact of stress abatement programs on reducing employees' accidents and their costs'. *American Journal of Health Promotion*, 1, 25–32.

Terry, D. J. (1994). 'Determinants of coping: the role of stable and situational factors'. *Journal of Personality and Social Psychology*, 66, 895–910.

Tunnecliffe, M. R., Leach, D. J., Tunnecliffe, L. P. (1986). 'Relative efficacy of using behavioural consultation as an approach to teacher stress management'. *Journal of School Psychology*, 24, 123–131.

Warr, P. (1987). 'Job characteristics and mental health'. In P. B. Warr (ed.), *Psychology at Work*. London: Penguin.

Chapter 8

Brands

For most of us choice abounds, with a profusion of brands pervading many aspects of our lives. It is difficult to think of markets which are not typified by several brands vying for buyers' attention. Even though brands have been around for a long time (for example, Coca-Cola was launched in 1887) it is only recently that brands have become a much discussed issue. In some quarters branding is now thought to be synonymous with marketing. So what exactly are brands? And how do they come to be such a dominant feature of modern marketing?

In this edited extract from their book *Creating Powerful Brands*, Leslie de Chernatony and Malcolm McDonald provide their own definition of a brand and through numerous examples show the characteristics and the types of brand that practitioners employ. They argue that brand planning is an important but often neglected aspect of creating powerful brands.

Understanding the branding process

Leslie de Chernatony and Malcolm H. B. McDonald

SUMMARY

The purpose of this chapter is to provide an overview of the key issues involved in planning for brand success. It begins by explaining that successful branding is more than merely the use of names, then goes on to discuss the concept of the brand, brand categorization in the 1990s and the importance of brand planning.

BRAND SUCCESS THROUGH INTEGRATING MARKETING RESOURCES

When BMW drivers proudly turn the ignition keys for the first time in 'the ultimate driving machine', they are not only benefiting from a highly engineered car with an excellent performance, but are also taking ownership of a symbol that signifies the core values of exclusivity, performance, quality and technical innovation. Purchasers of a Prudential insurance policy are not just buying the security of knowing that damage to their home through unforseen events can rapidly and inexpensively be rectified. They are also buying the corporate symbol of the face of Prudence reminding them of the added values of heritage, size and public awareness, inspiring confidence and sustained credibility. Likewise the data processing manager buying an IBM computer, is not just buying a device that rapidly computes data into a format that is more managerially useful, but is also buying the security of a back-up facility and commitment to customer satisfaction signified by the three letters of IBM.

While these purchasers in the consumer, service and industrial markets have bought solutions to their individual problems, they have also paid a price premium for the added values provided by buying *brands*. In addition to satisfying their core purchase requirements, they have bought an augmented solution to their problem, for which they perceive sufficient added value to warrant paying a premium over other alternatives that might have satisfied their buying needs.

The added values they sought, however, were not just those provided through the presence of a brand name as a differentiating device, nor through the use of brand names to recall powerful advertising. Instead, they perceived a total entity, the *brand*, which is the result of a coherent marketing approach which uses all elements of the marketing mix. A man does not give a woman a box of branded chocolates because she is hungry. Instead, he selects a brand that communicates something about his relationship with her. This, he hopes, will be recognized through the pack design, her recall of a relevant advertising message, the quality of the contents, her chiding of him for the price he paid and her appreciation of the effort he took to find a retailer specializing in stocking such an exclusive brand. The same goes for a woman buying a man a special box of cigars.

These examples show that thinking of branding as being 'to do with naming products', or 'about getting the right promotion with the name prominently displayed', or 'getting the design right', is too myopic. In the mid 1980s, we came across Scottowels when doing some work in the kitchen towels market. Managers in the company thought that this was a branded kitchen towel, but consumers perceived this as little more than another kitchen towel with a name added – one stage removed from being a commodity. It had a brand name, but because the rest of the marketing mix was neglected, it had to fight for shelf space on the basis of price and was ultimately doomed because of the vicious circle driven by minimum value leading to low price.

There are hundreds of examples of well-known brand names that have failed commercially. There are even some which are reviled by the public. Such unsuccessful brands are examples of a failure to integrate all the elements of marketing in a coherent way.

Thus, branding is a powerful marketing concept that does not just focus on one element of the marketing mix, but represents the result of a carefully conceived array of activities across the whole spectrum of the marketing mix, directed towards making the buyer recognize relevant added values that are unique when compared with competing products and services and which are difficult for competitors to emulate. The purpose of branding is to facilitate the organization's task of getting and maintaining a loyal customer base in a cost-effective manner to achieve the highest possible return on investment. In other words, branding should not be regarded as a tactical tool directed towards one element of the marketing mix, but rather should be seen as the result of strategic thinking, integrating a marketing programme across the complete marketing mix.

Neither is this a concept that should be regarded as more appropriate for consumer markets. Indeed, the concept of branding is increasingly being applied to people and places, such as politicians, pop stars, holiday resorts and the like, whilst it has always been equally relevant to the marketing of products and services. Were this not so, organizations such

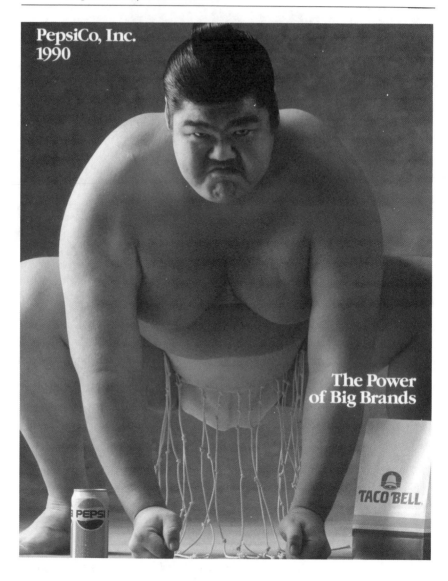

Exhibit 8.1 With a commitment to an integrated and coherent marketing approach to branding, PepsiCo Inc. are proud of their enhanced profitability from brands.

Source: Reproduced with kind permission of © PepsiCo Inc. 1991, Purchase, New York

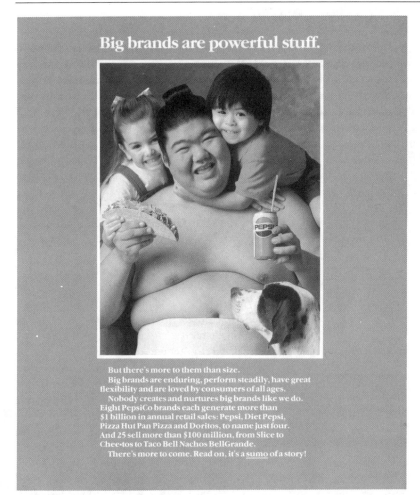

Big brands are powerful stuff.

But there's more to them than size.
Big brands are enduring, perform steadily, have great
flexibility and are loved by consumers of all ages.
Nobody creates and nurtures big brands like we do.
Eight PepsiCo brands each generate more than
$1 billion in annual retail sales: Pepsi, Diet Pepsi,
Pizza Hut Pan Pizza and Doritos, to name just four.
And 25 sell more than $100 million, from Slice to
Chee-tos to Taco Bell Nachos BellGrande.
There's more to come. Read on, it's a sumo of a story!

Exhibit 8.1 (continued)

as IBM would be unable to charge significantly higher prices for their computers, which compete so successfully with technically more advanced machines selling at lower prices. Strategic branding is concerned with evaluating how to achieve the highest return on investment from brands, through analysing, formulating and implementing a strategy that best satisfies users, distributors and brand manufacturers. It is only recently that a strategic perspective on branding has emerged, with firms beginning to recognize that they are sitting on valuable assets that need careful attention, as we shall see in the next section.

THE CONCEPT OF THE BRAND

Successful brands, that is those which are the focus of a coherent blending of marketing resources, represent valuable marketing assets. During the 1980s the value of brands was ironically brought to the attention of marketers by the financial community. For example, in 1985 Reckitt and Colman acquired Airwick Industries and put on its balance sheet £127 million as the financial value resulting from the intangible benefits of goodwill, heritage and loyalty conveyed by the newly acquired brand names. While this may have been one of the opening shots to make organizations aware of the financial value of brands, it was Rank Hovis McDougal who really brought the brand debate to life. They announced in 1988 that they had put £678 million on their balance sheet as the valuation of their brand names. In the same year Jacobs Suchard and Nestle fought for the ownership of Rowntree. At the time of the takeover battle it was estimated that Rowntree's tangible net assets were worth around £300 m, yet Nestle won control by paying £2.5 bn. This difference of £2.2 bn represented the value that Nestle saw in the potential earnings of strong brands such as Kit Kat, Polo, Quality Street and After Eight Mints!

Thus, because consumers recognize and appreciate the added values of successful brands, they are able to sustain a higher price premium over equivalent commodity items and generally generate healthy profits.

The ultimate assessor of the real value of a brand, however, is not the manufacturer or the distributor, but the buyer or the user. Marketers are able to develop strategies to convey added values to purchasers, but because of what is called the 'perceptual process', the target audience may well focus on only a part of the available information and 'twist' some of the messages to make them congruent with their prior beliefs. For example should a wallpaper paste manufacturer show an apparently incompetent DIY householder mixing paste in a television commercial in an attempt to communicate the smoothness and ease of application of their brand of wallpaper paste, they run the risk of some consumers interpreting the brand as being 'suitable for idiots'. This is one example of the perceptual process.

It is imperative to recognize that while marketers instigate the branding process (i.e. branding as an input), it is the buyer or the user who forms a mental vision of the brand (i.e. branding as an output), which may be different from the intended marketing thrust. While marketers talk about the branding effort they are undertaking, they should never lose sight of the fact that the final form of the brand is the mental evaluation held by the purchasers or users. Branding, then, needs to be appreciated in terms of both the input and the output process.

Drawing on the points discussed so far, we can better clarify the term 'brand' through our definition:

A successful brand is an identifiable product, service, person or place, augmented in such a way that the buyer or user perceives relevant unique added values which match their needs most closely. Furthermore its success results from being able to sustain these added values in the face of competition.

Later we review the plethora of brand definitions, some of which provide a helpful insight for the practitioner, but none of which fully describe the concept. Our definition above recognizes that brands exist in both product (consumer and industrial) and service domains and even relate to people, for example pop stars, and places, for example the marketing of cities as tourist attractions.

Brands are successful when developed with a clear statement of intent about the product's or service's purpose, the specific group of customers the brand is targeted at and a commitment to equipping the brand with the right types of resources to achieve the stated purpose. For example, Coca-Cola's success is partly attributable to a clear positioning as a refreshing, fun-type drink, targeted at teenagers and backed by a tradition of quality and continual consumer communication.

Brands deliver a variety of benefits, which for ease can be classified as satisfying buyers' rational and emotional needs. Successful brands are those which have the correct balance in terms of their ability to satisfy these two needs. For example, cigarette smokers have a variety of rational needs such as seeking the best value, or best taste, or best quality, or a certain aroma or achieving relaxation, etc. The extent to which different brands satisfy particular rational needs will be assessed by the consumer trying different brands, examining the packaging, looking at the shape of the cigarette, considering its price, etc. Besides these rational needs they will also be seeking to satisfy emotional needs, such as prestige, or distinctiveness, or style, or social reassurance, etc. The extent to which different brands satisfy these emotional needs will be evaluated by consumers recalling promotions, or assessing who smokes different brands, or considering what situations different brands are consumed in, etc. To succeed, the marketer must understand the extent to which their brand satisfies rational and emotional needs and then develop marketing programmes accordingly.

Some may question whether the rational dimension dominates industrial branding and therefore whether there is any need to consider emotional aspects at all. Our work has shown that emotion plays an important role in the industrial brand selection process. For example, some office services managers do not just consider the rational aspects of office furniture brands they are about to buy, but also seek emotional reassurance that the correct brand decision might reaffirm their continual career development or that they have not lost credibility amongst colleagues through the wrong brand choice.

Exhibit 8.2 The travel firm is taking advantage of the brand benefits offered by Queensland Tourist Commission, with permission, The Port Philip Co.

CHARACTERISTICS OF BRANDS

Our definition of a brand adheres to a model which shows the extent to which a product or service can be augmented to provide added value to increasing levels of sophistication. This model views a brand as consisting of four levels:

- generic
- expected
- augmented
- potential

The *generic* level is the commodity form that meets the buyer's or user's basic needs, for example the car satisfying a transportation need. This is the easiest aspect for competitors to copy and consequently successful brands have added values over and above this at the *expected* level.

Within the *expected* level, the commodity is value engineered to satisfy a specific target's minimum purchase conditions, such as functional capabilities, availability, pricing, etc. As more buyers enter the market and as repeat buying occurs, the brand would evolve through a better matching of resources to meet customers' needs (e.g. enhanced customer service).

With increased experience, buyers and users become more sophisticated, so the brand would need to be *augmented* in more refined ways, with added values satisfying non-functional (e.g. emotional) as well as functional needs. For example, promotions might be directed to the user's peer group to reinforce his or her social standing through ownership of the brand.

With even more experience of the brand, and therefore with a greater tendency to be more critical, it is only creativity that limits the extent to which the brand can mature to the *potential* level. For example, grocery retail buyers regarded the Rowntree confectionery brands as having reached the zenith of the *augmented* stage. To counter the threat of their brands slipping back to the *expected* brand level, and therefore having to fight on price, Rowntree shifted their brands to the *potential* level by developing software for retailers to manage confectionery shelf space to maximize profitability. Experienced consumers recognize that competing items are often similar in terms of product formulation and that brand owners are no longer focusing only on rational functional issues, but are addressing the *potential* level of brands by promoting more intangible, emotional factors.

To succeed in the long run, a brand must offer added values over and above the basic product characteristics, if for no other reason than that functional characteristics are so easy to copy by competitors. In the services sector, when all other factors are equal, this could be as simple as a correctly spelt surname on the monthly bank statement. In the industrial market, it could be conveyed by the astute sales engineer presenting the brand as a no-risk purchase (due to the thoroughness of testing, the credibility of the organization, compliance with British Standards, case histories of other users, etc.). It is most important to realize that the added values must be relevant to the customer and not just to the manufacturer or distributor. Car manufacturers who announced that their brands had the added value of electronic circuits emitting 'computer speak' when seat belts were not worn didn't take long to discover that this so-called benefit was intensely disliked by customers. In the retail banking sector, customers perceive added value when a full quota of clerks are present to serve, rather than a teller's cheerful face to greet the customer after a ten-minute wait resulting from inadequate staffing levels.

Buyers perceive added value in a brand because they recognize certain clues which give signals about the offer. In industrial markets, for example, buyers evaluate brands on a wide variety of attributes, rather than just on price. As a consequence, price is rarely the most important variable influencing the purchase decision. So it is not unusual for a buyer to remain loyal to a supplier during a period of price rises. However, if the price of a brand rises and one of the signalling clues is weak (say, poor reliability of delivery) compared with the other signalling clues (say, product quality), the buyer may perceive that the brand's value has diminished and will therefore be more likely to consider competitive brands. A further example of the need to provide consistency of signalling clues about brands is that of an advertising agency which produced an advertisement targeted at businesspeople, to portray the added value of in-flight comfort. Depth interviews amongst businesspeople revealed strong feelings about the poor quality of the advertisement and a concomitant rejection of any belief that such a company could deliver in-flight comfort. Sophisticated consumers recognized the high predictive capability of a clue (poor advertising) and rejected the brand's added value.

If brands are to thrive, their marketing support will have been geared towards providing the user with the maximum satisfaction in a particular context. Buyers often use brands as non-verbal clues to communicate with their peer groups. In other words, it is recognized that people do not use brands only for their functional capabilities, but also for their badge or symbolic value. It has been observed that people take care over their selection of clothes, since according to the situation, their brand of clothes is being used to signal messages of propriety, status or even seduction. Buyers choose brands with which they feel both physical and psychological comfort in specific situations. They are concerned about selecting brands which reinforce their own concept of themselves in specific situations. A very self-conscious young man may well drink a particular brand of lager with his peer group because he believes it will convey an aspect of his lifestyle; whilst at home alone his brand consumption behaviour may well be different, since he is less concerned about the situational context.

It is worth noting that this phenomenon has been recorded by many researchers. For example, it has been found that for cars and clothing, people were more likely to buy brands which they perceived were similar to their own concept of themselves. Where marketers have grounds for believing that their brands are being used by consumers as value-expressive devices, they need to be attuned to the interaction of the marketing mix with the user's environment and provide the appropriate support. In some instances this may involve targeting promotional activity to the user's peer group, to ensure that they recognize the symbolic messages being portrayed by the brand.

Whilst this issue of appreciating the buyer's or user's environment relates to consumer markets, it is also apparent in industrial markets. One researcher found that in a laboratory with a high proportion of well-educated scientists, there was a marked preference for a piece of scientific equipment that had a 'designer label' cabinet, over the same equipment presented in a more utilitarian manner. In a highly rational environment, scientists were partly influenced by a desire to select a brand of equipment which they felt better expressed their own concept of themselves.

Finally, our definition of a brand adopts a strategic perspective, recognizing that unless the added value is unique and sustainable against competitive activity, the life time will be very short. Without such a strategic perspective, then, it is questionable whether it is viable to follow a branding route. [. . .] It is our contention that unless brand instigators have a sustainable differential advantage, they should seriously consider the economics of following a manufacturer's brand route and consider becoming a supplier of a distributor's brand. In such situations it is more probable that the firm will follow a more profitable route by becoming a distributor brand supplier (i.e. a supplier of own label products). [. . .]

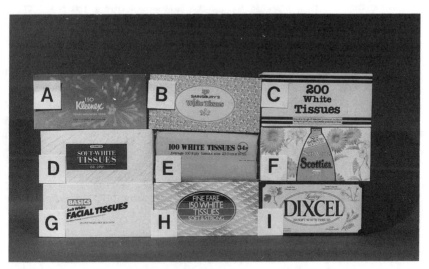

Exhibit 8.3 A 1985 example of branded (A, F, I), own label (B, D, H) and generic (C, E, G) facial tissues

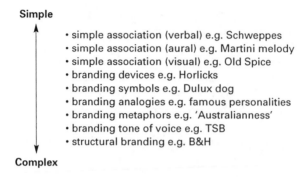

Simple

- simple association (verbal) e.g. Schweppes
- simple association (aural) e.g. Martini melody
- simple association (visual) e.g. Old Spice
- branding devices e.g. Horlicks
- branding symbols e.g. Dulux dog
- branding analogies e.g. famous personalities
- branding metaphors e.g. 'Australianness'
- branding tone of voice e.g. TSB
- structural branding e.g. B&H

Complex

Figure 8.1 Langmaid and Gorden's (1988) brand typology

BRANDING IN THE 1990s: BRAND CATEGORIZATION

An advertising perspective

[. . .] Two well-known researchers recently pointed out that the problem with branding is the surprising number of creative directors, planners, account handlers and clients who have a kindergarten knowledge of branding processes and mechanisms. They are rightly critical of those who regard branding merely as a process to ensure that the name on a product or service is highly visible. Based on a consideration of advertisements, they classified brands into nine categories, each representing a role in advertising, varying from simple through to complex branding. For example, at the simple end of the scale there are those brands which operate through straightforward association with the advertising slogan (e.g. the classic 'Sch . . . you know who'). By contrast, at the most complex end of the spectrum, they identify structural branding, in which for example, objects (scissors, hedge trimmers, etc.) coloured either purple or white are shown in order to ensure a link with Silk Cut cigarettes. Figure 8.1 shows the researchers' (Langmaid and Gordon) interpretation of brand types.

However, whilst their typology is of value to advertisers, its overt advertising bias restricts its value as an aid in evaluating how to employ the other elements of the marketing mix.

An output process

Our research and work with marketing executives have shown that there are other interpretations of the role played by brands, which we will now make explicit, all of which will be addressed in more detail in subsequent chapters. However, a key problem with many of these interpretations, is that they place too much emphasis on branding as something that is done to consumers, rather than branding as something consumers do things *with*. It is wrong, in other words, to focus on branding as an *input* process. Clearly we need to consider carefully how marketing resources are being used to support brands, but it is crucial to understand the *output* process as well, since, as mentioned earlier, the final evaluation of the brand is in the buyer's or user's mind. Consumers are not just passive recipients of marketing activity. They consume marketing activity, sometimes with a large subconscious appetite, twisting messages to reinforce prior expectations.

Several highly regarded branding advisers stress the importance of looking at brands as perceptions in consumers' minds, a notion which is comparatively easy to accept and which reinforces the conclusion about the importance of what consumers take out of the process rather than what marketers put into it. Whilst it is clear that marketers design the firm's offer, the ultimate judge about the nature of the brand is the consumer. When buying a new brand, consumers seek clues about the brand's capabilities. They try to evaluate the brand through a variety of perceptual evaluations, such as its reliability, or whether it's the sort of brand they feel right with, or whether it's better than another brand, so that a brand becomes not the producer's, but the consumer's idea of the product. The result of good branding is a perception of the values of a product, or service, interpreted and believed so clearly by the consumer, that the brand adopts a personality. This is so well recognized, that products with little apparent functional differences are regarded as different purely because of the brand personality. For example, while many organizations provide charge cards, American Express is 'the one you don't leave home without'. Parker pens have a personality of their own, as do Singapore Airlines, Fosters lager, and countless other brands around the world.

Thus, recognizing the inherent flaw when marketers focus upon branding as an input process, we have highlighted eight different types of brands that practitioners employ.

An eight-category typology

1 Brand as a sign of ownership

An early theme, given much prominence in marketing circles, was the distinction between brands on the basis of whether the brand was a manufacturers' brand or a distributors' brand ('own label', 'private label'). Branding was seen as being a basis of showing who instigated the marketing for that particular offering and whether the primary activity of the instigator was production (i.e. manufacturers' brand) or distribution (distributors' brand). However, this drew a rather artificial distinction, since nowadays consumers place a far greater reliance on distributor brands

– particularly when brands such as Benetton and Marks & Spencer are perceived as superior brands in their own right. In fact, some would argue that with the much greater marketing role played by major retailers and their concentrated buying power, the concept of USP (Unique Selling Proposition) should now be interpreted as 'Universal Supermarket Patronage'! With the much greater marketing activity undertaken by distributors, this typology does little more than clarify who instigated the marketing.

2 Brand as a differentiating device

The historical review earlier in this chapter indicated that, at the turn of the century, a much stronger emphasis was placed on brands purely as differentiating devices between similar products. This perspective is still frequently seen today in many different markets. Yet with more sophisticated marketing and more experienced consumers, brands succeed not only by conveying differentiation, but also by being associated with added values. For example, the brand Cadbury's Dairy Milk not only differentiates this from other confectionery lines, but is a successful brand since it has been backed by a coherent use of resources that deliver the added value of a high quality offering with a well-defined image. By contrast the one man operation, 'Tom's Taxi Service', is based upon branding as a differentiating device, with little thought to communicating added values.

Small firms seem to be particularly prone to the belief that putting a name on their product or service is all that is needed to set them apart from competitors. They erroneously believe that branding is about having a prominent name, more often than not based around the owner's name. Yet there is ample evidence that brands fail if organizations concentrate primarily on developing a symbol or a name as a differentiating device. Brands will succeed if they offer unique benefits, satisfying real consumer needs. Where an organization has reason to believe that their competitors are marketing brands primarily as differentiating devices, there is an opportunity to develop a strategy which gets buyers to associate relevant added values with their brand name and hence gain a competitive advantage.

3 Brand as a functional device

Another category of brands is that used by marketers to communicate functional capability. This stemmed from the early days of manufacturers' brands when firms wished to protect their large production investments by using their brands to guarantee consistent quality to consumers.

As consumers began to take for granted the fact that brands represented consistent quality, marketers strove to establish their brands as being associated with specific unique functional benefits.

A brief scan of advertisements today shows the different functional

THE
CLOSER
YOU GET
TO AN
IBIZA
THE
MORE
IT
LOOKS
UNDER-
PRICED.

With the host of standard
features on the SEAT Ibiza SXi, you'd
be forgiven for thinking the price was
a mistake.

Obvious features such as:
reclining front seats with integral
head restraints, split/folding rear
seats, tinted electric windows, tinted
glass sunroof, internally adjustable
twin door mirrors, rear window wash/
wipe, central door locking, 4-speaker
stereo radio/cassette, double rear
spoilers, alloy wheels and low profile
tyres.

And the not so obvious: 100 bhp
System Porsche engine with Bosch
jetronic fuel injection, four wheel
independent suspension, transverse
engine front wheel drive, laminated
windscreen, 9-stage paint process,
12 month unlimited mileage and
6 year anti-perforation corrosion
warranties.

So with prices of the 11 model
Ibiza range starting from £5199* you'll
want to hurry to your nearest
SEAT Dealer or call free-
phone 0800 521382 for your
free Ibiza information pack.

SEAT
Volkswagen Group

*PRICE CORRECT AT TIME OF GOING TO PRESS. INCLUDES CAR TAX AND VAT BUT EXCLUDES ON THE ROAD CHARGES. MODEL ILLUSTRATED - SXi (£8545.00)

Exhibit 8.4 Stressing the functional capability of the brand
Source: Courtesy NWA

attributes marketers are trying to associate with their brand, for example:
VAX, emphasizing the carpet-cleaning features of its less-than-aesthetic
vacuum cleaner; SEAT, striving to convey a good value-for-money proposition; Polycell, seeking the association of DIY simplicity; and Castrol
GTX, representing 'high technology' engine protection. Firms adopting
the view that they are employing brands as functional communicators
have the virtue of being customer driven, but clearly run the risk of an

Exhibit 8.5 VAX positioned as a functional brand
Source: VAX Appliances Ltd., with permission

excessive reliance on the functional (rational) element of the consumer choice, as all products and services also have some degree of emotional content in the buying process. For example, a Post Office campaign run in 1990 for a predominantly functional brand, advertised the emotional

If you don't want your burning passion to arrive lukewarm, send it in a Swiftpack.

Whether you want to send your burning passion or the hottest of gossip, Swiftpacks take flight before they have a chance to cool.

The distinctive Swiftpack international express envelopes receive VIP treatment, being handled separately from ordinary mail to enable a speedy arrival.

They're available from your local Post Office from only £2.05p. Isn't someone extra special worth that little extra?

International
*By Air, By Land, By Swiftpack,
By Hand.*

Exhibit 8.6 Balancing the functional and emotional elements in branding
Source: Royal Mail, with permission

dimension using the slogan 'If you don't want your burning passion to arrive lukewarm, send it in a Swiftpack.'

4 Brand as a symbolic device

In certain product fields (e.g. perfume and clothing) buyers perceive significant badge value in the brands, since it enables them to communicate something about themselves (e.g. emotion, status, etc.). In other words, brands are used as symbolic devices, with marketers believing that brands are bought and used primarily because of their ability to help users express something about themselves to their peer groups, with users taking for granted functional capabilities.

Where consumers perceive the brand's value to lie more in terms of the non-verbal communication facility (through the logo or name), they spend time and effort choosing brands, almost with the same care as if choosing a friend. It is now accepted that consumers personify brands and when looking at the symbol values of brands, they seek brands which have very clear personalities and select brands that best match their actual or desired self-concept.

For example, in the beer market, there are only marginal product differences between brands. Comparative consumer trials of competing beer brands without brand names present showed no significant preferences or differences. Yet, when consumers repeated the test with brand names present, significant brand preferences emerged. On the first comparative trial, consumers focused on functional (rational) aspects of the beers and were unable to notice much difference. On repeating the trials with brand names present, consumers were able to use the brand names to recall distinct brand personalities and the symbolic (emotional) aspect of the brands influenced preference.

Through being a member of social groups, people learn the symbolic meaning of brands. As they interpret the actions of their peer group, they then respond, using brands as non-verbal communication devices (e.g. feelings, status). To capitalize on symbolic brands, therefore, marketers must use promotional activity to communicate the brand's personality and signal how consumers can use it in their daily relationships with others. Nonetheless, whilst there are many product fields where this perspective of brands is useful, it must also be realized that consumers rarely consider just the symbolic aspect of brands. Research by the authors of this book across a wide variety of product fields, ranging from chipboard to watches, showed that consumers often evaluated brands in terms of both a symbolic (emotional) and a functional (rational) dimension. Marketers should, therefore, be wary of subscribing to the belief that a brand acts *solely* as a symbolic device.

5 Brand as a risk reducer

Many marketers believe that buying should be regarded as a process whereby buyers attempt to reduce the risk of a purchase decision. When a person is faced with competing brands in a new product field, they feel risk. For example, uncertainty about whether the brand will work, whether they will be wasting money, whether their peer group will disagree with their choice, whether they will feel comfortable with the purchase, etc. Successful brand marketing should therefore be concerned with understanding buyers' perceptions of risk followed by developing and presenting

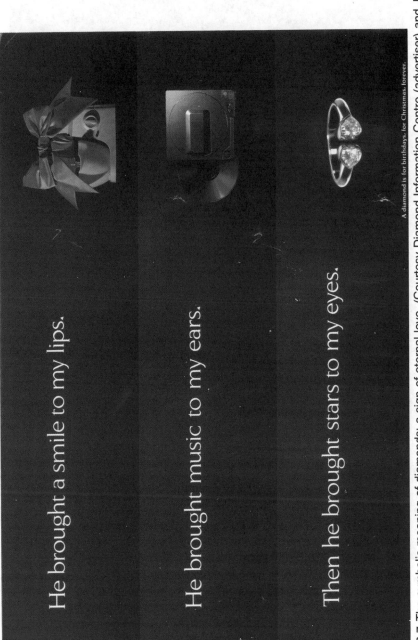

He brought a smile to my lips.

He brought music to my ears.

Then he brought stars to my eyes.

A diamond is for birthdays, for Christmas, forever.

Exhibit 8.7 The symbolic meaning of diamonds: a sign of eternal love. (Courtesy Diamond Information Centre (advertiser) and J. Walter Thompson (agency).

Exhibit 8.7 (continued)

the brand in such a way that buyers feel minimal risk. An example of an industry appreciating perceived risk is the pharmaceutical industry. One company has developed a series of questions which its sales representatives use to evaluate the risk aversion of doctors. When launching a new drug, the company focuses sales presentations initially on doctors with a low risk aversion profile.

To make buying more acceptable, buyers seek methods of reducing risk by, for example, always buying the same brand, searching for more information, only buying the smallest size, etc. Research has shown that one of the more popular methods employed by buyers to reduce risk is reliance upon reputable brands. Some marketers, particularly those selling to organizations rather than to final consumers, succeed with their brands because they find out what dimensions of risk the buyer is most concerned about and then develop a solution through their brand presentation which emphasizes the brand's capabilities along the risk dimension considered most important by the buyer. This interpretation of branding has the virtue of being output driven. Marketers, however, must not lose sight of the need to segment customers by similar risk perception and achieve sufficient numbers of buyers to make risk reduction branding viable.

6 Brand as a shorthand device

Glancing through advertisements today, one becomes aware of brands whose promotional platform appears to be based on bombarding consumers with considerable quantities of information (e.g. Guardian Royal Exchange's Choices pension plan). These brands are used as shorthand devices by consumers to recall from memory sufficient brand information at a later purchasing time. There is merit in this approach, as people generally have limited memory capabilities. To overcome this, they bundle small bits of information into larger chunks in their memory, and use brand names as handles to recall these larger information chunks. By continuing to increase the size of these few chunks in memory, buyers in consumer, industrial and service sectors can process information more effectively. At the point of purchase, they are able to recall numerous attributes by interrogating their memory.

There is, none the less, the danger of concentrating too heavily on the quantity, rather than the quality of information directed at purchasers. It also ignores the perceptual process which is used by buyers to twist information until it becomes consistent with their prior beliefs – an error fatally overlooked by the short-lived Strand cigarette brand.

7 Brand as a legal device

With the appearance of manufacturer's brands at the turn of this century, consumers began to appreciate their value and started to ask for them by name. Producers of inferior goods realized that to survive they would have to change. A minority, however, changed by illegally packaging their inferior products in packs that were virtually identical to the original brand.

Exhibit 8.8 Positioning the brand as a risk reducing device
(with permission, Bradford & Bingley Building Society)

To protect themselves against counterfeiting, firms turned to trademark registration as a legal protection. Some firms began to regard the prime benefit of brands as being that of legal protection, with the result that a new category of branding appeared. Within this group of brands, marketers direct their efforts towards effective trademark registration along with consumer education programmes about the danger of buying poor grade brand copies. For example, the pack details on Matchbox products boldly state that 'Matchbox is the trademark of the Matchbox group of companies

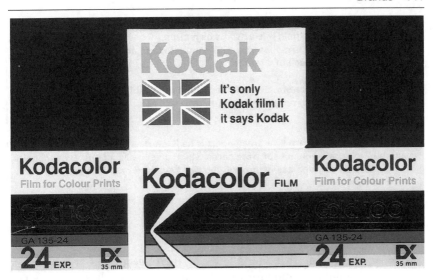

Exhibit 8.9 A successfully protected brand

and is the subject of extensive trademark registrations', while Kodak packs all carry the advice 'It's only Kodak film if it says Kodak.'

Yet again, however, whilst clearly there is a need to protect brands, brand owners also need to adopt a more strategic approach to developing ways of erecting defensive barriers, besides being reliant only on legal redress.

8 Brand as a strategic device

Finally, more enlightened marketers are adopting the view to which we subscribe, which is that brands should be treated as strategic devices. The assets constituting the brand need to be audited, the forces affecting the future of the brand evaluated and by appreciating how the brand achieved its added value, a positioning for the brand needs to be identified such that the brand can be successfully protected and achieve the desired return on investment. To take full advantage of brands as strategic devices, a considerable amount of marketing analysis and brand planning is required, yet many firms are too embroiled in tactical issues and so do not gain the best possible returns from their brands. All the strategic issues associated with capitalizing on strategic branding are covered in this book.

A good example of successful branding through majoring upon a differential advantage and ensuring the sustainability of such an advantage was seen in a colour supplement advertisement by Sharp in 1990. Figure 8.2 shows the main points presented in the advertisement. This organization

The Sharp IQ leads the field in electronic organizers. A compact way to store and retrieve information, it provides you with complete time and information management at the touch of a button.

Of course it has its imitators. Some limited by their capabilities. Others restricted by their memory. Many requiring computer literacy. Most of them vulnerable to obsolescence.

But what keeps the Sharp IQ a breed apart is its IC card technology: a simple system of integrated circuit software cards which give the IQ infinite expandability. All operated quickly and easily through the IQ's keyboard or an integral touch-sensitive pad.

Figure 8.2 Advertisement for Sharp IQ

evaluated the forces that could impede their electronic organizer and developed a unique position for their brand that is difficult for competitors to copy. The technology of the IC card gave the brand a competitive edge. In a true strategic style, the firm had developed a brand which it had differentiated from its competitors and had used its corporate strengths to satisfy customer need better than competitors. [. . .]

THE IMPORTANCE OF BRAND PLANNING

As the previous sections have shown, brands play a variety of roles and for a number of reasons satisfy many different needs. They are the end result of much effort and by implication represent a considerable investment by the organization. With the recent interest in the balance sheet value of brands, companies are beginning to question whether their financially valuable assets in the form of brands are being effectively used to achieve high returns on investment. To gain the best return from their brands, firms must adopt a broad vision about their brands and not just focus in isolation on tactical issues of design and promotion. Instead, they need to audit the capabilities of their firm, evaluate the external issues influencing their brand (briefly overviewed in the next section) and then develop a brand plan that specifies realistic brand objectives and the strategy to achieve them.

Brand planning is an important but time-consuming activity, which, if undertaken in a thorough manner involving company-wide discussion, will result in a clear vision about how resources can be employed to sustain the brand's differential advantage. Unfortunately, it is only a minority of organizations who undertake thorough brand planning. Without well-structured brand plans there is the danger of what we call brand 'vandalism'. Junior brand managers are given 'training' by making them responsible for specific brands. Their planning horizons tend to be in terms of a couple of years (i.e. the period before they move on) and their focus tends to be on the tactical issues of advertising, pack design and tailor-made brand promotions for the trade. At best this results in 'fire fighting' and a defensive rather than offensive brand plan. The core values of the brand are in danger of being diluted through excessive brand extensions. For example, one of the key core values of the Ribena brand is vitamin C, yet by extending the brand into other fruits (e.g. Strawberry) this is weakening the brand's proposition and potentially weakening the brand's strength.

Internally, organizations may be oblivious to the fact that they are hindering brand development. Clearly, by not preparing well-documented strategic brand plans, firms are creating their own obstacles to success. Some of the characteristics that internally hinder any chance of brand success are:

- Brand planning is based on little more than extrapolations from the previous few years.
- When it doesn't look as if the annual budget is going to be reached, quarter 4 sees brand investment being cut (i.e. advertising, market research, etc.)
- The marketing manager is unable to delegate responsibility and is too involved in tactical issues.
- Brand managers see their current positions as good training grounds for no more than two years.
- Strategic thinking consists of a retreat once a year, with the advertising agency and sales managers, to a one-day meeting concerned with next year's brand plans.
- A profitability analysis for each major customer is rarely undertaken.
- New product activity consists of different pack sizes and rapidly developing 'me-too' offers.
- The promotions budget is strongly biased towards below-the-line promotional activity, supplemented only occasionally with advertising.
- Marketing documentation is available to the advertising agency on a 'need to know' basis only.

Brand strategy development must involve all levels of marketing management and stands a better chance of success when all the other relevant internal departments and external agencies are actively involved. It must progress on the basis of all parties being kept aware of progress.

British Airways exemplify the notion of brand development as an integrating process, having used this to achieve a greater customer focus. For example, the simple operation of taking a few seats out of an aircraft can be done with confidence, as engineering are consulted about safety implications, finance work out the long-term revenue implication, scheduling explore capacity implications and the cabin crew adjust their in-flight service routines. [. . .]

CONCLUSIONS

This chapter has provided an overview of the key issues involved in planning for the future of brands. It has also shown that brands succeed when marketers regard them as the end result of a well-integrated marketing process. To view branding as naming, design or advertising, is too myopic and such a perspective will shorten the brand's life expectancy. Branding is about the communication of relevant added values for which buyers are prepared to pay a price premium and which competitors find difficult to emulate.

With the advent of distributor' brands, more experienced buyers and increasingly sophisticated marketing techniques, eight different types of brands were identified: a sign of ownership of the branding process; a differentiating device; a communicator of functional capability; a device which enables buyers to express something about themselves; a risk-reducing device; a shorthand communication device; a legal device; and a strategic device. To capitalize upon the asset represented by their brand, firms need to adopt strategic brand planning as a way of life. [. . .]

REFERENCES AND FURTHER READING

Langmaid R., Gordon W. (1988). 'A great ad – pity they can't remember the brand – true or false'. In *31st MRS Conference Proceedings*. London: MRS, pp. 15–46
Levitt T., (1970). 'The morality of advertising'. *Harvard Business Review*, (July–Aug.), 84–92.
Levitt T., (1980). 'Marketing success through differentiation of anything'. *Harvard Business Review*, (Jan.–Feb.), 83–91.
McDonald M. (1989). *Marketing Plans*. Oxford: Heinemann.
Meadows R. (1983) 'They consume advertising too'. *ADMAP*, **19**, (July–Aug.), 408–13.
Murphy J. (1990). 'Brand valuation – not just an accounting issue'. *ADMAP*, **26**, (April), 36–41.
Patti C., Fisk R. (1982) 'National advertising, brands and channel control: an historical perspective with contemporary options'. *Journal of the Academy of Marketing Science*, **10**, (1), 90–108.
Pitcher A. (1985). 'The role of branding in international advertising'. *International Journal of Advertising*, **4**, (3) 241–6.
Porter M. (1985). *Competitive Advantage* New York: Free Press.
Room A. (1987). 'History of branding'. In *Branding: A Key Marketing Tool*. Murphy J., ed.) Basingstoke: Macmillan.

Chapter 9

Organizational capability

The concept of organizational capability provides a refreshing reassertion of the complexity of effective organization. Capability is a *systemic* property: it can be cultivated over time, but not bought-in, designed or decreed. So taking capability seriously has far-reaching implications. It challenges popular nostrums like Business Process Re-engineering, and the management-by-exhortation that so often passes for culture-building. It highlights the importance of accumulated know-how and experience, established working relationships, and painstaking attention to systems and procedures, especially as these involve the integration of separate areas of functions. In the following edited version of a longer article, George Day uses the capability approach to explore what it means in reality to be 'market-driven', and contrasts this perspective with the more familiar competitive forces approach to business strategy.

The capabilities of market-driven organizations

George S. Day

The marketing concept has been a paradox in the field of management. For over 40 years managers have been exhorted to 'stay close to the customer', 'put the customer at the top of the organizational chart', and define the purpose of a business as the creation and retention of satisfied customers.[1] Companies that are better equipped to respond to market requirements and anticipate changing conditions are expected to enjoy long-run competitive advantage and superior profitability.

Throughout much of its history, however, the marketing concept has been more an article of faith than a practical basis for managing a business.[2] Little was known about the defining features or attributes of this organizational orientation, and evidence as to the antecedents and performance consequences was mainly anecdotal. Consequently, managers had little guidance on how to improve or redirect their organizations' external orientation toward their markets.

Fortunately, this situation is changing following a 'rediscovery' in the late 1980s (Dickson 1992; Webster 1988). In the last five years, a number of conceptual and empirical studies have appeared that more clearly describe what a market orientation is and what it consists of. According to this emerging literature, market orientation represents superior skills in understanding and satisfying customers (Day 1990). Its principal features are the following:

- A set of beliefs that puts the customer's interest first (Deshpandé, Farley, and Webster 1993),
- The ability of the organization to generate, disseminate, and use superior information about customers and competitors (Kohli and Jaworski 1990), and
- The coordinated application of interfunctional resources to the creation of superior customer value (Narver and Slater 1990; Shapiro 1988b).

In addition, a modest but growing body of empirical evidence supports the proposition that a market orientation is positively associated with superior performance (Deshpandé, Farley, and Webster 1993; Jaworski and Kohli 1992; Narver and Slater 1990; Ruekert 1992). [. . .]

THE CAPABILITIES APPROACH TO STRATEGY

Two perspectives on competitiveness

How does a business achieve and maintain a superior competitive position? This question is at the heart of the strategy development process and largely defines the field of strategic management. One answer given by the emerging capabilities or resource-based theories cites two related sources of advantage: *Assets* are the resource endowments the business has accumulated (e.g., investments in the scale, scope, and efficiency of facilities and systems, brand equity, and the consequences of the location of activities for factor costs and government support); and *capabilities* are the glue that brings these assets together and enables them to be deployed advantageously. Capabilities differ from assets in that they cannot be given a monetary value, as can tangible plant and equipment, and are so deeply embedded in the organizational routines and practices that they cannot be traded or imitated (Dierkx and Cool 1989).

The competitive forces approach (Porter 1980) and the related entry deterrence approach (Ghemawat 1990), which have been the dominant paradigms in the strategy field (Teece, Pisano, and Shuen 1991), have a different answer to the question of how superior performance is achieved. These approaches put the emphasis on the intensity of competition in the industry and market segment that determines the profit potential. The firm seeks a position in an attractive market that it can defend against competitors. Although management's task is then to identify and develop the requisite capabilities, what really matters is achieving a defensible cost or differentiation position in an attractive market and keeping their rivals off balance through strategic investments, pricing strategies, and signals.

The capabilities approach, by contrast, locates the sources of a defensible competitive position in the distinctive, hard-to-duplicate resources the firm has developed (Itami 1987; Rumelt, Schendel, and Teece 1991). These resources, which are made up of integrated combinations of assets and capabilities, are cultivated slowly over time and limit the ability of the firm to adapt to change. Management's task is to determine how best to improve and exploit these firm-specific resources (Mahoney and Pandian 1992), although in times of turbulence the challenge of developing new capabilities comes to the fore (Barney 1991; Wernerfelt 1984).

Defining and identifying capabilities

[. . .]As noted previously, capabilities are complex bundles of skills and accumulated knowledge, exercised through organizational processes, that enable firms to coordinate activities and make use of their assets.[3] Capabilities are manifested in such typical business activities as order fulfillment, new product development, and service delivery. One well-known capability is Wal-Mart's cross-docking logistics system (Stalk, Evans and Shulman 1992). It is part of a broader 'customer pull' system that starts with individual stores placing their orders on the basis of store-movement data. These orders are gathered and filled by suppliers in full truckloads. The loads are delivered to Wal-Mart's warehouses, where they are sorted, repacked, and dispatched to stores. The transfer from one loading dock to another takes less than 48 hours, sharply cutting the usual inventory and handling costs.

Capabilities and organizational processes are closely entwined, because it is the capability that enables the activities in a business process to be carried out. The business will have as many processes as are necessary to carry out the natural business activities defined by the stage in the value chain and the key success factors in the market. Thus, the necessary business processes of a life insurance company will be different from the processes found in the microprocessor fabricator. Each of the processes has a beginning and end state that facilitates identification and implies all the work that gets done in between. Thus, new product development proceeds from concept screening to market launch, and the order fulfilment process extends from the receipt of the order to payment.

Because capabilities are deeply embedded within the fabric of the organization, they can be hard for the management to identify. One way to overcome this problem is to create detailed maps of the sets of process activities in which the capabilities are employed (Hammer and Champy 1993). These maps usually show that capabilities and their defining processes span several functions and several organizational levels and involve extensive communications.

Capabilities are further obscured because much of their knowledge component is tacit and dispersed. This knowledge is distributed along four separate dimensions (Leonard-Barton 1992): First are the accumulated employee *knowledge* and *skills* that come from technical knowledge, training, and long experience with the process. The second dimension is the knowledge embedded in *technical systems*, comprising the information in linked databases, the formal procedures and established 'routines' for dealing with given problems or transactions (Nelson and Winter 1982), and the computer systems themselves. Third and fourth are the *management systems* and the *values* and *norms* that define the content and interpretation of the knowledge, transcend individual capabilities, and unify these capabilities into a cohesive whole. The management systems represent the formal and informal ways of creating and controlling knowledge. The values and norms that dictate what information is to be collected, what types are most important, who gets access to the information, how it is to be used, and so forth are a part of the overall culture.[4]

Distinctive capabilities

Every business acquires many capabilities that enable it to carry out the activities necessary to move its products or services through the value chain. Some will be done adequately, others poorly, but a few must be superior if the business is to outperform the competition. These are the distinctive capabilities that support a market position that is valuable and difficult to match. They must be managed with special care through the focused commitment of resources, assignment of dedicated people, and continued efforts to learn, supported by dramatic goals for improvement.

The most defensible test of the distinctiveness of a capability is whether it makes a disproportionate contribution to the provision of superior customer value – as defined from the customer's perspective – or permits the business to deliver value to customers in an appreciably more cost-effective way. In this respect a distinctive capability functions like a key success factor. Clearly, for example, Honda's prowess with fuel-efficient, reliable, and responsive small displacement engines and drive trains adds a great deal of value and sets their cars apart from the competition. Other examples are Motorola's mastery of continuous quality improvement and rapid product development and Federal Express's ability to manage integrated transaction processing systems.

Customers are unlikely to be aware of or interested in the underlying processes that yield the superior value they receive. Thus, one of the critical management tasks is to decide which capabilities to emphasize, which is dictated by how they choose to compete. Consider how Marriott Hotels is able to consistently receive the best ratings from business travelers and meeting planners for high-quality service. They are certainly as capable as Hyatt, Hilton, and others at selecting good sites, opening new hotels smoothly, and marketing them well (Irvin and Michaels 1989). What consistently sets them apart and reveals a distinctive service capability (actually a set of linked capabilities each performed outstandingly well) is a 'fanatical eye for detail'. This begins with a hiring process that systematically recruits, screens, and selects from as many as 40 applicants for each position and continues through every hotel operation; for example, maids follow a 66–point guide to making up bedrooms. The effective management of these linked processes, within an organizational culture that values thoroughness and customer responsiveness, creates a distinctive capability that gives

Marriott employees clear guidance on how to take the initiative to provide excellent customer service.

Another test asks whether the capability can be readily matched by rivals. Because distinctive capabilities are difficult to develop, they resist imitation. K Mart knows full well what Wal-Mart has accomplished with its logistics system and can readily buy the hardware and software, but it has been unable to match the underlying capability. First, Wal-Mart's capability is embedded in a complex process that harmonizes an array of skills and knowledge and involves considerable learning over many years. Second, Wal-Mart's processes are not readily visible because they cut across different organizational units. Third, because much of the collective knowledge that makes up the coordination skills is tacit and dispersed among many individuals, a competitor could not acquire the requisite knowledge simply by staffing with the best available people (Bartmess and Cerny 1993).

Another attribute of distinctive capabilities is that they are robust and can be used in different ways to speed the firm's adaptation to environmental change (Boynton and Victor 1991; Prahalad and Hamel 1990). Honda, for example, has been able to apply its companywide mastery of engine and drive train technology development and manufacturing processes to create distinctive capabilities in a variety of related markets like generators, outboard marine engines, and lawn mowers. It is less clear whether Honda's distinctive capability in dealer management (Stalk, Evans, and Shulman 1992), which was used to develop a network of better managed and financed motorcycle dealers than the part-time dealers of competitors, also aided its entry into new markets. On the one hand, Honda's skill at managing dealers has been of value in the auto market, where Honda dealers consistently receive high ratings for customer satisfaction. It is harder to say whether the logic of Honda's diversification into related markets was really guided by a desire to exploit this dealer management capability. More likely it was the ability to gain a multiplier effect by integrating both distinctive capabilities that shaped the moves into new markets.

The capabilities of a corporation that span and support multiple lines of business, such as those that Honda has deployed, are commonly called *core competencies*. Each of the separate business units draws on these corporatewide resources to quickly and effectively develop some or all of the distinctive capabilities it needs to attain a superior competitive position in its served markets. These core competencies are also different from both business and corporate assets (see Figure 9.1).

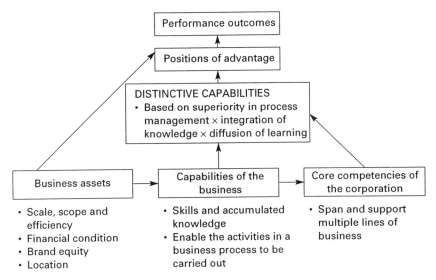

Figure 9.1 Sources of competitive advantage and superior performance

Capabilities and performance

The strategic importance of capabilities lies in their demonstrable contribution to sustainable competitive advantages and superior profitability. A sizeable literature has recently emerged to explain how capabilities serve as a source of competitive advantage and also accounts for the durability of these advantages (Amit and Schoemaker 1993; Peteraf 1993). The durability of capabilities-based advantages stems from

1 their scarcity,
2 their relative immobility, either because they cannot be traded or are much more valuable where they are currently employed than they would be elsewhere, and
3 the difficulty that competitors face in understanding and imitating them (Reed and De Fillippi 1990).

What if a business has no distinctive capabilities? In other words, it is no more proficient with any of its essential processes than the average of its rivals and is unable to distinguish itself favorably along any dimensions that are important to its target customers. If the industry is at a stalemate and none of its rivals has a meaningful advantage, then the profits of the business will settle at the level of the industry average (Porter 1980). In the more likely event that different competitors have mastered different capabilities and can offer higher quality, more responsive service, or more innovative products, then a parity business has no recourse but to lower its prices to offset the lack of benefits. Thus, a direct connection exists between the mastery of distinctive capabilities and superior profitability. [. . .]

Marketing sensing as a distinctive capability

Every discussion of market orientation emphasizes the ability of the firm to learn about customers, competitors, and channel members in order to continuously sense and act on events and trends in present and prospective markets. In market-driven firms the processes for gathering, interpreting, and using market information are more systematic, thoughtful, and anticipatory than in other firms. They readily surpass the ad hoc, reactive, constrained, and diffused efforts of their internally focused rivals.

A behavioral definition of a market orientation as 'the organization-wide generation of market intelligence, dissemination of its intelligence across departments, and organization-wide responsiveness to it' (Kohli and Jaworski 1990, p. 6), captures the essence of a market sensing capability. Each element of this definition describes a distinct activity having to do with collecting and acting on information about customer needs and the influence of technology, competition, and other environmental forces. Narver and Slater (1990) offer another definition in the same spirit. They distinguish three behavioral components: *customer orientation* – the firm's understanding of the target market; *competitor orientation* – the firm's understanding of the long-run capabilities of present and prospective competitors; and *interfunctional coordination* – the coordinated utilization of company resources to create superior customer value.

An alternative to this behavioral perspective holds that a market orientation is part of a more deeply rooted and pervasive culture. For this purpose, Deshpandé and Webster (1989, p. 3), following Davis (1984), define culture as 'the pattern of shared values and beliefs that gives the members of an organization meaning, and provides them with the rules for behavior.' A market-driven culture supports the value of thorough market intelligence and the necessity of functionally coordinated actions directed at gaining a competitive advantage. An absence of these shared beliefs and values would surely compromise the activity patterns advocated by the behavioral perspective.

The process of market sensing follows the usual sequence of information processing activities that organizations use to learn (Day 1994; Fioles and Lyes 1985; Huber 1991; Levitt and March 1988; Sinkula 1994). It can be initiated by a forthcoming decision or an emerging problem, such as explaining why performance is declining. In addition, established procedures for collecting secondary information may prompt further market-sensing activity. This step leads to the active acquisition and distribution of information about the needs and responses of the market, how it is segmented, how relationships are sustained, the intentions and capabilities of competitors, and the evolving role of channel partners. Before this information can be acted on, it has to be interpreted through a process of sorting, classification, and simplification to reveal coherent patterns. This interpretation is facilitated by the mental models of managers, which contain decision rules for filtering information and useful heuristics for deciding how to act on the information in the light of anticipated outcomes. Further learning comes from observing and evaluating the results of the decisions taken on the basis of the prior information. Did the market respond as expected, and if not, why not? Organizational memory plays several roles in this process: It serves as a repository for collective insights contained within policies, procedures, routines, and rules that can be retrieved when needed; a source of answers to ongoing inquiries; and a major determinant of the ability to ask appropriate questions.

Market-driven firms are distinguished by an ability to sense events and trends in their markets ahead of their competitors. They can anticipate more accurately the responses to actions designed to retain or attract customers, improve channel relations, or thwart competitors. They can act on information in a timely, coherent manner because the assumptions about the market are broadly shared. This anticipatory capability is based on superiority in each step of the process. It is achieved through open-minded inquiry, synergistic information distribution, mutually informed interpretations, and accessible memories.

Open-minded inquiry All organizations acquire information about trends, events, opportunities, and threats in their market environment through scanning, direct experience, imitation, or problem-solving inquiries. Market-driven organizations approach these activities in a more thoughtful and systematic fashion, in the belief that all decisions start with the market. The most distinctive features of their approach to inquiry are the following:

- *Active scanning* – All organizations track key market conditions and activities and try to learn from the departures from what is normal and expected. However, this learning is usually a top-down effect because information from the frontline employees is blocked. In market-driven organizations, these frontline contacts, who hear complaints or requests for new services and see the consequences of competitive activity, are motivated to inform management systematically.
- *Self-critical benchmarking* – Most firms do regular tear-down analyses of competitors' products and occasionally study firms for insights into how to perform discrete functions and activities better. Market-driven firms study attitudes, values, and management processes of nonpareils.
- *Continuous experimentation and improvement* – All organizations tinker

with their procedures and practices and take actions aimed at improving productivity and customer satisfaction. However, most are not very serious about systematically planning and observing the outcomes of these ongoing changes, so those that improve performance are adopted and others are dropped.

- *Informed imitation* – Market-driven firms study their direct competitors so they can emulate successful moves before the competition gets too far ahead. This investigation requires thoughtful efforts to understand why the competitor succeeded, as well as further probes for problems and shortcomings to identify improvements that would be welcomed by customers. Here the emphasis is more on what the competitor was able to achieve in terms of superior performance, features, and so forth, and less on understanding the capabilities of the competitor that resulted in the outcome.

Synergistic information distribution.   Firms often do not know what they know. They may have good systems for storing and locating 'hard' routine accounting and sales data, but otherwise managers have problems figuring out where in the organization a certain piece of information is known or assembling all the needed pieces in one place. This is especially true of competitor information, in which, for example, manufacturing may be aware of certain activities through common equipment suppliers, sales may hear about initiatives from distributors and collect rumors from customers, and the engineering department may have hired recently from a competitor.

Market-driven firms do not suffer unduly from organizational chimneys, silos, or smokestacks, which restrict information flows to vertical movements within functions. Instead, information is widely distributed, its value is mutually appreciated, and those functions with potentially synergistic information know where else it could be used beneficially.

Mutually informed interpretations.   The simplifications inherent in the mental models used by managers facilitate learning when they are based on undistorted information about important relationships and are widely shared throughout the organization (Senge 1990). These mental models can impede learning when they are incomplete, unfounded, or seriously distorted – by functioning below the level of awareness, they are never examined. A market-driven organization avoids these pitfalls by using scenarios and other devices (DeGeus 1988) to force managers to articulate, examine, and eventually modify their mental models of how their markets work, how competitors and suppliers will react, and the parameters of the response coefficients in their marketing programs.

Accessible memory.   Market-driven inquiry, distribution, and interpretation will not have a lasting effect unless what is learned is lodged in the collective memory. Organizations without practical mechanisms to remember what has worked and why will have to repeat their failures and rediscover their success formulas over and over again. Collective recall capabilities are most quickly eroded by turnover through transfers and rapid disbanding of teams. Data banks that are inaccessible to the entire organization can also contribute to amnesia. Here is where information technology can play an especially useful role.

Customer linking as a distinctive capability

As buyer-seller relationships continue their transformation, a customer-linking capability – creating and managing close customer relationships – is becoming increasingly important. At one time, standard purchasing practice emphasized arm's length adversarial bargaining with suppliers, aimed at achieving the lowest price for each transaction or contract. Not surprisingly, suppliers focused on individual transactions and gave little attention to the quality of the interface with the customer. They had little incentive to be open with buyers or develop superior or dedicated capabilities because they could easily lose the business to a competitor. The buyer, in turn, was unlikely to be aware of a supplier's costs and capabilities.

Now customers, as well as major channel members such as Ikea and Wal-Mart, are seeking closer, more collaborative relationships with suppliers based on a high level of coordination, participation in joint programs, and close communication links. They want to replace the adversarial model, which assumes that advantages are gained through cutting input costs, with a cooperative model that seeks advantage through total improvement and reduced time to market. This way of doing business suits their better suppliers, who confront intense competition that quickly nullifies their product advantages and powerful channels that control access to the market.

Despite recent emphasis on the establishment, maintenance, and enhancement of collaborative relationships, few firms have mastered this capability and made it a competitive advantage. Successful collaboration requires a high level of purposeful cooperation aimed at maintaining a trading relationship over time (Frazier, Spekman, and O'Neal 1988; Spekman 1988). The activities to be managed start with the coordination of inside-out and spanning capabilities, although these are not the means by which the relationship is managed. Instead, new skills, abilities, and processes must be mastered to achieve mutually satisfactory collaboration. These include the following.

Close communication and joint problem solving   Suppliers must be prepared to develop team-based mechanisms for continuously exchanging information about needs, problems, and emerging requirements and then taking action. In a successful collaborative relationship, joint problem solving displaces negotiations. Suppliers must also be prepared to participate in the customer's development processes, even before the product specifications are established.

Communications occur at many levels and across many functions of the customer and supplier organizations, requiring a high level of internal coordination and a new role for the sales function. When the focus is on transactions, the salesperson is pivotal and the emphasis is on persuading the customer through features, price, terms, and the maintenance of a presence. The sales function adopts a very different – and possibly subordinate – role in a collaborative relationship. It is responsible for coordinating other functions, anticipating needs, demonstrating responsiveness, and building credibility and trust.

Coordinating activities   In addition to the scheduling of deliveries, new management processes are needed for

1 joint production planning and scheduling,
2 management of information system links so each knows the other's requirements and status and orders can be communicated electronically, and
3 mutual commitments to the improvement of quality and reliability.

Manufacturer-reseller relations has become a fertile area for the development of collaborative management capabilities, with the major grocery product firms taking the lead. The objective of each party used to be to transfer as much of their cost to the other as possible. This approach led to dysfunctional practices such as forward buying to take advantage of manufacturer's promotional offers, resulting in excessive warehousing expenses and costly spikes in production levels. Traditionally, contacts between parties were limited to lower-level sales representatives calling on buyers who emphasized prices, quantities, and deals. Increasingly, manufacturers like Procter & Gamble and retailers like KMart are assigning multifunctional teams to deal with each other at many levels, including harmonizing systems, sharing logistics and product movement information, and jointly planning for promotional activity and product changes. The objectives of this collaborative activity are to cut total system costs while helping retailers improve sales.

Firms that have developed a distinctive capability for managing collaborative relationships find they have more integrated strategies. The integration begins with a broad-based agreement on which customers serve collaboratively (Anderson and Narus 1991). No longer is this choice left to the sales function, without regard to the impact on the manufacturing and service functions. The cross-functional coordination and information sharing required to work collaboratively with customers enhances shared understanding of the strategy and role of the different functions.

Although collaborative relationships are becoming increasingly important, they are not appropriate for every market or customer. Some customers want nothing more than the timely exchange of the product or service with minimum hassle and a competitive price. And because of the effort and resources required to support a tightly linked relationship, it may not be possible to do this with more than a few critical customers (Shapiro 1988a). Yet even when most relationships are purely transactional, there are still possibilities for gaining advantages by nurturing some elements of a linking capability with the organization. This process begins by analyzing which customers are more loyal or easier to retain and proceeds by seeking ways to maintain continuity with these customers through customized services or incentives. [. . .]

SUMMARY AND CONCLUSIONS

It is almost an article of faith within marketing that superior business performance is the result of superior skills in understanding and satisfying customers. This proposition has been partially validated by a growing body of research on the impact of a market orientation on business performance. This work has helped give a fuller picture of the attributes of market-driven organizations, highlighting the roles of culture, information utilization, and interfunctional coordination. These insights are not sufficient for managers, because they do not reveal how the superior skills were developed. All we see is the results of the organizational transformation. Now managers seek guidance on how to enhance the market orientation of the organization.

The emerging capabilities approach to strategy offers a valuable new perspective on how to achieve and sustain a market orientation. This approach seeks the sources of defensible competitive positions in the distinctive, difficult-to-imitate capabilities the organization has developed. The shift in emphasis to capabilities does not mean that strategic positioning is any less important (Porter 1991). On the contrary, the choice of which capabilities to nurture and which investment commitments to make must be guided by a shared understanding of the industry structure, the needs of the target customer segments, the positional advantages being sought, and the trends in the environment.

Two capabilities are especially important in bringing these external realities to the attention of the organization. One is the market sensing capability, which determines how well the organization is equipped to continuously sense changes in its market and to anticipate the responses to marketing actions. The second is a customer-linking capability, which comprises the skills, abilities, and processes needed to achieve collaborative customer relationships so individual customer needs are quickly apparent to all functions and well-defined procedures are in place for responding to them.

NOTES

1 The earliest proponent of the marketing concept was Peter Drucker (1954), who argued that creating a satisfied customer was the only valid definition of business purpose. Subsequent authors described the concept and its benefits, e.g., McKittrick (1957), Felton (1959), Barksdale and Darden (1971), Kotler (1977), Peters and Waterman (1982), Shapiro (1988b) and Webster (1992). These authors do not make careful distinctions among *customer oriented, market oriented,* and *market driven;* they lean toward *market-driven* to describe the orientation of a firm that stays close to its customers and ahead of its competitors – thus making competitive superiority an explicit element of the concept.
2 This state of affairs may explain why the marketing concept has had little influence on other management fields. Thus, a review of 'all variables that have been proposed seriously as indices of organizational effectiveness' (Campbell 1977) failed to mention customer satisfaction. Similarly, the notion of a market orientation is nowhere to be found in a discussion of competing principles of management presumed to be causally related to the effectiveness of organizations (Lewin and Minton 1986). During this period, however, discussions of organizational culture gave considerable weight to an 'external versus internal emphasis' as an influential aspect of a culture (Reynolds 1986).
3 Distinctions are frequently made between *competencies,* well-defined routines that are combined with firm-specific assets to enable distinctive functions to be carried out, and *capabilities,* the mechanisms and processes by which new competencies are developed (Teece, Pisano, and Shuen 1991). This implies that competencies are largely static, which seems a restrictive and unnecessary condition. Thus, for our purpose the terms are essentially interchangeable.
4 This role of culture is consistent with the organizational cognition paradigm from which the competing values model of culture is derived (Quinn 1988; Quinn and McGrath; Smircich 1983). This model has been successfully adapted to the study of cultures of market-driven organizations by Deshpandé, Farley, and Webster (1988).

REFERENCES

Amit, Raphael and Paul J. H. Schoemaker (1993), 'Strategic Assets and Organizational Rent', *Strategic Management Journal*, 14 (January), 33–46.
Anderson, James C. and James A. Narus (1991), 'Partnering as a Focused Market Strategy', *California Management Review* (Spring), 95–113.
Barksdale, Hiram C. and Bill Darden (1971), 'Marketers' Attitudes Toward the Marketing Concept', *Journal of Marketing*, 35 (October) 29–36.
Barney, Jay (1991), 'Firm Resources and Sustained Competitive Advantage', *Journal of Management*, 17, 99–120.
Bartmess, Andrew and Keith Cerny (1993), 'Building Competitive Advantage Through a Global Network of Capabilities', *California Management Review* (Winter), 78–103.
Boynton, Andrew C. and Bart Victor (1991), 'Beyond Flexibility: Building and Managing the Dynamically Stable Organization', *California Management Review* (Fall), 53–66.

Campbell, John P. (1977), 'On the Nature of Organizational Effectiveness', in *New Perspectives on Organizational Effectiveness*, P. S. Goodman and J. M. Pennings, eds. San Francisco; Jossey-Bass, 13–55.

Davis, Stanley M. (1984), *Managing Corporate Culture*. Cambridge, MA: Ballinger Publishing Co.

Day, George S. (1990) *Market-Driven Strategy: Processes for Creating Value*. New York: The Free Press.

—— (1994), 'Continuous Learning About Markets,' *California Management Review*, forthcoming.

DeGeus, Arie P. (1988), 'Planning as Learning', *Harvard Business Review*, 66 (March/April), 70–74.

Deshpandé, Rohit, John U. Farley, and Frederick Webster, Jr. (1993) 'Corporate Culture, Customer Orientation, and Innovativeness in Japanese Firms: A Quadrad Analysis', *Journal of Marketing*, 57 (January) 23–37.

Dickson, Peter R. (1992) 'Toward A General Theory of Competitive Rationality', *Journal of Marketing*, 56 (January), 69–83.

Dierckx, I. and K. Cool (1989), 'Asset Stock Accumulation and Sustainability of Competitive Advantage', *Management Science*, 35 (December), 1504–11.

Drucker, Peter F. (1954), *The Practice of Management*. New York: Harper & Row.

Felton, Arthur P. (1959) 'Making the Marketing Concept Work', *Harvard Business Review*, 37 (July/August), 55–65.

Fioles, C. M. and M. A. Lyles (1985), 'Organizational Learning', *Academy of Management Review*, 10 (October), 803–13.

Frazier, Gary L., Robert E. Spekman, and Charles R. O'Neal (1988), 'Just-in-Time Exchange Relationships in Industrial Markets', *Journal of Marketing*, 52 (October), 52–67.

Ghemawat, Pankaj (1990), *Commitment: The Dynamics of Strategy*. New York Free Press.

Grant, Robert M. (1991), 'The Resource-Based Theory of Competitive Advantage: Implications for Strategy Formulation', *California Management Review* (Spring), 114–35.

Hamel, Gary and C. K. Prahalad (1989), 'Strategic Intent', *Harvard Business Review*, 67 (May/June), 63–76.

Hammer, Michael and James Champy (1993) *Reengineering the Corporation: A Manifesto for Business Revolution*. New York: Harper Business.

Huber, George P. (1991) 'Organizational Learning: The Contributing Processes and the Literatures', *Organization Science*, 2 (February), 88–115.

Irvin, Robert, A. and Edward G. Michaels III (1989), 'Core Skills: Doing the Right Things Right', *The McKinney Quarterly* (Summer) 4–19.

Itami, Hiroyuki (1987), *Mobilizing Invisible Assets*. Cambridge, MA: Harvard University Press.

Jacob, Rahul (1993), 'TQM: More than a Dying Fad?' *Fortune* (October 18), 66–72.

Jaworski, Bernard and Ajay Kohli, (1993), 'Market Orientation: Antecedents and Consequences', *Journal of Marketing*, 57 (July), 53–70.

Kohli, Ajay K. and Bernard Jaworski (1990), 'Market Orientation: The Construct, Research and Propositions, and Managerial Implications', *Journal of Marketing*, 54 (April), 1–18.

Kotler, Philip (1977), 'From Sales Obsession to Marketing Effectiveness', *Harvard Business Review*, 55 (November/December), 67–75.

Leonard-Barton, Dorothy (1992), 'Core Capabilities and Core Rigidities: A Paradox in Managing New Product Development', *Strategic Management Journal*, 13 (Summer), 111–25.

Levitt, Barbara and James G. March (1988), 'Organizational Learning', *Annual Review of Sociology*, W. Richard Scott and Judith Blake, eds. Palo Alto, CA: Annual Reviews, Inc., 319–40.

Lewin, Arie Y. and John W. Minton (1986), 'Determining Organizational Effectiveness: Another Look, and an Agenda for Research', *Management Science*, 32 (May) 514–38.

Mahoney, John T. and J. Rajendran Pandian (1992), 'The Resource-Based View Within the Conversation of Strategic Management', *Strategic Management Journal*, 13 (June), 363–80.

McKitterick, J. B. (1957), 'What Is the Marketing Management Concept?' in *The Frontiers of Marketing Thought and Science*, Frank M. Bass, ed. Chicago: American Marketing Association, 71–92.

Narver, John C. and Stanley F. Slater (1990), 'The Effect of a Marketing Orientation on Business Profitability', *Journal of Marketing* 54 (October), 20–35.

Nelson, Richard R. and Sidney G. Winter (1982), *An Evolutionary Theory of Economic Change*. Cambridge MA: Harvard University Press.

Peteraf, Margaret A. (1993), 'The Cornerstones of Competitive Advantage: A Resource-Based View', *Strategic Management Journal*, 14 (March), 179–91.

Pfeffer, Jeffrey and Gerald R. Salancik (1978), *The External Control of Organizations: A Resource Dependence Perspective*. New York: Harper and Row.

Porter, Michael (1980), *Competitive Strategies*. New York: The Free Press.

—— (1991), 'Towards a Dynamic Theory of Strategy', *Strategic Management Journal*, 12 (Winter), 95–118.

Prahalad, C. K. and Gary Hamel (1990), 'The Core Competence of the Corporation', *Harvard Business Review* (May/June), 79–91.

Quinn, Robert E. (1988), *Beyond Rational Management*. San Francisco: Jossey-Bass.

—— and Michael R. McGrath (1985), 'Transformation of Organizational Cultures: A Competing Values Perspective', in *Organizational Culture*, Peter First, et al., eds. Beverley Hills, CA. Sage Publications.

Reed, Richard and Robert DeFillippi (1990) 'Causal Ambituity, Barriers to Imitation, and Sustainable Competitive Advantage', *Academy of Management Review*, 15 (1), 88–102.

Reynolds, Paul D. (1986), 'Organizational Culture as Related to Industry, Position and Performance: A Preliminary Report', *Journal of Management Studies*, 23 (May), 333–45.

Ruekert, Robert W. (1992), 'Developing a Market Orientation: An Organizational Strategy Perspective', *International Journal of Research in Marketing*, 9, 225–45.

Rumelt, Richard P., Dan Schendel, and David Teece (1991), 'Strategic Management and Economics', *Strategic Management Journal*, 12 (Winter), 5–30.

Senge, Peter M. (1990), *The Fifth Discipline: The Art and Practice of the Learning Organization*. New York: Doubleday.

Shapiro, Benson P. (1988a), 'Close Encounters of the Four Kinds: Managing Customers in a Rapidly Changing Environment', unpublished working paper, Harvard Business School.

—— (1988b), 'What the Hell is "Market Orientated"?', *Harvard Business Review*, 66 (November/December), 119–25.

——, V. Kasturi Rangan, and John J. Sviokla (1992), 'Staple Yourself to an Order,' *Harvard Business Review*, 70, (July/August), 113–22.

Sinkula, James M. (1994), 'Market Information Processing and Organizational Learning,' *Journal of Marketing*, 58 (January), 35–45.

Smircich, Linda (1983), 'Concepts of Culture and Organizational Analysis', *Administrative Science Quarterly*, 28 (September), 338–58.

Spekman, Robert, (1988), 'Strategic Supplier Selection: Towards and Understanding of Long-Term Buyer-Seller Relationship' *Business Horizons*, 24–36.

Stalk, George, Philip Evans, and Lawrence E. Shulman (1992), 'Competing on Capabilities: The New Rules of Corporate Strategy', *Harvard Business Review*, 70 (March/April), 57–69.

Teece, David J., Gary Pisano, and Amy Shuen (1991), 'Dynamic Capabilities and Strategic Management', working paper, University of California, Berkeley.

Webster, Frederick E., Jr. (1992) 'The Changing Role of Marketing in the Corporation', *Journal of Marketing*, 56 (October), 1–17.

Wernerfelt, Berger (1984), 'A Resource-Based View of the Firm', *Strategic Management Journal*, 5 (March), 171–80.

Chapter 10

Information management

With so much written and talked about information *technology* we often forget that information itself is the lifeblood of all organizations and the stuff with which all managers work. Whether a manager is concerned with human resource issues, marketing or research and development; or whether the organization's function is to transport passengers, manufacture televisions, collect taxes or to treat the sick, management at all levels has to manage the acquisition and processing of information, and must employ information in order to make decisions and put them into effect. In the first article in this section, Davenport, Eccles and Prusak emphasize that the way in which information is managed is a function of organizational politics. Information access and information flows are conditional on organizational structures and processes that themselves result from organizational politics. Taking as their pretext the notion that information is power, the authors propose five different models of information politics that illustrate the benefits and consequences of these adopted political regimes. Information and communication technologies used in support of particular forms of information politics are of course extremely powerful tools.

The second article explores how information can be managed strategically in conditions of rapid, frequent and unpredictable changes in the organization's environment. Under these conditions, organizations must strive to achieve what Boynton calls dynamic stability – the ability to react to changing markets and environmental demands whilst at the same time cumulatively building knowledge and organizational capabilities. He provides examples of the ways in which organizations can use information and communication technology to support the process of achieving dynamic stability and cope with conditions of rapid, unpredictable and frequent change.

Information politics

Thomas H. Davenport, Robert G. Eccles and Laurence Prusak

[...]
'Information is not innocent.'

(James March)[1]

During the past decade, many firms have concluded that information is one of their most critical business resources and that broadening information access and usage and enhancing its quality are key to improving business performance. The 'information-based organization', the 'knowledge-based enterprise,' and the 'learning organization,' forecasted by management experts, all require a free flow of information around the firm.[2] The computers and communications networks that manipulate and transmit information become more powerful each year. Yet the rhetoric and technology of information management have far outpaced the ability of people to understand and agree on what information they need and then to share it.

Today, in fact, the information-based organization is largely a fantasy. All of the writers on information-based organizations must speak hypothetically, in the abstract, or in the future tense. Despite forty years of the Information Revolution in business, most managers still tell us that they cannot get the information they need to run their own units or functions. As a recent article by the CEO of a shoe company put it: 'On one of my first days on the job, I asked for a copy of every report used in management. The next day, twenty-three of them appeared on my desk. I didn't understand them ... Each area's reports were greek to the other areas, and all of them were greek to me.'[3] A more accurate metaphor might be that these reports each came from a different city-state – Athens, Sparta, Corinth, Thebes, and Peloponnesus – each part of the organization but a separate political domain with its own culture, leaders, and even vocabulary.

We have studied information management approaches in more than twenty-five companies over the past two years. Many of their efforts to create information-based organizations – or even to implement significant information management initiatives – have failed or are on the path to failure. The primary reason is that the companies did not manage the politics of information. Either the initiative was inappropriate for the firm's overall political culture, or politics were treated as peripheral rather than integral to the initiative. Only when information politics are viewed as a natural aspect of organizational life and consciously managed will true information-based organizations emerge.

Furthermore, a good argument can be made – and there is increasing evidence for it – that as information becomes the basis for organizational structure and function, politics will increasingly come into play. In the most information-oriented companies we studied, people were least likely to share information freely, as perceived by these companies' managers. As people's jobs and roles become defined by the unique information they hold, they may be less likely to share that information – viewing it as a source of power and indispensability – rather than more so. When information is the primary unit of organizational currency, we should not expect its owners to give it away.[4]

This assertion directly contradicts several academic and popular concepts about how widespread information and information technology will affect organizations. These thinkers have hypothesized that as organizations make widespread use of information technology, information will flow freely and quickly eliminate hierarchy. Mention is rarely made in such accounts of the specter of information politics.[5] Although this optimistic view has widespread appeal, it is not what we see today in companies.

When owners of key information resist sharing it either outright or, more commonly, through bureaucratic maneuvres, they are often dismissed as unfair or opportunistic. Yet they may have quite legitimate reasons for withholding the information. Political behavior regarding information should be viewed not as irrational or inappropriate but as a normal response to certain organizational situations. Valid differences in interpretation of information, for example, may lead to apparently intransigent behavior. At an electronics company we once worked with, the marketing organizations for direct and indirect channels could never agree on what constituted a sale. Getting the product to the end-customer was direct marketing's sale; getting it to the distributor, even though it might return eventually, was how the indirect group wanted to measure its success. When the indirect channel was the dominant one for the company, this group's view of sales prevailed. Later, as more product moved directly to buyers, end-customer sales became the official definition. In information politics, might makes right. As a result of losing influence, however, the indirect group wanted to create its own sales databases and reports. Political disputes of this type will often arise when there is no consensus around the business's information needs.

One reason the stakes are so high in information politics is that more than information is at stake. In order to arrive at a common definition of information requirements, organizations must often address not just the information they use, but the business practices and processes that generate the information. Most firms have not recognized the linkage between processes and information, but there are a few exceptions. At a fast-growing specialty manufacturer, CEO-appointed information 'czars' are responsible for ensuring consistency in the information-generating activities of their areas. For example, the order-processing czar mandated common companywide practices for assigning customer and product numbers, recognizing revenue, and determining contract prices. At IBM, eighteen key business processes (e.g., 'customer fulfillment') are being redesigned to build a new information infrastructure. Out of each new process will come information on its performance – how long it takes, how much it costs, how satisfied the customer is with it – as well as the more traditional results-oriented information such as sales and profitability. At Dow Chemical, managers believe there must be common financial processes around the world in order to create common measures of financial performance. [. . .]

Our purpose is to help companies understand information politics and manage them. In the next section, we classify the major models of information politics we have seen in client companies and firms we have studied. Following that, we present a set of approaches to managing information politics at both a strategic and a day-to-day level.

MODELS OF INFORMATION POLITICS

We have identified five information models (or, to continue the political metaphor, 'states') that are representative of the practices we have observed (see Table 10.1). Three of these, technocratic utopianism, anarchy, and feudalism, are less effective than the other two, monarchy and federalism.[6] After we define each model, we will evaluate their relative effectiveness along the dimensions of information quality, efficiency, commonality, and access.

Any organization is likely to have proponents for more than one of these models. Sometimes the models conflict, and sometimes one model predominates. Table 10.2 shows the distribution of models among the companies we studied. The first step in managing information more effectively and realistically is explicitly recognizing these existing models and then choosing a single desired state. Maintaining multiple models is confusing and consumes scarce resources. Once a model has been selected, an organization can manage the daily politics of information, just as an alderman manages a ward.

Technocratic utopianism

Many companies have a strong bias toward approaching information management from a technological perspective. This approach eschews information politics, assuming that politics are an aberrant form of behavior. It is usually driven by a firm's information systems (IS) professionals, who see themselves as the custodians, if not the owners, of the firm's information. Their technological efforts to alleviate information problems often involve a considerable amount of detailed planning and revolve around modeling and efficient use of corporate data. Their goal is to plan a technology infrastructure that can deliver information to each individual's desktop and then to build databases with the correct structure to store this information without redundancy. Some technical efforts around information management are reasonable; however, when the technological approach to information predominates, the company's model of information management can be described as technocratic utopianism.

Although neither the IS professionals nor the users may be consciously creating a technocratic utopia, there is an underlying assumption that technology will resolve all problems and that organizational and political issues are nonexistent or unmanageable. In fact, information itself – its content, use, and implications for managing – receives little attention in this model. The focus is instead on the technologies used to manipulate the information.

We found technocratic utopianism, either by itself or alongside another model, in almost a third of the firms we analyzed. The model usually coexists, however uneasily, with other models; in fact, the technocratic utopian model is often held by a small group of technologists supported by many technical journals, consultants, and technology vendors. While the technologists plan a utopia around the free flow of information, the senior executives for whom they work usually ignore, or are ignorant of, their efforts. Because these technical models are difficult for nontechnologists to understand, managers outside the IS function are rarely active participants. If a technocratic utopia is the only political model, it is probably because senior managers have abdicated their roles in selecting and managing information.

Technocratic utopians often have three factors in common: they focus heavily on information modeling and categorization; they highly value emerging hardware and software technologies; and they attempt to address an organization's entire information inventory.

A key emphasis in most technocratic utopias is information modeling and categorization. Once a unit of information is represented in an 'entity-relationship model' or a 'data-flow diagram', all problems in managing it have been solved, according to the extreme utopians. They consider such modeling and categorization a key aspect of the engineering of information

Table 10.1 Models of information politics

Technocratic Utopianism	A heavily technical approach to information management stressing categorization and modeling of an organization's full information assets, with heavy reliance on emerging technologies.
Anarchy	The absence of any overall information management policy, leaving individuals to obtain and manage their own information.
Feudalism	The management of information by individual business units or functions, which define their own information needs and report only limited information to the overall corporation.
Monarchy	The definition of information categories and reporting structures by the firm's leaders, who may or may not share the information willingly after collecting it.
Federalism	An approach to information management based on consensus and negotiation on the organization's key information elements and reporting structures.

(indeed, 'information engineering' is an established discipline within the IS profession). In this ideal world, information flows like water, and the only task is to construct appropriate canals, aqueducts, and dams in order for information to flow freely to those who need it. Information sometimes feels as common in organizations as water; since it is so plentiful, there is a natural instinct to try to channel it rather than drown in it.

Information engineering is important, of course, but the political aspects cannot be neglected. Information may flow like water, but in the real world even water doesn't flow without political assistance. Those knowledgeable about the back-room politics involved in bringing water to Los Angeles or about Robert Moses's political steamrolling in New York's water management will understand the role of politics in managing a 'natural' resource like information.[7]

Technologists also frequently assert that new forms of hardware and software are the keys to information success. Executives often hear that they will get the information they need 'when our new relational database system is installed' or 'when our new network is complete'. The coming panacea for many organizations is object-oriented technologies, in which information is combined with application functions in reusable modules. Too often, however, when the silver bullet arrives it does not have the intended effect. No technology has yet been invented to convince unwilling managers to share information or even to use it. [. . .]

Finally, utopians focus on all information throughout the corporation – at least all that can be captured by a computer. A common example is the creation of an 'enterprise model' – a structured inventory and categorization of all data elements used throughout the firm. Such modeling exercises often take years and yield vast amounts of detail. Although their purpose is often to eliminate redundant date storage, they often yield little real business value. Several MIT researchers have chronicled their failure.[8]
[. . .]

Technocratic utopians assume that managing information is an exercise without passion. Their rallying cry is an uninspiring, 'Data is a corporate asset'. They believe, consciously or unconsciously, that information's value for business decisions is not only very high but also self-evident. They assume that employees who possess information useful to others will share it willingly. They assume that information itself is valueless, or at least that its value is the same to all organizational members. If they are conscious of the relationship between information access and hierarchy, they assume that those high in the hierarchy would not restrict the free flow of information for any reason other than corporate security. These assumptions resemble human behavior found only in utopias.

Anarchy

Some firms have no prevailing political information model and exist in a state of anarchy. Rarely do organizations consciously choose this state, in which individuals fend for their own information needs. Information anarchy usually emerges when more centralized approaches to information management break down or when no key executive realizes the importance of common information. Information anarchy was made possible – and much more dangerous – by the introduction and rapid growth of the personal computer. Suddenly individuals and small departments could manage their own databases, tailoring their own reports to their own needs at any time and at minimal cost.

Although several firms we researched have allowed anarchy to survive, we found only one firm that had consciously chosen it. This software firm had previously tried to develop an overall information management structure by asking key managers what information they needed to run the business. When the firm could not achieve consensus, it determined that a bottom-up structured exchange of documents across its network, using a new software technology developed for this purpose, would yield all of the required information. Even here, however, an alternative information model flourished in some quarters; as one senior executive put it, 'I get all the information I need in breakfast meetings with the CEO.'

The long-term shortcomings of information anarchy are obvious. Technologists might worry that so much redundant information processing and storage is inefficient, but anarchy has more serious shortcomings. When everyone has his or her own database, the numbers for revenues, costs, customer order levels, and so on will diverge in databases throughout the company. Although anarchy is seldom chosen consciously, its effects are not uncommon; we know of several firms in which it was the source of late or inaccurate quarterly earnings reports. A firm cannot survive for long with such information discrepancies. The desire for information that leads to anarchy should quickly be harnessed into a more organized political model.

Feudalism

The political model we most often encountered was feudalism. In a feudal model, individual executives and their departments generally control information acquisition, storage, distribution, and analysis.[9] These powerful executives determine what information will be collected within their realms, how it will be interpreted, and in what format it will be reported to the 'king' or CEO. They can also decide what measures are used to understand performance as well as what 'language', by which we mean a common vocabulary, is used within the realm. Different realms often end up with different languages, and the subsequent fragmenting of information authority diminishes the power of the entire enterprise – just as the growth of powerful noblemen and their entourages inhibited the king's power in medieval times.

Feudal actions diminish the central authority's power to make informed decisions for the common good. Key measures of the enterprise's health often are not collected, reported, or even considered beyond roll-up of financial outcomes, further diminishing the central authority's power. Corporatewide performance is of interest only to those within corporate headquarters, and its indicators may poorly reflect what is actually happening around the firm.

Feudalism flourishes, of course, in environments of strong divisional autonomy. When divisions have their own strategies, products, and customers, it is almost inevitable that their information needs will differ. Furthermore, they may also be reluctant to fully disclose potentially negative information at the corporate level.

At a major consumer electronics firm's U.S. subsidiary, the feudalism was quite overt. The firm was organized along product lines; product division heads were informally referred to as 'barons'. Each had his or her own financial reporting system, with only the most limited amounts of data shared with the subsidiary head. [. . .]

At a large consumer goods firm organized by distribution channel, each channel had its own measures of performance that it thought were important. This information autonomy had prevailed for years and was tolerated because the firm had long been profitable using any set of measures. A new CEO arrived at a time when profits were down, and he felt he had no way to manage across the entire firm. He mandated the development of a common information architecture. Unfortunately, the IS group charged with this initiative began to create a technocratic utopia. We suspect that the feudal culture will eventually prevail. [...]

Despite these battles in feudal environments, some degree of cooperation can emerge. Powerful executives can create strategic alliances to share information or establish a common network or architecture, just as feudal lords banded together to build a road or common defense wall, go to war, or plan a marriage for mutual enrichment. [...]

Monarchy

The most practical solution to the problems inherent in the feudal model is to impose an information monarchy. The CEO, or someone empowered by the chief executive, dictates the rules for how information will be managed. Power is centralized, and departments and divisions have substantially less autonomy regarding information policies.

Much depends on the approach the 'monarch' takes to managing the realm's information. A more benign monarch (or enlightened despot, as they were called in the eighteenth century) will tilt toward freer access and distribution of key information and may attempt to rationalize and standardize the parameters used to measure the state's health and wealth. This top-down model may be most appropriate for firms that have difficulty achieving consensus across business units.

The rapidly growing specialty manufacturer mentioned above is an example. The CEO, who felt that information flow was critical to developing a flexible organization, decreed a policy of 'common information' to bring about access to consistent information by all who needed it. [...] This top-down approach is an example of enlightened monarchy at its best, since the action was taken not in response to a specific crisis but as a well-considered response to a broad organizational objective.

A progressive further step is a constitutional monarchy. Constitutional monarchy can evolve directly from feudalism or from the more despotic forms of monarchy. It is established by a document that states the monarch's limitations, the subjects' rights, and the law's authority. As a model for information management, this means that dominion is established over what information is collected, in what form, by whom, and for what ends. The chart of accounts becomes the realm's Magna Carta ('great charter'), a document establishing rules that will be enforced by processes and enabled by an information technology platform. A common vocabulary is developed so that the information's meaning is consistent and has integrity throughout the firm. The financial functions at both Digital and Dow

Chemical are establishing constitutional monarchies for financial information, with strong support from the CEOs. [...]

Federalism

The final information state, federalism, also has a number of desirable features, and in today's business environment, it is the preferred model in most circumstances. Its distinguishing feature is the use of negotiation to bring potentially competing and noncooperating parties together. Federalism most explicitly recognizes the importance of politics, without casting it in pejorative terms. In contrast, technocratic utopianism ignores politics, anarchy is politics run amok, feudalism involves destructive politics, and monarchy attempts to eliminate politics through a strong central authority. Federalism treats politics as a necessary and legitimate activity by which people with different interests work out among themselves a collective purpose and means for achieving it.

Firms that adopt or evolve into this model typically have strong central leadership and a culture that encourages cooperation and learning. However, it takes tough negotiating and a politically astute information manager to make the federalist model work. Such an information manager needs to have the CEO's support (although not too much support, or a monarchy emerges) as well as the trust and support of the 'lords and barons' who run the divisions. He or she needs to understand the value of information itself as well as of the technology that stores, manipulates, and distributes it. Such skills are not widely distributed throughout organizations, even (or perhaps especially) among IS executives.

An executive who has this perspective can then use cooperative information resources to create a shared information vision. Each realm contracts with the executive and with other realms to cede some of its information assets in return for helping to create a greater whole. This is a genuine leveraging of a firm's knowledge base.

At IBM, the former head of corporate information services, Larry Ford, concluded that the firm needed to manage information in a dramatically new way. Ford and his organization produced an information strategy that focused on the value that information can bring to all of IBM. The strategy was refined and ratified by all of the senior executives, and now Ford, his staff, and the divisional IS executives have gone out into the field to negotiate with senior managers about sharing their information with others in the company. 'Would you share your product quality data with the service organization? How about sales?' Eventually all the important information will be in easy-to-access 'data warehouses.' Information management at IBM has become very personal politics, like the ward politician campaigning door to door.

Table 10.2 Models observed in research sites

25 Companies Studied	Federalism	Monarchy	Technocratic Utopianism	Anarchy	Feudalism
Chemicals					
Company A			✓		✓
Company B	✓	✓			
Company C	✓		✓		
Computers					
Company A	✓			✓	✓
Company B	✓		✓		
Consumer Goods					
Company A			✓		✓
Company B					✓
Direct Marketing		✓			
Electronics					
Company A					✓
Company B					✓
Entertainment					✓
Financial Services		✓		✓	✓
Gas Transmission		✓			
Information Services					
Company A			✓		
Company B	✓				✓
Insurance					
Company A		✓	✓		
Company B	✓				✓
Company C					✓
Medical Supplies					
Company A			✓		
Company B	✓				✓
Office Products	✓		✓		
European Office Products			✓		
Software					
Company A		✓		✓	
Company B				✓	
Specialty Manufacturing		✓			
Total	8	7	9	4	12

Of course, the politician has only so much time to ring doorbells. A division may have hundreds of important data elements that need to be shared. IBM is finding that the time to educate and persuade information owners of their responsibilities is the biggest constraint to implementing a federalist model. Ford's departure from IBM to head a software firm may also place the federalist initiative at risk.

MANAGING INFORMATION POLITICS

Given these options for building an information polity, how do firms begin to effectively manage information? The first step is to select the preferred information model, as discussed in the next section. Following that, we present other principles of politically astute information management, including matching information politics to organizational culture, practising technological realism, electing the right information politicians, and avoiding empire-building.

Select an information state   The first step in managing information politics is figuring out which models people in the firm hold, which model currently predominates, which is most desirable, and how to achieve it. As we have noted, adopting multiple models will needlessly consume scarce resources and will confuse both information managers and users. Therefore, a firm should choose one model and move continually toward it, however long it takes.

We believe that there are only two viable choices among the five models: monarchy and federalism. In a business culture that celebrates empowerment and widespread participation, federalism is preferable, but it is harder to achieve and takes more time. Federalism requires managers to negotiate with each other in good faith while avoiding the temptation to use and withhold information destructively. Most firms we know of profess a desire to move toward a federalist model. But a firm that has difficulty getting consensus from its management team on other issues may find that federalism is impossible; a benevolent monarchy may be almost as effective and easier to implement.

Table 10.3 summarizes our assessments of the five political models along four dimensions:

1 commonality of vocabulary and meaning;
2 degree of access to important information;
3 quality of information – that is, its currency, relevance, and accuracy; and
4 efficiency of information management.

These dimensions can be useful for evaluating a firm's current model and its effectiveness.

Commonality refers to having a set of terms, categories, and data elements that carry the same meaning throughout the enterprise. The desirability of common discourse may appear obvious, but in our experience it does not exist in many large firms. Even the definition of what a 'sale' is can be variously interpreted by different divisions, to say nothing of more ambiguous terms such as 'quality', 'performance', and 'improvement'.[10]

The degree of information access is another good indicator of political

Table 10.3 Ranking alternative models of information politics

	Federalism	Monarchy	Technocratic Utopianism	Anarchy	Feudalism
Commonality of Vocabulary	5	5	3	1	1
Access to Information	5	2	3	4	1
Quality of Information	3	2	1	2	2
Efficiency of Information Management	3	5	3	1	3
Total	16	14	10	8	7

Note: 5 = high   3= moderate   1 = low

culture. Many firms proclaim that all employees should have the information they need to do their work well. However, in making the choices about who actually needs what information, firms are making political decisions, whether or not they acknowledge it. The technocratic utopians focus less on what information is accessed by whom and more on the mechanisms of distribution.

In many ways the quality of information is the most important of these indicators. Information quality is achieved through detailed attention to its integrity, accuracy, currency, interpretability, and overall value. As with other types of products, the quality of information is best judged by its customers. Even companies that declare themselves as firmly in the Information Age, however, rarely have measures or assessments of their information's quality.

Efficiency is often the objective of technologists who wish to minimize redundant data storage. The incredible improvements in price-performance ratios for data storage technologies have reduced this issue's importance somewhat. However, there is still the human factor. Multiple measures of the same item take time to analyze and synthesize. Effective management requires focusing on a few key performance indicators. Computers and disk drives may be able to handle information overload, but people still suffer from it.

Federalism has the potential to be effective on all four dimensions of information management. A common vocabulary emerges through negotiations between levels and units. This makes possible the widespread access and distribution of meaningful information, which is then used for the benefit of the whole enterprise. Federalism strikes a balance between the unintegrated independence of the feudal baronies and the undifferentiated units under monarchy. Although satisfying all constituencies may require gathering more information than is absolutely necessary (hence decreasing efficiency), and the necessary compromises may reduce quality, federalism scores higher in the minds of the managers we interviewed than any other model.

Because federalism explicitly acknowledges the important positive role that information politics can play, it is apt to be the most effective model for companies that rely on individual initiative for generating collective action. This is most likely to be the case for companies operating in complex and rapidly changing competitive environments, which create a high level of uncertainty. The federalist approach supports both autonomy and coordination. Accomplishing it, of course, requires negotiating skills and the willingness of managers to take the time to negotiate. Not all companies have executives with the ability or the commitment to do this. The temptation always exists to look to a strong monarch to resolve the endless negotiations by fiat, to fall prey once more to the alluring utopian vision painted by the technologists, to fall back into a nasty and brutish condition of feudal conflict, or to dissolve into the chaos of anarchy. Firms may want to pursue alternative models, in case federalism fails. In fact, as Table 10.2 shows, many of the firms pursuing federalism were also pursuing other models, either consciously or implicitly as a backup strategy. Sooner or later it is obviously best to settle on one model, though most firms find this difficult.

An information monarchy solves some of the problems of managing information throughout the enterprise. A strong, top-down approach ensures that a common language – in both vocabulary and meaning – underlies the information generated. Little unnecessary information is collected or distributed, guaranteeing a high level of efficiency. The monarch and his or her ministers mandate and oversee the right processes to generate the right information to be used in the right way – all enhancing information quality, at least as they perceive it. These advantages, however, are often gained at the expense of information access. It is the rare monarch who had enough democratic ideals to make information as broadly available as in a federalist state.

Technocratic utopianism focuses on using information technology to dramatically improve data distribution. Efficiency is high, at least in terms of a lack of data redundancy. Information access is also relatively high, at least for technologically oriented users. Because technocratic utopians do not concern themselves with the processes that produce information, the quality of information remains low. Further, the quality of information usage is inhibited by technocratic efforts such as complex data modeling that are often not understood or appreciated by line managers. As a result, the information produced by computer systems and the information actually used to manage the company are decoupled. Although this model scores high in principle, many of these initiatives fail. Commonality, access, and efficiency in a failed utopian scheme may actually be as low as in feudalism or even lower.

Although few executives would consciously adopt anarchy, it is not the lowest-scoring model. Commonality and efficiency are the lowest possible, of course, but at least individuals have easy access to the data they need. The customer controls information, thus its quality is likely to be high – unless the customer is an executive trying to take an organizationwide perspective.

Feudalism is the least effective political model along these dimensions. The existence of strong, independent, and often warring fiefdoms prevents the development of a common vocabulary and shared meaning. The feudal lords restrict access to and distribution of information under their authority. Feudalism gets only middling marks for quality; it may be high for individual divisions, but it is low from the corporate perspective. Finally, because some information is duplicated around the organization, efficiency is also only moderate. Feudalism is the least desirable yet the most common state in the organizations we researched; when more difficult and effective models fail, it is easy to fall back into the feudal state. [. . .]

Match information politics to your organizational culture [. . .] Information policies, we have found, are among the last things to change in an organization changing its culture. We have never seen increased information flow leading to elimination of a management layer or a greater willingness to share information. When these latter changes happen, they happen for reasons unrelated to information: restructurings, tighter cost control, external events (eg., the 1970s' oil shocks or the current banking crisis), and so forth. Several companies, however, state that their new organization could not have survived without new information policies. Phillips Petroleum, for example, radically reduced its management ranks after a raider-forced restructuring. A new information policy was the key to its functioning.[11]

We observed this relationship between organizational culture and information politics in two computer companies. One firm was a fast-growing personal computer (PC) manufacturer when we studied it; since then, its growth has slackened. The other firm was a large manufacturer of several types of computers that was experiencing financial problems when we visited it. Their cultures seemed similar at first glance; they both had tried to develop cultures in which information was shared freely throughout their organizations with little regard to level or function. However, two key aspects of their cultures – their organizational structures and their relative financial success – had led to radically different information politics.

The PC firm had a traditional functional structure. According to the executives and employees we interviewed, information flowed relatively freely in the company. The firm had an explicit ethic of open communications, stressing early notification of problems and a 'don't shoot the messenger' response. As a key US executive stated, 'Someone in international can request any piece of data and ask us to explain it. Allowing others access to information requires a lot of trust, but that trust seems to exist here.' However, the firm is beginning to face more difficult competitive conditions, as PCs increasingly become commoditized. In more difficult times, with new management, the open information environment may not persist.

The other firm had a 'networked' organization, with ad hoc teams assembling to address specific tasks. This structure, which made the firm flexible and responsive, also seemed to hinder the flow of important information. Several managers we interviewed reported that hoarding of valuable information was common. The ad hoc teams often resisted sharing their unique information. The managers we interviewed speculated that this was because a team that shares its information fully may lose its reason to exist. This is particularly true during the economically difficult times now facing the company. If an organizational structure is defined by information nodes, then those who freely surrender information may lose their place in the structure. Put more broadly, in the information-based organization, information becomes the primary medium of value and exchange, and who would give it away for free? [. . .]

Not surprisingly, in an era of mergers, acquisitions, and global management, most large organizations have multiple political cultures. A newly acquired firm may resist adopting the information-sharing norms of its acquirer. [. . .] Poorly performing divisions will rarely be as enthusiastic about new information reporting initiatives as long-term strong performers. And geographic differences affecting the willingness to share information are legendary; how many times has it been uttered, 'We're having problems getting data from our French subsidiary.'

Practice technological realism   Although technology will not lead us to an information utopia, there are still important technological factors to consider. Information engineering should be highly focused, information should be in units that managers can understand and negotiate with, and technology platforms should be as common as possible.

Previously we pointed out the folly of trying to engineer an organization's entire information inventory. We (and other researchers) believe that focused, less ambitious information management objectives are more likely to succeed, given that the volume of information in corporations is too great to be rigorously categorized and engineered.[12] [. . .]

It is also important to acknowledge that not all information will be managed through technological means, just as most of the water around us does not run through our water meters. Only about 5 percent to 10 percent of the information in most firms is in electronic form. According to a recent study of information use by managers, even computer-based data are often preceded by word-of-mouth renditions of the same information.[13] The verbal and visual information that informs all of us is not totally unmanageable, but it cannot be modeled and categorized through technological means. [. . .]

Elect the right information politicians Along with having a suitable political culture and technology environment, companies desiring to change their information politics must elect (or otherwise get into office) the right information politicians. We find that the information politician role -- not the owner of information but the manager with primary responsibility for facilitating its effective use – is still up for grabs in many companies, despite some pretenders to the throne. In one fast-growing software company, for example, problems with information flow were widespread, but no one below the CEO took any ownership of the problem.[14] One would assume that CIOs would own this domain, but until now they have not necessarily been the best choice.

Until recently, most CIOs were selected for technical acumen rather than political skills. Few would have embarked on initiatives to improve the way information – not just information technology – is used and managed. Only a few IS function heads have the political clout to persuade powerful barons to share their information for the good of the entire kingdom. Still, this is changing. At companies such as IBM, Xerox, Kodak, and Merrill Lynch, recent CIOs have been fast-track executives with records of managing important non-technology aspects of the business. If these nontechnical managers can master the considerable technical challenges in creating an information infrastructure, they will likely have the skills and influence to bring about a political environment in which the information can be shared and used. [. . .]

The CEO is perhaps best positioned to lobby for a particular information environment; indeed, in an information monarchy, the CEO is the only politician who counts. In more democratic environments, such as federalism, the CEO must appreciate the importance of information and communicate it throughout the firm. The time demands of day-to-day information negotiation may require that the CEO delegate political authority to other managers. [. . .]

Avoid building information empires Because information is such a powerful tool, federalist organizations will inherently resist or distrust managers who try to build an empire by controlling information. Concentration of all responsibility for collecting, maintaining, and interpreting information in one person, regardless of position, is too much power in any organization with democratic leanings. In fact, the concept of information ownership is antithetical to federalist information management. Rather, companies should institute the concept of information stewardship – responsibility for ensuring data quality – with ownership by the corporation at large. Stewardship of information, again perhaps at the document level rather than for individual data elements, should be assigned widely throughout the organization.

The IS organization should be particularly careful to avoid building an information empire. It may already wield considerable power by virtue of its technical custody of information. [. . .]

CONCLUSION

Explicitly recognizing the politics of information and managing them constructively is a difficult, complex, and time-consuming task. It will not happen by itself, nor will the problem go away. Effectively managing information politics requires a shift in organizational culture; new technology and even new executives alone are not enough to make this happen. Information management must become something that all managers care about and most managers participate in. They must view information as important to their success and be willing to spend time and energy negotiating to meet their information needs. As in real democracies, democratic information models like federalism require informed participation of all organizational citizens.

Unless the politics of information are identified and managed, companies will not move into the Information Age. Information will not be shared freely nor used effectively by decision makers. No amount of data modeling, no number of relational databases, and no invocation of 'the information-based organization' will bring about a new political order of information. Rather, it will take what politics always take: negotiation, influence-exercising, back-room deals, coalition-building, and occasionally even war. If information is truly to become the most valued commodity in the businesses of the future, we cannot expect to acquire it without an occasional struggle.

REFERENCES

1 J. G. March, *Decisions and Organizations* (Cambridge, Massachusetts: Basil Blackwell, 1988).
2 For example: M.S. Scott Morton, The *Corporation of the 1990s: Information Technology and Organizational Transformation* (New York: Oxford University Press, 1991); P. G. W. Keen, *Shaping the Future: Business Design through Information Technology* (Boston: Harvard Business School Press, 1991); and D.R. Vincent, *The Information-Based Corporation: Stakeholder Economics and the Technology Investment* (Homewood, Illinois: Dow Jones—Irwin, 1990).
3 J. Thorbeck, 'The Turnaround Value of Values', *Harvard Business Review*, January-February 1991, pp. 52–62.

4 J. Pfeffer, *Power in Organizations* (New York: Harper Business, 1986).
5 See articles in W.G. McGowan, ed., *Revolution in Real-Time: Managing Information Technology in the 1990s* (Boston: Harvard Business School Press, 1991). A notable exception to the apolitical perspective is found in M.L. Markus, 'Power, Politics, and MIS Implementation', Communications of the ACM 26:6 (June 1983): 434–444.
6 A term similar to 'technocratic utopianism' has been defined, without reference to information management, by Howard P. Segal. See: H. P. Segal, *Technological Utopianism in American Culture* (Chicago: University of Chicago Press, 1985).
7 See R.A. Caro, *The Power Broker: Robert Moses and the Fall of New York* (New York: Random House, 1975); and *Chinatown*, the film.
8 See D. L. Goodhue, J. A. Quillard, and J. F. Rockart, 'Managing the Data Resource: A Contingency Perspective', *MIS Quarterly* (September 1988), 373–392; and D.L. Goodhue, L. Kirsch, J. A. Quillard, and M. Wybo, 'Strategic Data Planning: Lessons from the Field' (Cambridge, Massachusetts: MIT Sloan School of Management, Center for Information Systems Research, Working Paper No. 215, October 1990).
9 Some interesting examples of feudalism, again largely outside the information management context, are described in: J. Pfeffer, *Managing with Power* (Boston: Harvard Business School Press, 1991).
10 Some of the reasons for these discrepancies are described in: S. M. McKinnon and W. J. Bruns, Jr., *The Information Mosaic* (Boston: Harvard Business School Press, 1992).
11 L. M. Applegate and C. S. Osborn, 'Phillips 66 Company: Executive Information System', 9–189–006 (Boston: Harvard Business School, 1988).
12 See Goodhue et al. (1988) and Goodhue et al. (1990).
13 McKinnon and Bruns (1992).
14 J. Gladstone and N. Nohria, 'Symantec', N9–491–010 (Boston: Harvard Business School, 1990, revised 4 February 1991).

Achieving dynamic stability through information technology

Andrew C. Boynton

Most firms have learned how to deal with periodic changes in market demand and production technologies. The world is perpetually changing in one way or another, and success means adapting to that change. But what happens when a firm is suddenly faced with *frequent, rapid, unpredictable change* in its competitive environment – in its markets, in customer demands, in technologies, in competitive boundaries, in products and processes, all at the same time? The fact is, change on this scale is not something most firms or managers are equipped to deal with effectively. Yet for many, this type of change in the competitive environment is increasingly prevalent. Just how are managers faced with these particular competitive conditions supposed to respond?

In a previous article, 'Beyond Flexibility: The Dynamically Stable Organization', my co-author and I broadly discussed the emergence and increased presence of these competitive conditions, as well as the overall impact of these conditions on a firm's strategies and structures.[1] We suggested that managers facing these types of changing conditions must learn how to create organizations that are *dynamically stable* – organizations capable of serving the widest range of customers and changing product demands (dynamic), while building on long-term process capabilities and the collective knowledge of the organization (stable).[2] My purpose in this present article is to further clarify these concepts for managers by focusing on one of the most critical steps to achieving a state of dynamic stability – *the strategic management of information*.

THE CHANGING COMPETITIVE ENVIRONMENT

[. . .] For many firms, today's competitive environment is changing dramatically in two important ways: in terms of markets and product demands; and in terms of available process capabilities. First, customers are demanding greater product choice and customization; product life cycles are getting shorter and shorter; market boundaries are rapidly shifting; demands for globalization and technological innovation are becoming the rule, not the exception. In order to keep pace with this change, firms are finding that they must be able to build and deliver high-quality, customized goods and services, but at the same time keep costs down and get products to market quickly.[3]

At the same time, these changes in competitive requirements are paralleled by changes in process technologies and process know-how management – more specifically, these changes include advances in information technology that give firms the power to build a stable base of process capabilities that are at the same time flexible, efficient, and long-term.[4] At the heart of these process developments are technological advances in information technology – not advances in increased speed or memory capacity, but in increased *modularity, flexibility, applicability*, and *reusability* of hardware and software environments. In short, the result of these two simultaneous changes in competitive conditions – rapidly changing, unpredictable customer demand paralleled by evolving process expertise and technologies – is increased pressure on firms to compete aggressively and simultaneously on both a low-cost and product-differentiation position.

Not surprisingly, firms are also realizing that this strategic response requires the rise of organizational forms that are not just a combination of structures that were appropriate for strategies that attempted to balance and trade-off between low cost and differentiation. Many firms and their managers have begun to design organizations that are *dynamically stable* – organizations based on long-term process experience and collective organizational know-how that are strategically designed to respond to rapid and unpredictable market demands. In essence, they are creating firms that combine the best of both worlds. Not surprisingly, information technology is often an important resource behind this type of organization.

INFORMATION MANAGEMENT FOR DYNAMIC STABILITY: A CORE RESOURCE

How is the management of information at the very heart of what it means to achieve dynamic stability? To answer this question, we need first to understand the role of 'core' knowledge and competencies in the dynamically stable firm.

The move toward firms becoming both efficient and highly responsive to market change by focusing on a stable platform of firm-specific know-how or process technologies has been recognized recently by a number of experts. In particular, the concept of 'core' capabilities or competencies and their relationship to strategic advantage plays a central role in emerging strategic thinking.[5] According to Prahalad and Hamel, core competencies are 'the collective learning in the organization, especially how to coordinate diverse production skills and integrate multiple streams of technologies'.[6]

For example, Corning Inc. views its knowledge about glass and ceramic processes as a core strategic resource. Management commonly refers to this firm-specific know-how as Corning's 'treasury of process knowledge' and continuously invests in its enhancement. Although Corning produces thousands of different products, strategic success is based not on products but on the firm's core competencies, namely its collective knowledge about ceramic and glass processes.

With this notion of 'core competencies' in mind, we can now identify three specific information management challenges facing the firm trying to achieve dynamic stability:

- The first challenge involves how we define the firm in terms of its primary function or objectives. Most firms have traditionally been defined by their products or services. Given the changing nature of competition, for many firms that definition is no longer possible. The definition (and success) of many firms must now be based on *learning, experience, and knowledge.* That is to say, in managing for dynamic stability, the focus of competitive advantage is on 'knowing' and the collective knowledge about the firm's process capabilities. What are the information implications of this for managers? Because knowledge, experience, and organizational capabilities are the focus of competitive advantage, managers must be able to rapidly identify new ways to tap quickly into and use information about product and process know-how resident throughout the firm. This is particularly critical for global firms that must manage across large 'boundaries', both geographical and organizational.
- The second challenge involves coping with today's changing markets and products. New competitors are often entering the playing field, new technologies are changing the rules of the game, and customer expectations are increasingly becoming more sophisticated. Given these changes, what are the information implications for managers? The effect of these changes is that rapid and unpredictable market change must be matched with *timely information flow to senior managers* so they can assess product demand and application, as well as evaluate process use and optimize its application. In the dynamically stable firm, information about external market and product conditions, both of the firm and its competitors, must be readily accessible to senior managers.
- The third challenge involves the horizontal, cross-functional, or cross-organizational flow of information. In today's shifting market environment, firms need to apply learning, knowledge, and experience differently to changing product requirements, and do so fast and at low cost. As a result, firms simply cannot control information in the same narrow way anymore. The confining 'stovepipe' design and information structure characteristic of so many firms will no longer suffice. Instead,

information to encourage flexible cross-functional and cross-organizational process management is required. Moreover, firms can no longer afford to build a new information control system each time product requirements shift – today's rapid and unpredictable market change prohibits it. Today, managers need information processing capabilities that are *flexible, reusable, re-combinable, and open to links* with other systems within the firm as well as with external constituencies, such as suppliers or customers. The fact is today's changing markets require improved information flow, and a faster, more flexible IT system to improve coordination and control of process capabilities.

By clearly understanding the importance of the management of information to achieving dynamic stability, and by taking advantage of recent advances in information technology, organizations and their managers now have both the knowledge and the advanced capabilities to develop systems that specifically address these three information management challenges facing the dynamically stable firm. In particular, managers need to think in terms of building three distinct yet interrelated types of information systems: *systems of scope, vertical systems*, and *horizontal systems* (see Exhibit 10.1). While the information challenges posed by these three types of systems are not conceptually new (firms have been struggling with similar information challenges for years), a discussion here of specific information management challenges and subsequent information technology-enabled system requirements will help sharpen the focus on the specific organizational and strategic requirements posed by dynamic stability.

Systems of scope

In order for managers to effectively respond to rapid, unpredictable market change, it is essential that they be able to quickly tap into their firm's knowledge-base of product and process. Take, for example, the situation of one European-based manufacturer of electronic car components we studied. Although the firm is a recognized world-leader in the design, manufacture, and marketing of its products (the firm operates in global markets and has manufacturing facilities throughout Europe and Asia), we discovered that the firm's ability to share knowledge within the organization was severely limited. Customer marketing couldn't answer questions about new products being offered in other countries. Even though the firm has a well-funded competitive intelligence group, managers were unable to access information on the latest competitor product lines. Nor did managers within product design have access to knowledge about the latest product trends, even though specific information resided in individual marketing offices throughout Europe. Within manufacturing, managers

Systems of scope
(a system of 'knowing')

Information systems which allow process and product managers to rapidly develop, gather, store, and disseminate information across all boundaries about markets, products, or process capabilities. Systems of scope are designed to maintain stable, permanent reservoirs and conduits of knowledge about internal capabilities or experience as well as the capabilities of competitors. They are designed to be dynamically responsive for managers who have a need to know and must be able to access firmwide knowledge in response to local, fast-changing business environments.

Requirements:

- Need to reach *all* managers in order to provide the necessary information to build or use organizational know-how and process capabilities.
- Must be *fast* and be able to reach instantaneously into all areas of the firm.
- Should be open to *self-design* and a wide variety of information requirements.

Vertical Systems
(a system of 'knowing')

Information systems that allow an organization to rapidly acquire, store, and provide timely access to real-time information about market change, product change, and process use and allocation for purposes of evaluating and allocating the use of process capabilities in the face of rapid market change (related to classic control systems).

Requirements:

- Should not reach all managers – just those senior managers involved with resource allocation decisions for products.
- Should not allow for 'self-design.' Should have a very specific design, one that is tapped into and collects specific information on product movement and process use, analyzing specifically for product/process evaluation and optimization.

Horizontal Systems
(a system of 'doing')

Cross-functional or cross-organizational information processing capabilities that are flexible, reusable, modular, general purpose, and open to links with other platforms that exist inside or outside the organization. Horizontal systems cut laterally across functions and departments so that process capabilities can be combined and recombined to support rapid and flexible product and service delivery. Horizontal systems coordinate, control, and integrate information and technologies across different boundaries.

Requirements:

- Must be designed specifically with change in mind – change in product specifications, customer requirements, and service needs. Attention to open architectures, modularity, flexibility, reusability, and other capabilities that allow future change are essential within the design process of horizontal systems.

Exhibit 10.1 Systems of scope, vertical systems, and horizontal systems

didn't have access to information about what factories had excess production capacity, and thus often had to invest in duplicate resources.

Unfortunately, the challenges faced at this firm are similar to challenges managers are facing everywhere: basic but important questions that are directly related to knowledge that already *exists* somewhere in the organization are, for some reason, very difficult to get answered. The question, then, is just how does a firm develop, collect, store, and disseminate firmwide knowledge in order to assure that important questions involving information that already exists somewhere in the organization get answered in a timely, efficient manner? The answer is *systems of scope* – information systems which allow managers within the organization to rapidly develop, gather, store, and disseminate information across all boundaries about markets, products, or process capabilities. Systems of scope are designed to maintain stable, permanent reservoirs and conduits of knowledge about internal capabilities or experience as well as the capabilities of competitors. They are designed to be dynamically responsive for managers who have a need to know and must be able to access firm-wide knowledge in response to local, fast-changing business environments.[7]

In the dynamically stable firm, systems of scope play a critical role for both product and process managers. Fist, product managers facing rapidly shifting markets need to be able to anticipate and respond to market change as soon as possible. Systems of scope provide timely and accessible information about not only markets and products, but also about what resources (know-how/process capabilities) are available within the firm to meet product demands. For example, if a salesperson at Du Pont in Germany wants to sell gaskets to an auto company, that salesperson currently must look up the parts in a German inventory catalogue. When Du Pont integrates its mainframe and minicomputers into a global network in the mid-1990s, that salesperson will be able to find not only gaskets, but also information about many other products, even those under development. With this system of scope, Du Pont salespersons will have access to not only information located in Germany, but to *all* the knowledge stored within Du Pont on a global basis. The evolving systems at Du Pont illustrate the power that IT systems can have in helping organizations build a firm-wide knowledge-base that can be utilized by product managers around the globe to respond to their own unique information requirements.

Systems of scope also play a critical role for process managers. In the dynamically stable firm, process managers must be able to focus on developing process capabilities that are responsive to the changing environment, i.e., process capabilities that are general purpose, flexible, reusable, and cost competitive. Systems of scope provide process managers with insights into product requirements and thus process needs throughout the entire organization, not just one product in one division. In addition, process managers need to know not only what today's range of product demand is, but also what tomorrow's might be in order to develop process capabilities that are responsive to these needs. Thus, it is vital that process managers be able to tap into product information, and communicate with product managers above, next to, and below them in the organization.

For example, Digital Equipment has developed a central data base designed to capture, maintain, and disseminate knowledge on an as-needed basis to project managers throughout the corporation. This system permits project managers to examine and evaluate a wide-range of solutions developed world-wide in the organization, in the possibility that these solutions might be of value to a particular project at hand. Before the development of this central data base, process managers had to rely on relatively inefficient methods of information sharing such as trips abroad and meetings. They didn't know what was going on elsewhere in the organization, and the information flows to keep them up to date were slow and pre-designed: sometimes they got the information they needed, sometimes they didn't. With its newly developed systems of scope, Digital now maintains a 'pool' of information about process capabilities, a pool that can be accessed by process managers around the globe to speed up the development and production of a wide range of other products and processes.

Given the purpose of systems of scope, there are a number of basic design implications that affect managers which must be considered. First, systems of scope need to reach *all* managers in order to provide the necessary information to build or use organizational know-how and process capabilities. Why is this? If the system is limited to managing only certain types of information for certain managers for certain problems, it won't be able to harness the full knowledge of the firm in order to respond to market changes. Thus, systems of scope must be designed in a way that allows all managers to share information and knowledge.

Second, systems of scope must be *fast*. The 'old' methods of sharing information – ships and planes, telephones, even modern fax machines and Federal Express – are just not quick enough and not thorough enough to substitute for an entire communication exchange system that must, by definition, be able to reach instantaneously into all areas of the firm. The dynamically stable firm must be able to collect and store a wide variety and amount of information in a systematic and efficient manner, in both simple ways (such as electronic mail) and more complicated ways (such as permanent electronic reservoirs of firm-wide knowledge).

Third, systems of scope should not only provide access to managers throughout the firm, but they should also be open to *self-design* and a wide variety of information requirements. In an environment of frequent change, product and process managers need to be able to tap into a broad set of information about the firm, and thus have the ability to make individual decisions about what information is needed, when it is needed, and how it is to be used. It is also important that systems of scope tap into important information that exists outside the firm, such as the market's response to product or service quality and important trends in business or economic conditions. Therefore, systems of scope must be able to increase the firm's knowledge-base, not just by providing access to important information generated inside the firm, but by providing managers with information that is generated outside the firm and has important ramifications to the firm's strategy or operational positioning.

In summary, systems of scope allow process and product managers to rapidly develop, gather, store, and disseminate information about markets, products, or process capabilities across a multitude of boundaries. They are specifically designed to maintain stable, permanent reservoirs of firm-wide knowledge about internal capabilities or experience, as well as knowledge about the capabilities of competitors. Systems of scope must be dynamically responsive and open to self-design for managers who must access firmwide knowledge in response to local, fast-changing business environments.

Vertical systems

In addition to maintaining stable, permanent reservoirs of firm-wide knowledge about internal capabilities and experience through systems of scope, the dynamically stable firm also needs to:

- maintain real-time information about market response to products and services;
- maintain real-time information about production capabilities and schedules; and
- be able to integrate this information so senior managers can assess product demand and process capability application, as well as evaluate process use and optimize its application.

Take, for example, the situation faced by one customer electronics manager we talked with. This particular manager told us that overseeing the allocation of manufacturing resources used to be a job she delegated, when product life cycles were longer and new products were introduced three or four times a year. Now, the situation is painfully different. The manager personally spends 30 to 40 percent of her time tracking product performance and then making production and distribution resource allocation decisions. In short, her firm's existing information systems simply do not provide rapid enough market information, nor does the information she receives provide accurate or rapid enough insights into the use of the firm's manufacturing and distribution resources. As a result, meeting after meeting is required to make decisions about what products to introduce when and how to produce them. To solve the problem, her firm is investing in a vertical information system that will integrate manufacturing capacity and distribution information with near real-time product sales information. With this new information system in place, the firm will be able to increase product introductions and be confident that it is taking advantage of and maximizing available manufacturing and distribution resources.

Vertical systems, then, are those that allow an organization to rapidly acquire, store, and provide timely access to real-time information about market change, and process use and allocation for purposes of evaluating and allocating the use of process capabilities in the face of rapid market change. In many ways, vertical systems play a role similar to classic control systems. Unlike classic control systems, however, which are unable to cope with supporting decisions under rapid, unpredictable change, vertical systems built for the dynamically stable firm are purposefully designed to allow timely and effective decision making in the face of rapidly changing products and services. In addition, vertical systems are specifically designed for senior managers who need to control and allocate resources as well as track products.

For example, Frito Lay has a vertical 'executive information system' that has drastically cut (from a matter of months to a matter of weeks) the time it takes senior managers to evaluate new product introductions. Frito Lay's vertical system collects large amounts of process and product data by arming its 10,000–person sales force with hand-held computers. Information is collected and made available daily via easy-to-use display software located on senior managers' desks world-wide. This vertical system allows for both rapid product decisions and flexible, responsive process allocation by linking new product performance in the market with manufacturing and distribution process capabilities. In this way, Frito Lay is able to evaluate and then optimize the use of existing capabilities for fast changing products in a dynamic market. [. . .]

Given the purpose of vertical systems, there are a number of basic design implications which must be considered. First, as stated above, vertical systems do not need to reach all managers. In fact, they *should not* reach all managers – just those senior managers involved with resource allocation decisions for products. Second, vertical systems should not allow for 'self-design.' They should have a very specific design, one that is tapped into and collects specific information on product movement and process use, analyzing specifically for product/process evaluation and optimization. [. . .] As important as it is to design vertical systems for 'ease of use' by managers, it is equally important that a firm's systems be efficiently tied into key market and production systems in order to provide the important information that enables market change to be matched with the allocation of firm-wide process knowledge and capabilities.

In summary, vertical systems take advantage of information technology capabilities that allow for near real-time integration of product sales and process information into a single data base. This enables almost instantaneous evaluation of how process capabilities are being applied to changing product requirements. In turn, this information allows senior managers to re-configure and change the product/process mix to optimize the organization's use of process capabilities. More than ever before, firms are recognizing the importance of vertical information systems that supply managers with direct and rapid access to market information and allow rapid resource allocation decisions.

Horizontal systems

While systems of scope and vertical systems are important systems of 'knowing' (because they involve the developing, gathering, storing, and dissemination of various types and levels of information), the dynamically stable firm also needs a system of 'doing' – that is to say, a system that coordinates, controls, and integrates information and technologies across different boundaries.

In today's market environment, firms need to apply technologies differently to changing product requirements, and do so fast and at low cost. Today, firms need cross-functional or cross-organizational information processing capabilities, or *horizontal systems*, that are flexible, reusable, modular, general purpose, and open to links with other platforms that exist inside or outside the organization. What do horizontal systems look like and do? Horizontal systems cut laterally across functions and departments so that process capabilities can be combined and recombined to support rapid and flexible product and service delivery. Under conditions of heavy product demand, differing combinations of information processing requirements are necessary to produce and deliver products or services. As product requirements rapidly change, so must information processing systems. In many instances, horizontal systems not only increase speed to market and the firm's ability to provide greater customized products, but also increase the efficiency and effectiveness of important process activities.

For example, the vertical process allocation system at Frito Lay referred to earlier is fully integrated with production systems, raw material procurement, distribution, manufacturing, and marketing. All of these areas are in fact connected by rapid information flow made possible by well thought out horizontal information systems, allowing Frito Lay to combine resources across functions in order to increase product introductions. Faced with shorter product life cycles, increased competition, and the need to allocate manufacturing capabilities across rapidly changing product requirements, Frito Lay has found that integrated systems are vital to enabling managers to respond dynamically to changing markets in an efficient manner. [. . .]

What are the design implications for horizontal systems? Horizontal systems require more than just that the organization 're-engineer' existing process capabilities to be streamlined cross-functionally and to focus on rapid and customized product delivery. A system, for instance, that dramatically reduces the product time to market for a single specific product may provide a source of competitive advantage in the short term, but when product specifications change – and they will – that very same information system may function to lock the organization into old ways of managing the business. In the dynamically stable firm, horizontal systems must be designed specifically, with change in mind – change in product specifications, customer requirements, and service needs. Thus, attention to open architectures, modularity, flexibility, reusability, and other capabilities that allow future change are essential within the design process of horizontal systems.

In summary, horizontal systems reach out across functional and even organizational boundaries, enabling key, general-purpose processes and knowledge to be combined and recombined quickly and efficiently in order to meet dynamically changing product specifications.

TAKING THE RIGHT PATH TO DYNAMIC STABILITY

There are many reasons why firms have had trouble implementing, or even thinking about, information systems that meet the challenges of dynamic stability. However, one main reason is that many firms attempting to achieve dynamic stability choose the 'wrong path' – that is, they try to get there by using existing information systems and architectures. Why would this be a problem?

Consider for a moment what most firm's information processing structures are based on. Most firms' existing information architectures are built upon years of system development to support a wide range of administrative, support, and product applications geared towards *very particular competitive conditions*. For a majority of firms, these systems have been built to support the tenets of mass production – functional specialization, hierarchal structure, inflexibility to change – resulting in vertical tunnels of information, each managed by local managers acting as feudal lords. For many other firms, systems have been built to support the tenets of invention – constant innovation, product variety, decentralized structure. Not that there is anything inherently wrong with either of these designs. For the demands of mass production, a focus on functional specialization and information isolation is the right organizational formula; for the demands of invention, a focus on innovation and decentralization is also the right formula. The problem is, however, that the demands on many organizations and managers have changed, and so must the way information is handled.

While the information challenges we have talked about in general are not new, they become particularly acute when attempting to compete under today's conditions of rapid, unpredictable market changes from a cost-efficient process base, especially for firms competing on a global basis. The simple fact is that the 'old' information processing capabilities aren't designed to meet today's challenge of managing an organization's knowledge and technological capabilities, and responding to the dual competitive requirements of rapid product customization and production/distribution efficiency. As a result, any attempt to apply information systems designed to support mass production or product invention to rapidly changing markets that demand *both* low cost and differentiation usually results in neither flexibility nor efficiency, but most likely in organizational chaos.

Thus, the challenge of implementing systems geared towards dynamic stability becomes not simply a technical 'system' challenge, but primarily an *organizational change challenge* as firms attempt to transform systems, structures, and processes designed and used to compete under one set of conditions, to another set of systems, structures, and processes designed to compete under very different conditions.

Case in point: In the early 1980s Citibank wanted to improve market responsiveness in its consumer banking group. Because information systems were seen as the critical resource in executing day-to-day decisions and tactics at Citibank, decentralizing key information processing capabilities to as low a level of responsibility and control as possible was thought to be the quickest way to turn the organization around and make it more responsive to a changing market. This decentralization strategy, designated 'Project Paradise', was executed by directly taking existing information processing technologies, systems, and know-how specifically designed for stable and slow-changing product markets, and applying them to competitive conditions of more rapid, unpredictable market change. Of course, Project Paradise turned out to be more of a hell than a paradise. Rather than achieving improved market responsiveness, Citibank found itself drowning in a sea of useless systems, unable to collect, store, disseminate, or analyze vital information. The people, procedures, and other systems not associated with the decentralization simply couldn't cope with the change. Business couldn't get done. Realizing it was on the wrong path to improving organizational responsiveness, Citibank quickly re-centralized its information management processes.

The failure of 'Project Paradise' illustrates an important lesson for today's managers about the right path to dynamic stability. While Citibank was correct in thinking that information had to be managed very differently to achieve market responsiveness, its attempt to take information systems designed for efficiently supporting relatively standard products and services and simply distributing these systems to remote operating facilities and managers did not take into account the real information management challenges posed by Citibank's new competitive environment. In essence,

Citibank confused changing its information technology structure with what really had to be changed to achieve market responsiveness: its organizational structure.

Consider some of the characteristics of Citibank's organization before Project Paradise: stovepipes of information for each functional area, computer systems centrally designed and managed, reward systems designed to ensure efficient operations, control systems designed to monitor standard products and services, people trained as specialists. Then along comes Project Paradise, and suddenly the information structures, flows, and ownership necessary to support these organizational characteristics and systems have been changed. In effect, the information structure created by Project Paradise no longer 'fit' with other vital organizational components. The internal consistency that existed among the component parts to effectively support efficient operations was now gone. The result was predictable – political battles, resistance to the new systems, service quality problems – in a word, organizational chaos.

The lesson learned at Citibank and many other firms is that changing information systems (especially dramatic change like Project Paradise) is equivalent to *major organizational change*, and must be seen as such. Managers attempting to move their organization along the right path must remember that information systems are a large component of organizational designs intended to support a particular competitive strategy. In fact, these components may work very well together, even if the strategy and the design of the firm no longer meets external competitive requirements. However, when components are suddenly changed to meet changing competitive requirements – such as information flows and ownership patterns – the likelihood that resistance and confusion will occur rises markedly. Implementation failure is imminent.

How can such problems be avoided? For starters, all too often specialists from a firm's MIS function are assigned responsibility to manage and lead the conceptualization and implementation of new information systems. However, conceptualizing and implementing the kinds of information systems necessary to achieve dynamic stability requires that line or general managers, with the formal authority and political clout, not only take the lead in formulating the requirements for such systems, but also take the lead in making the systems happen. To the best of their ability these managers (working as senior partners with IT specialists) must carefully assess how new information systems, especially systems attempting to dramatically shift the organization in a new direction, fit within the existing set of overall organizational procedures and systems, and then make decisions to ensure consistency in how information is used throughout the organization. One way to achieve this is to first develop a clear vision of what the future organization must look like, making sure that senior line or general managers are in charge of creating the vision. Achieving this vision should be approached like a major organizational design change, so that all inter-related and interdependent systems and processes – not just IT related systems – are examined closely.

In addition to developing a clear understanding and vision of how the new information system will 'fit' with other elements within the organiz-ation, many different levels of management should be involved with the change process. This multi-level involvement should be used throughout the change process to help formulate both the vision and the detailed implementation plans. Continuous experimentation and learning is also an important ingredient to change. Rather than attempting to implement one gargantuan project effort designed to dramatically change a firm, firms should implement a series of smaller projects consistent with the ultimate vision. Finally, managers need to realize that these projects inherently provide for organizational learning and adjustment. If executed properly, they create an environment where the proposed vision is progressively 'bought into' throughout the organization, and where learning takes place at the same time change is occurring.

In summary, understanding that transformation to dynamic stability must follow a carefully thought out 'right path' is a critical step to success for firms attempting to position themselves to compete in today's competi-tive environment. Corning and Frito Lay are examples of firms taking the right path to dynamic stability. Each is investing in and carefully designing information architectures that are stable and efficient platforms, yet simultaneously provide flexible, general purpose, information processing capabilities. These firms did not try to leap-frog existing capabilities with-out thinking through the organizational design issues and consequent infor-mation challenges required for dynamic stability. In each case, careful engineering or re-engineering of process capabilities positioned the firm and its managers to meet the dual competitive challenges of product differ-entiation and low cost required by dynamic stability. In each case, the firm thought of new information systems as a way to help with a larger organizational change effort.

One final word about pursuing the right path. It should be clear by now that achieving dynamic stability is not a one-shot deal. After a firm positions itself for dynamic stability, continuous enhancement to core pro-cess capabilities is required. Making continuous enhancements requires that firms have policies allowing for financial investments to be made in process capabilities that are not simply associated with short-term, known product requirements, but that are capable of responding to rapidly and unpredict-ably shifting product requirements. This requires continuous enhancement of information technology that can best meet future needs for scope, vertical, and horizontal systems in order to achieve efficient flexibility in a competitive environment earmarked by unpredictable product demand.

CONCLUSION

Designing and managing the dynamically stable firm is a significant challenge. Firms and managers wishing to get on the 'right' path to dynamic stability need to think carefully about what they are doing. They first need to ask: Is dynamic stability right for this firm? Does my firm truly face increasingly rapid and unpredictable product demand? Does my firm face competitive pressures to compete on both low-cost and on innovation and differentiation, equally and aggressively? Does my firm face the requirement to achieve 'flexible efficiency', combining the best of both mass production and innovation? If the answer to any of these questions is yes, then the manager next needs to ask: What transformations in my organization are required to meet these contradictory demands? In particular, managers need to think fully about the management of information in their firms, since the management of information is at the heart of dynamic stability. Is my firm locked into managing information to achieve only the efficiencies of mass production or the innovation required for product differentiation? Does my firm require new information structures designed specifically for dynamic stability? If the answer is *yes*, then thinking through the information requirements posed by scope, vertical, and horizontal systems can help lead managers to a new understanding of the relationship between the firm's IT systems and competitive advantage.

Dynamic stability may not be right for every firm. But when it is, research tells us that carefully managing information is the best start down the 'right' path to dynamic stability.

ACKNOWLEDGEMENTS

The author would like to thank Mark Eaker, Thomas McMillan, Bart Victor, and three anonymous reviewers for their important insights during preparation of this article. The research on which this article is based was made possible in part by support from IBM's Advanced Business Institute.

REFERENCES

This article is based on a three-year-old and ongoing research project conducted by the author and sponsored by International Business Machine Corporation's Advanced Business Institute. The ideas presented here are based on a number of sources, including field research, personal contact with managers in a number and variety of organizations, understanding of current literature, and exposure to cases and teaching material. The author has met with a number of managers from a dozen firms based in several countries and on multiple continents. The firms are from several industries, including health care, consumer products, telecommunications, financial services, and industrial manufacturing.

1 Andrew C. Boynton and Bart Victor, 'Beyond Flexibility: The Dynamically Stable Organization', *California Management Review*, 34/1 (Fall 1991): 53–66.
2 Process capabilities includes broadly the management, manufacturing, procurement, delivery, service, marketing, sales and other necessary functions and activities associated with the creation, production, and distribution of an organization's products or services. Changing product demands involves the demands for new products or services placed on a firm; for example, the changes firms face in markets that results from competitor moves, shifting customer preferences, or from the firm entering new geographical or national markets.
3 I am not the first to make this claim. Others eloquently discuss the rise of new, fundamental requirements for today's organizations attempting to combine low-cost advantages with rapid market response. See Stanley M. Davis, 'Mass Customizing', in *Future Perfect* (Reading, MA: Addison-Wesley, 1987); Michael L. Dertouzos, Richard K. Lester, Robert M. Solow, and the MIT Commission on Industrial Productivity, *Made in America: Regaining the Productive Edge* (Cambridge, MA: The MIT Press, 1989); Piore and Sabel, op. cit. Michael J. Poire and Charles F. Sabel, *The Second Industrial Divide* (New York, NY: Basic Books, 1984).
4 Process technologies and know-how management refers broadly to human, manufacturing, distribution, service, marketing, and financial capabilities within a firm. The focus in this article is on information and information technology which can play an important role in the organization and management of these capabilities throughout an entire firm.
5 The concept of core process capabilities and their relationship with strategic advantage has been discussed by a number of authors and plays a central role in emerging strategic thinking. See David J. Teece, 'Economics of Scope and the Scope of the Enterprise', *Journal of Economic Behavior and Organization* (1980); C. K. Prahalad and Gary Hamel, 'The Core Competence of the Corporation,' *Harvard Business Review* (May/June 1990); James Brian Quinn and Penny C. Paquette, 'Technology in Services: Creating Organizational Revolutions,' *Sloan Management Review* (Winter 1990).
6 Prahalad and Hamel, *op. cit.*
7 The term 'Systems of Scope' was derived from the requirements of [the] firm to apply its know-how and competencies to achieve scope economies in a rapidly changing market environment.

Chapter 11

Models of management

We need models of management in order to represent and distinguish between different, but more or less coherent and viable, ways of getting things done. Such models allow us to recognize the limits of the applicability of particular management theories and prescriptions, and help to distinguish between what are *unsatisfactory* arrangements and what are simply *different* arrangements. Needless to say, mapping and explaining the huge variety of organizational forms – which is what the following articles do – is not easy.

Roland Calori is Professor of Business Policy at the Groupe École Superiore de Commerce de Lyon, one of Europe's leading business schools. His article is based on interviews with fifty-one top managers of forty large international companies with headquarters or major operating units in Europe. Some of these managers were Europeans, some Japanese and some North American.

The research team wanted to discover whether the idea of a distinctive European style of management is purely wishful thinking. They concluded that beyond the diversity of management philosophies, structures and practice found across Europe, there are some common characteristics which form the ingredients of a European model of management.

Diana Pheysey offers a thorough exposition of current ideas on organizational design. It is densely packed with typologies of cultures, values and structures, some of which, such as those of Charles Handy, are well known, while others will be less familiar. The strength of her paper lies in the way she combines the various models in order to explore the relationships between different aspects of organizations, and to sketch out some of the ways that organizations change as they grow.

Cultures and organizational design

Diana Pheysey

1 MODELS FOR DESIGNING ORGANIZATIONS

[...] We are familiar with designs in architecture, art, manufacturing, civil engineering, landscaping and many other fields. Things are usually designed before they are made. But organizations are designed whilst they operate. Their structure has to serve changing tasks, so we could more accurately speak of an on-going *process* of *re*design. This is usually the responsibility of managers at the top level. These managers have to see that the structure is appropriate to ideological, economic and order goals.

Goals of sharing and involvement require a structure where people are COLLABORATIVE. Goals of control and legality require a structure that can marshall PRODUCTIVE resources in an orderly and EFFICIENT way. Goals of competition require that the structure encourages people to be INNOVATIVE so that new challenges can be met.

These requirements are listed in Figure 11.1 which also sets out five tasks which organizations must undertake if the values listed in capital letters are to be achieved.

The first *entrepreneurial* task is to secure agreement on what to make or whom to serve. The decision on the product or clientele will include the technology. Second, materials, equipment and workers have to be obtained and used: the *engineering* task. Third, future requirements for staff, equipment and finance must be predicted, and fourth, *administration* must be set up so that regulative control can be maintained.

The importance of the tasks varies in sequence, in what Miles and Snow (1978) call an 'adaptive cycle', in which the entrepreneurial, engineering and administrative problems follow each other as firms seek to maintain or modify their market strategies. The task numbered 5 is therefore to balance the structure to changing conditions. Miles and Snow indicate that cycle duration is variable, so that at times two or more cycles may coincide. In fact all the problems are always present in some degree. The entrepreneurial problems shown on the right involve relations with the outside world, while the problems on the left are internal.

For an EFFICIENT organization	For an INNOVATIVE organization
4 The structure must be such that the organization can formalize working arrangements and keep administrative control, using **role culture** procedures (the 'administrative' problem)	3 The structure must be such that the organization can prepare for future management requirements, using appreciation and an **achievement culture** (the 'entrepreneurial' problem)

5 The structure must be such that the organization can achieve BALANCE, shifting emphasis according to needs

For an PRODUCTIVE organization	For an COLLABORATIVE organization
2 The structure must be such that the organization can obtain operational control over resources using a **power culture** orientation (the 'engineering' problem)	1 The structure must be such that the organization can choose and serve an appropriate clientele using appreciation as in **support cultures** (the 'entrepreneurial' problem)

Notes: The values are in capital letters. The numbers represent the stages in Greiner's life cycle when a particular value will be appropriate to emerging needs. The terms in parentheses are those of Miles and Snow (1978).

Figure 11.1 Design tasks for achieving five organizational values

Five types of *organizational design* that help the five tasks just described are shown in Figure 11.2. They refer to the design of a whole organization, rather than to its constituent parts. The examples are discussed in order. We then relate the idea of an adaptive cycle in organizational design to ideas from the previous chapters.

1.1 Entrepreneurial and self-managed forms

Entrepreneurial clusters

[...] In the West there have been numerous studies of entrepreneurs, some of which are listed in the bibliography. An entrepreneur gets personally involved in a host of activities while seeking to build a discrete business. However, he or she also needs to involve other people (bankers, customers, suppliers and so on). This is useful in giving the entrepreneur knowledge of possible product markets. Werbner (1985) gives an example – the social network of Manchester Pakistanis.

> Brothers, kinsmen and fellow villagers often follow one another into market trading or manufacturing. They create 'entrepreneurial chains'. Pakistanis of similar origins are concentrated in certain sections of the industry ... Tarik's son had worked at weekends and in the school

Emphasis on internal stability

4 Classic or *full bureaucracy*,
   or **temple** HIERARCHY
   (compatible with role
   culture)

Emphasis on external
uncertainty

3 Decentralized,
   collegiate
   or **matrix** or
   MARKET forms
   (compatible with
   achievement culture)

5 Hybrid or
   multidivisional forms,
   transnational
   corporations
   (compatible with
   mixed cultures)

2 Traditional ADHOCRACY,
   a centralized form;
   the pyramid or **web**
   (compatible with power
   culture)

1 Entrepreneurial
   cluster, or CLAN
   or *implicitly
   structured form*;
   self-management
   (compatible with
   support culture)

Figure 11.2 Models of organization
Notes: The terms in bold type are those used by Handy 1985. Those in italics
are from Pugh *et al.* 1968, those in capitals from Quinn and McGrath 1985.

holidays for various Pakistani rag-trade manufacturers. Several of his
school friends came from families that had small factories, so he could
buy 'lines' of clothing at a discount direct from the factory. This gave
him the edge in starting his first market stall.

(Werbner 1985:411)

Tarik himself was made redundant and handed his redundancy money to
his son to help him to establish himself. Soon the son co-opted his father
into the business. They formed the nucleus of a cluster, in which relationships are built on trust and people tend, by mutual agreement, to do what
they are best at. Decision-making is intuitive and control appreciative. Coordination in such an organization is achieved through informal
understanding. Beyond the activities entailed by legal requirements, there

is little formal structure. Norms are implicit in what people do rather than explicit in written job descriptions. Pugh and his colleagues (1968) coined the term *implicitly structured* for organizations which scored low on three dimensions which they measured – impersonal control, structuring of activities and concentration of authority. Such organizations do not specialize, standardize or formalize their arrangements. The absence of formality is countered by the strength of personal ties, as between Tarik and his son. Even when entrepreneurs attach themselves as subcontractors (or extrapreneurs) to large sponsoring organizations, the ties are based on trust, as are the ties of an entrepreneur who builds a cluster inside a 'host' organization (an 'intrapreneur'). The activities of the cluster are geared to serving the chosen customers or clients, whether small or large. Decisions are *ad hoc* and taken by persons on the spot. Relationships are friendly. The cluster is consistent with support culture values.

Self-management forms

This form of organization is more self-conscious about its internal structure than is the entrepreneurial. An example is given by Bloor (1986) who worked as a novice staff member in a half-way house for disturbed adolescents in the UK. He says it was permissive and egalitarian. [. . .]

The key therapeutic device seems to have been the morning coffee group (a cluster) where people were confronted with the consequences of their behaviour by other residents, or by staff. Such a unit also has close ties with the outside world from which young people are referred and to which they go.

Another example was a Chinese factory during the Cultural Revolution. The Revolutionary Committee had three links to the outside world – the representatives from the state, the army and the party. The workers' management teams seem to have been clusters in which, according to Lockett (1983), some workers were in charge of equipment and maintenance, others in charge of tools and implements, others of labour and welfare matters and yet others of production planning. These teams exercised some supervision of managers who were expected to do manual work, on a regular basis, in order to appreciate the problems faced by workers.

Here, as in the entrepreneurial forms, authority is diffuse and relationships informal despite a variety of tasks. Status differences are minimized. These conditions are compatible with support culture values.

1.2 Centralized structures

The cluster is often followed by the centralized form. Greiner explained that, as organizations grow, it becomes difficult to resolve internal disagreements unless someone is willing to take a strong line. This central person may be the charismatic founder of the voluntary organization or the owner-manager in the entrepreneurial cluster.

The task that is addressed by centralization is that of gaining operational control. This can be done in several ways. Rezazadeh (1961) suggests that the term centralization (versus decentralization) contains three different ideas. First there is *concentration* (versus dispersal) of authority. There is a single source of authority instead of many sources. Second there is *absolutism* (versus autonomy). Commands or rules are enforceable instead of being optional. Finally the rules have '*universal*' scope. They apply to everyone, not just to particular persons. In practice these three aspects of centralization may be found to different degrees and in different combinations.

The owner who manages the small firm may be the sole source of authority. In the UK most owner-managers are men, but more women are now starting their own businesses. By custom and practice 'bosses' are able to take all major decisions. Though they tend to give orders *ad hoc* as problems arise, they can enforce them. There are few rules, but all the subordinates are known to the boss, and the rule of obedience applies to everyone.

Handy calls this typical power culture structure in a small firm a 'web', with the spider at the centre. Another metaphor is the hub of a wheel from which the spokes radiate outwards. The most common metaphor for the centralized structure is the pyramid, with power at its apex. Where the organization is small enough to be one 'tribe', and the pyramid is relatively flat, such centralization can have a unifying effect. It was common in the West until the middle of this century and, according to Lammers and Hickson (1979) and to Hofstede (1980a), it is traditional in developing countries. The associated values are status, obedience and control. By the time the organization has grown to about a thousand employees, however, the chief executive is likely to be overloaded, especially if there are external problems demanding attention.

The centralized form keeps internal order through vertical channels of communication, concentrated authority and deferential relationships. But the design has the weakness that a successor to the chief executive may not be found. Managers below the apex have been excluded from knowledge of the business as a whole. They have been confined by the structure to a geographical area, or to one function (probably either manufacturing or sales), or to one stage of operations (for example spinning or weaving) or to one product line (for example brand A or brand B). No one but the chairman and managing director has the whole picture (see Figure 11.3). Thus, when change is sought, 'new blood' may have to be brought in from outside if those below the chief executive are unwilling to accept increased responsibility. At all events, the design changes to a decentralized form, and the culture changes also.

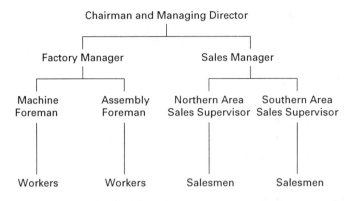

Figure 11.3 A centralized form of organization

1.3 Decentralized structures

The entrepreneurial clusters and self-managed forms (see Section 1.1) operate with dispersed sources of authority, freedom to challenge decisions and limited scope for rules, partly because they are small and partly because they have support cultures which encourage co-operation. We now look at forms of decentralization in larger organizations with achievement cultures, which value creativity, competition and independence.

Decentralized profit centres

A department, division, subsidiary or any unit defined by a market, or a technique to serve that market, can be turned into a profit centre with freedom to decide its own policy and strategies for reaching given goals. The task of the top managers (above unit level) is to determine long-term policies for the whole company, manage corporate finances and arbitrate among profit centres (Figure 11.4). The scope of the autonomy of each

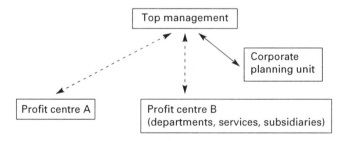

Figure 11.4 A decentralized form of organization
Note: – – – indicates that top management has only partial control over profit centres

profit centre is limited to its own particular operations, but there it can enforce its own decisions and, from the parent business's point of view, those decision sources are dispersed. The advantages of this type of decentralization are as follows:

- top managers are freed from having to make short-term decisions;
- it provides intrinsic satisfactions to those who head the profit centres;
- it is flexible because it puts decision-making closer to the scene of action.

There are also disadvantages or difficulties, however:

- it requires capable managers;
- the centre head may maximize short-run profits at the expense of corporate long-term goals;
- provision of support services to each centre may add to administrative costs;
- there are centrifugal tendencies which top management may not be able to curb.

Collegiate structure

This is the form of 'bottom up' decision-making that is found in many academic institutions. The faculty members serve on committees which decide the policies for their own departments. Departments are represented on the supreme decision-making bodies. However, there can be antagonism and 'rubbish bin' decisions to the extent that the term 'organized anarchy' has been applied to universities. Wilson (1985) describes 'Chaos College' where the innovations pursued by each department were at the expense of the integrity of the whole college. Some departments have much more influence than others because of their popularity with powerful outside interests – funding bodies, employers, schools and so on. However, the advantages of the decentralized profit centres can also apply to collegiate forms where major goals are shared.

Matrix structure

The collegiate form has sometimes been combined with the matrix (Figure 11.5). The latter co-ordinates activities at the point where they intersect. Each position in the matrix has at least two reporting links. In a college there may be differentiation by subject taught and by type of course – undergraduate, postgraduate, short-course students and so on. A teacher of mathematics who is responsible to the professor of maths for pursuit of scholarship in mathematics may be teaching maths to engineers and responsible to a director of undergraduate engineering courses for

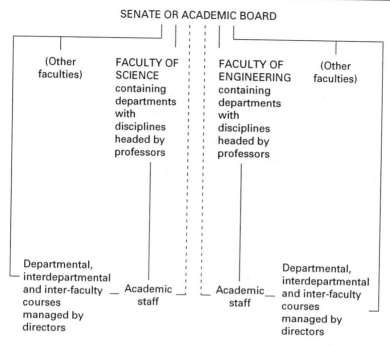

Figure 11.5 An example of matrix structure
Note: solid line reporting relationships; broken line, upwards representation

collaboration with specialists from other disciplines in furthering the aims of the course. The industrial equivalent of the 'subject-by-course' matrix would be the 'functional-by-product' matrix where, for example, a training specialist may report to both a personnel manager and a manufacturing manager. Matrix organizations may have dual assignments for certain managers, or a joint-planning process that spans the parts of the organization that are stable and those that change frequently. The Faculty Boards in the University example deal with five-year plans and frequent redesign of courses.

A power culture, because of its emphasis on central control and superior authority, has difficulty with a matrix structure. Similarly, a role culture does not approve the unscheduled meetings which help the smooth working of a matrix. The support culture may operate within a matrix, but it is the achievement culture which is most compatible with matrix structure requirements. Co-ordination is focused on *unlike* contributions to a common task, for example mathematicians and engineers to a degree course. (A support culture may emphasize the common interest in teaching but not give due weight to the different resource needs of the two subjects). Galbraith (1971) suggests that a reason for using a matrix form is that previous attempts at co-ordination have not succeeded. The matrix may be used as a part of a flexible bureaucracy (see below).

Flexible bureaucracy

Bureaucracy is often thought of as 'rule by bureaucrats' or officials. A 'classic bureaucracy' resembles this image (see Section 1.4 below). But the term 'flexible bureaucracy' is used by Lammers and Hickson to describe an organization where there are dispersed decision sources, local variations in rules and only partial enforcement. Indeed, among units, there may be relations which are similar to market relations in the economy, with parts of the organization charging other parts for services or for goods supplied. Raybould (1985) describes the Coats Patons group of companies in 1985 in terms which suggest a decentralized bureaucratic structure.

> More people have had some element of their pay related to individual or company performance, or a combination of the two. The form of involvement varies enormously, from factory floor productivity schemes, added-value schemes, plant-wide profit-sharing and executive bonus schemes to a group-wide savings-related share option scheme.... Local autonomy, organization into smaller units, improved communication and concentration on the personal element in relationships has helped to provide greater awareness ... in the involvement and participation of the workforce.
>
> (Raybould 1985: 42)

This organization would be bureaucratic on measures of specialization, standardization and formalization, developed by Pugh *et al.* (1969), but it is decentralized, not centralized, and the type of culture is one of achievement rather than role. Lammers and Hickson state that the flexible bureaucracy is characteristic of Anglo-Saxon countries, whereas the classic bureaucracy is more characteristic of Latin countries.

Before we consider the classic bureaucracy, let us summarize the design features of decentralized forms, since four variants have been described. What they have in common is that activities are spread across numerous occupations and sometimes across sites also. Dispersed centres of authority get power over their own operating decisions. Specialists of different occupations may be jointly responsible for common tasks, for example through task forces or project teams or committees, and persons may report to more than one superior. Decisions of broad scope which are taken by the top policy makers may still be challenged from below, and the scope of rules may be modified to allow for local circumstances.

1.4 Classic bureaucracy

Classic bureaucracies are said by Weber (1947) to have a *rational-legal* basis. This is because there are rational grounds for the division of labour, and because each official is employed under a contract that is legal in form. Classic bureaucracies grew out of the *line and staff* type of organization which was developed by armies. The front line soldiers do the fighting (called by systems theorists the 'primary task'). They are supported by staff in specialized units who transport and maintain their equipment, cook their food, pay their wages, treat casualties and so on. [. . .]

Most bureaucracies are large and have tall hierarchies. It is often assumed that they will be government agencies. But they can be found in businesses also when the centralized flat pyramid has grown tall. Pugh and his colleagues suggest that administrative control is exercised impersonally through appeal to procedures, and so a role culture is suitable. [. . .]

A problem with bureaucracies is described by Lawrence and Lorsch (1967). People whose work is divided into separate specialisms come to have different priorities. They start serving different goals. Some need immediate results, others a long-term perspective. This growing apart is known as *differentiation*. The greater the amount of differentiation, the greater is the requirement for integration, or pulling together. The internal boundaries need to be regulated, so that all parts work for the overall goals and not solely for subunit goals. This necessity leads to *hierarchy*. In the army the hierarchy extends from the private to the general. Each officer has his own command and is responsible for unique results. The whole organization has a pyramid shape. Argenti (1968) argues that the pyramid is at its best when it is flat, allowing rapid communication up and down, but many pyramids have grown tall.

> A manufacturing company is essentially an organization that buys components or materials, adds something to them in the production department that increases their value and sells them. These three functions, buying, production and selling, are the activities from which the company earns its profits – in some types of company a fourth activity must be added, namely transporting and distributing. . . . An advisory department's task is to comment upon how these physical operations are being done . . . (as the accounts department does with its costing system), or how it should be done (as the work study officer does) or what should be done in the future (as research, or planning, or marketing departments do). So important is it to choose the right thing to do and to do it in the right way that the actual task of doing it is gradually becoming of less importance.
>
> (Argenti 1968: 148)

The number of services has proliferated. There are often several hierarchies of different lengths, depending on the type of occupation. The pyramid cannot easily accommodate them all, neither can the 'temple' – Handy's (1985) term for a classic bureaucracy. The pillars of Handy's temple, the different functions, are kept separate from bottom to top. The board of directors is like the Grecian pediment, which can unify a stable structure but which falls when there is an earthquake. Bureaucratic procedures may be so geared to regulation that the variety in the environment cannot be met through extra appreciation.

Hannan and Freeman (1977, 1984) believe that the past successes of temple structures are an obstacle to redesign from within. Upwards accountability means that each level is monitored by the level above. This hierarchy leads to structural inertia. Performance which has served in the past gets repeated. For this reason, when circumstances change, classic bureaucracies do not transform themselves but may die and be replaced by newer organizations.

Fligstein (1985), however, reports research that suggests that it is not the inertia of the structure so much as the inertia of those who occupy the institutional roles in the structure that prevents adaptation.

Where the classic design ceases to serve, the designers can choose a flexible form or a hybrid form, and this frequently occurs. Pugh and his colleagues (1968) used the term 'full bureaucracy' instead of 'classic' because they believed they had discovered several partial forms. They drew profiles of particular organizations indicating the degree to which they resembled the classic case. They correlated the number of employees with their measures of concentrated authority, impersonal controls, levels of specialization, standardization and formalization. The more employees there were, the more likely it was that a full bureaucracy would be found. (Conversely, the fewer the employees, the more likely it was that the organization would be only 'implicitly structured'.) The classic bureaucracy is, then, an attempt to control large concerns through hierarchical decision-making and impersonal relationships. It usually has a role culture.

1.5 Hybrid forms

A hybrid is a mixed form likely to be found in very large concerns. Figures 11.1 and 11.2 together suggest that a hybrid is an attempt to achieve balance between preparing for the future (by appreciation) and keeping operational and technical control (by regulation).

National hybrids

State enterprises may be hybrids, as may any concerns that are large enough to be operating in several environments. The activities, decision-making, authority patterns and relationships are all varied. The hybrid concern is attempting to run 'steady state' operations where conditions are stable, while maintaining a readiness to innovate in unstable conditions.

There are many ways in which organizations can grow into hybrids. Public bodies may be set up by legislation and extended through government or local finance. Businesses may plough back their profits into extending their operations, they may borrow more finance, they may take over or merge with other businesses. Some organizations seek to remain distinctive by staying in one industry, and so they grow by taking over their supplier or their outlets (vertical integration). Other organizations may grow territorially, or by extending their clientele, while continuing to provide the same service. Organizations known as conglomerates have grown by diversifying into areas of business unrelated to their previous ones.

A conglomerate may have a holding company form at the centre (a legal device through which a small central office manages the portfolio of investments) and subunits that operate as independent companies. Alternatively, the centre may be the locus for long-range planning and finance, with divisions elsewhere based either on products or territory.

Whatever the design, the directors have to ensure dividends for the owners, who may be large institutions (such as pension funds) whose stake is a purely financial one. [. . .]

> The capitalist corporation is indeed the only major human organization in our present society which has owners who may buy and sell it as a piece of property.
>
> (Ellerman 1983: 271)

[. . .] The problem of organizational democracy, or how the boards of businesses can represent many 'constituencies', is especially acute when the conglomerate is a transnational corporation (TNC), or a multinational enterprise (MNE).

Transnational hybrids

Firms have

> initially sought foreign markets for their domestically produced products in order to further utilize productive capacity. If their products sell well in host countries, the parent firm may then establish regional marketing operations in these areas to assure a continuing market. Finally, in order both to achieve transportation economies and to further relations with host governments, production facilities may be constructed in these host countries through direct investment or joint ventures.
>
> (Miles and Snow, 1978: 132)

The TNC which has been successful will move into yet more countries, and become multinational. It is both a strategic and a design decision how far such an MNE decentralizes its operations, training indigenous managers to assume responsibility, and how far it reserves all major positions to nationals of the owning group.

Let us look further at the power which the boards of MNEs can wield. Dunning outlines some of the consequences of the present system. He says that where

> disposition [of resources] is decided by private capital in promotion of its own goals, it does not follow that the resulting distribution of output will be consistent with that which the countries in which the MNEs operate are seeking. This new international division of labour is certainly accelerating the relocation of some industrial sectors from older to newer industrialized countries.
>
> (Dunning 1985: 15)

The MNE can open up operations or close them down according to the perceptions of its top managers of what will serve its objectives as it seeks global profits for its investors. If it pulls out of a country it can sometimes adversely affect not only its own workforce but also that country's economy. Thus a lot of power is being exercised.

Dunning is particularly concerned with the structural changes at national level in Britain which have been affected by the decisions of MNEs on where, and in what, to invest.

Technological innovation has made communication over large distances quick and reliable. Investment in one country may well be financed from profits made in another part of the world. In what Patterson and Stevenson (1986) call 'the firm of the future' there will be computer integrated manufacturing with a core of 'permanent' staff at any given place, but also a periphery of temporary workers who can be called upon to supplement the core, possibly working from their own homes in another country.

Another fairly recent development is that trade, which used to be carried on between separately owned organizations, can now be conducted under the umbrella of common ownership. According to the United Nations (which created a Commission on TNCs in 1974), over 30 per cent of world trade in 1985 was intra-firm.

Marlow comments:

> Multinationals are very nearly in the position of being unloved and unwanted; that this is not quite the case is because of their actual and potential contribution to the provisions of goods and services and the creation of wealth so desperately needed by one third of mankind.
>
> (Marlow 1984: 301)

Perhaps the problem is not so much who owns the MNEs as how to make sure that others who have legitimate interests are also influential. This leads to consideration of the role of governments and of the international community.

Dunning points out that in the nineteenth century government intervention helped industry to settle by providing public utilities, but in the late twentieth century the equivalent attractions are airports, motorways, colleges and universities and an efficient economic system. He cites Japan as

> the classic example of a case in which industry and government can work harmoniously together to promote a positive and yet well articulated policy towards both inward and outward MNE activity.
>
> (Dunning 1985: 18)

Many countries do not have the economic power that Japan can wield, which is why the United Nations set up its Commission. That body, at the time of writing, has not been able to agree more than a draft code for regulating the activities of MNEs, though member countries of the Organization of Economic Co-operation and Development (OECD) have signed a code to prevent the worst abuses. It seems likely that MNEs will also find themselves more and more constrained by the 'instruments' that the European Community will develop.

Indeed, Marlow (1984) thinks that a new breed of corporate leaders must reconcile some of the conflicts attributable to the success of MNEs. Part of the design for MNEs in the 1990s should be 'a well-established multi-national secretariat representing the considered views and interests of multi-nationals the world over'. (p. 304).

After the MNE we need to be able to design the 'pro-world' enterprise. The United Nations is a candidate, but its future shape and resourcing is not yet clear. We shall have to learn fast how to tackle global problems and international emergencies.

2 DISCUSSION: A SEQUENCE OF DESIGNS

Quinn and Cameron (1983) summarize eight models of organizational 'life cycles', each of which has an entrepreneurial stage, a collectivity stage (similar to the adhocracy), a stage where structure is elaborated (and decentralized) and a formalization of control (bureaucratic) stage. But there is great variation in how long any stage may last. They comment that

> none of the models is concerned with organizational decline and death.... This may be because in mature organizations ... life cycle models break down.... In the small group literature however it has been found that groups frequently return to earlier stages.
>
> (Quinn and Cameron 1983: 40)

For organizations we might consider a learning-cycle rather than a life-cycle model. There are experiences to be reflected upon, inferences to be made and modifications to structure to be introduced. These changes form the basis for more reflection. When problems recur, new elements can be distinguished from familiar ones and new solutions tried. A learning cycle is not just 'going round in circles'. It is more like an upward spiral of developing capabilities.

How might the capabilities of organizations be judged? Quinn and Cameron produced a summary of effectiveness criteria which includes the values shown in capital letters in Figure 11.1. They think organizations are judged differently at different stages in their 'lives' (or learning cycles). They cite the case of a Development Center for treatment of the mentally disabled. Its first head was a charismatic psychiatrist. The Center was entrepreneurial and the staff had 'almost missionary dedication and zeal'. The Center was praised for this COLLABORATION and for the INNO-VATIONs in its programme. However, some years later, a series of adverse newspaper reports criticized the Center for INEFFICIENCY and inade-quate accounting for public monies. The New York State's Department of Mental Hygiene, the Center's parent department, intervened, insisting on more formalization. The psychiatrist left soon after, and a more adminis-tratively minded person, who emphasized control, was appointed as head. Staff morale dropped and more staff left. The initial support and achieve-ment culture was replaced by a power and role culture.

According to the competing values approach of Quinn and McGrath (1985), two aspects of the environment are critical in determining the most appropriate structure and culture. The first is the degree of uncertainty or certainty, and the second is the degree to which an immediate response is required, the urgency, or intensity in their terms, of environmental demands. The entrepreneurial cluster or clan can deal with high uncertainty, but a more centralized approach is needed to deal with high uncertainty combined with high intensity. A more decentralized approach can respond to urgent operating situations, provided that these are not combined with high uncertainty also. The hierarchical form of the classic bureaucracy is best suited to conditions in which there is neither high intensity nor high uncertainty.

Greiner (1972) suggested that each new design is an attempt to rectify the problems created by the previous one. It is a form of incremental decision-making. Touraine suggested that the desire on the part of indi-viduals for autonomy to pursue their own self-interests is in conflict with the need for unity in the system, and so the design swings first one way and then the other. Skinner and Winckler (1980) posited three types of goals which are best realized by different types of power. From their descriptions we can surmise that the cluster would be best for ideological goals, the centralized or bureaucratic forms for order goals and the decent-ralized or hybrid forms for economic goals.

Whoever is taking redesign decisions will be forced to make tradeoffs. Some values can only be realized at the expense of others. A productive and efficient concern may be profitable in the short run, satisfying present customers and shareholders. If it does not organize for new product development, however, it will lose potential customers and decline. Products have a life cycle for which an organization must be prepared. Thus the timing of organizational redesign is as important as the model chosen. There is no perfect or permanent solution, only small or large transformations. An organization has many different 'stake-holders' whose interests may conflict. The power to back such interests is unequal.

3 SUMMARY

Organizational design is the creation of structures which provide for activities, decision-making authority and relationships at work. To create the type of organization desired (for example one which is externally and internally innovative, productive, efficient and collaborative) there are four main areas to consider. What is the organization trying to do? How is it to do it? What administrative arrangements does it need now, or might it need for the future? These four areas are addressed through five different types of organizational design: the cluster or self-managed group, the centralized concern, decentralized forms of various kinds, the classic bureaucracy and hybrid forms. Over a long period of time all of these designs may succeed one another in the same enterprise.

The entrepreneurial cluster is suited to close scanning of the market. It is egalitarian, informal and friendly. So is the self-managed group. Both are compatible with a support culture.

The centralized form is an attempt to unify and control operations once the enterprise has too many employees to rely on agreement among them. It concentrates decision-making in one or two offices, has vertical communication and has deferential relationships consistent with a power culture.

The decentralized structures use dispersed decision-making in an attempt to locate decisions near the points where action occurs. Relationships tend to be dictated by the nature of the work being done. Different professions may be expected to collaborate for common goals. The achievement culture is suited to these structures.

The classic bureaucracy uses numerous specialists whose activities are co-ordinated by a hierarchy in which each level is accountable to the level above. Relationships are formal and governed by regulations. The role culture is likely to be most compatible here.

Hybrid cultures are attempts to deal simultaneously with problems of internal control and external responsiveness – issues discussed in cyclical theories. One form of hybrid, the multinational corporation, is large

214 Emergent concepts and issues

enough to be able to influence national economies for good or ill. International bodies such as the OECD and the United Nations are concerned with the legal framework governing corporations. It is impossible to attain all desired values through organizational design. There have to be tradeoffs. Other things being equal, **culture affects organization design through a preference for centralized or decentralized forms.**

REFERENCES

Argenti, J (1968) 'The pyramid, the ladder and the matrix', *Management Decision* 2 (3): reprinted in Folkertsma, B. (ed.) *Handbook for Managers*, London: Kluwer Harrap, 1972.
Bloor, M. (1986) 'Who'll make the tea?', *New Society* 75 (1205): 185–6.
Dunning, J. H. (1985) 'Multinational enterprise and industrial restructuring in the U.K.', *Lloyds Bank Review* 158: 1–19.
Ellerman, D. P. (1983) 'The employment relation, property rights and organizational democracy', in Crough, C. and Heller, F. A. (eds) *International Yearbook of Organizational Democracy*, New York: Wiley.
Fligstein, N. (1985) 'The spread of the multi-divisional form among large firms, 1919–1979', *American Sociological Review* 50: 377–91.
Galbraith, J. R. (ed.) (1971) *Matrix Organizations: Organization Design and High Technology*, Cambridge, MA: MIT Press.
Greiner, L. E. (1972) 'Evolution and revolution as organizations grow', *Harvard Business Review* 50 (4): 37–46.
Handy, C. B. (1985) *Understanding Organizations*, 3rd edn, London: Penguin.
Hannan, M. and Freeman, J. (1977) 'The population ecology of organizations', *American Journal of Sociology* 92: 929–64.
——'Structural inertia and organizational change', *American Sociological Review* 49: 149–64.
Hofstede, G. (1980a) *Culture's Consequences*, Beverley Hills, CA: Sage.
Lammers, C. J. and Hickson, D. J. (eds) (1979) *Organizations Alike and Unlike: International and Inter-institutional Studies in the Sociology of Organizations*, London: Routledge & Kegan Paul.
Lawrence, P. R. and Lorsch, J. W. (1967) *Organization and Environment*, Boston, MA:, Harvard University Press.
Lockett, M. (1983) 'Organizational democracy and politics in China', in Crough, C. and Heller, F. (eds) *International Yearbook of Organizational Democracy* vol. 1, New York: Wiley, ch. 28.
Marlow, H. (1984) *Success: Individual, Corporate and National, Profile for the Eighties and Beyond*, London: Institute of Personnel Management.
Miles, R. E. and Snow, C. C. (1978) *Organizational Strategy, Structure, and Process*, New York: McGraw-Hill.
Patterson, C. and Stevenson, D. (1986) 'Why the factory of the future is the challenge of today', *Personnel Management* 18 (3): 46–50.
Pugh, D. S., Hickson, D. J., Hinings, R. and Turner, C. (1968) 'Dimensions of organization structure', *Administrative Science Quarterly* 13: 65–105.
Pugh, D. S., Hickson, D. J. and Hinings, C. R. (1969) 'An empirical taxonomy of work organization structures', *Administrative Science Quarterly* 14: 115–26.
Quinn, R. E. and Cameron, K. (1983) 'Organizational life cycles and shifting criteria of effectiveness: some preliminary evidence', *Management Science* 29 (1): 33–51.

Quinn, R. E. and McGrath, M. (1985) 'The transformation of organizational cultures: a competing values perspective', in Frost, P. J., Moore, L. F., Louis, M. R., Lundberg, C. C. and Martin, J. (eds) *Organizational Culture*, New York: Praeger.

Raybould, J. (1985) 'Ten years of decentralization', *Personnel Management* 17 (6): 40–43.

Rezazadeh, R. (1961) 'The concept of centralization', *Revista International de Sociologia* 27 (11): 425–30.

Skinner, G. W. and Winckler, E. A. (1980) 'Compliance succession in rural communist China: a cyclical theory', in Etzioni, A. and Lehman, E. W. (eds) *A Sociological Reader on Complex Organizations*, 3rd Edn, New York: Holt, Rinehart & Winston.

Touraine, A. (1971) *The Post-Industrial Society* trans. by L. Mayhew, New York: Random House.

Weber, M. (1947) *The Theory of Social and Economic Organization*, New York: Free Press.

——(1968) *Economy and Society*, vols I-III, New York: Bedminster Press.

Werbner, P. (1985) 'How immigrants can make it in Britain', *New Society* 73 (1186): 411–13.

Wilson, E. K. (1985) 'What counts in the death or transformation of an Organization?', *Social Forces* 64 (2): 259–80.

The diversity of management systems

Roland Calori

The idea that good scientific management is universal spread when the US economy and American business schools dominated the world in the 1960s. Since then, recognition of the diversity of good management practices has grown, even in the United States. The dominant assumption now is that management philosophies and practices should fit the sociological context in which they are placed (Hofstede, 1993). The change in the dominant paradigm coincided with the success of Japanese firms world-wide and the differences that managers and researchers could observe between the US and Japanese systems. The contrast between the two systems is striking. It is presented briefly below before focusing on Europe, because comparisons with the two other zones of the triad helps in understanding specific European characteristics. We will first build comparisons from the existing literature, and then analyze and synthesize the views of the directors in our study.

1 CONTRASTING THE US AND THE JAPANESE SYSTEMS OF MANAGEMENT

The Art of Japanese Management by Richard T. Pascale and Anthony G. Athos (1981) was one of the most respected books – along with those of Ohmae (1976) and Ouchi (1981) – to describe the subtleties of the Japanese management system as an alternative to the dominant American model.

For Pascale and Athos the best firms are characterized by a fit between seven elements – the famous 7Ss: strategy, structure, systems, skills, style, staff (people) and shared superordinate goals. The Americans are similar to the Japanese in the way they manage 'hard' components of the 7Ss: strategy, structure and systems. The Japanese are different from the Americans in the way they heed and manage the soft components: skills, style, staff and especially shared superordinate goals. Their culture helps them value interdependence as a mode of relationship, whereas the Americans value independence. In Japan the 'self' is considered as an obstacle to development; individuals define their identity by the group to which they belong. American society, on the other hand, is built upon the importance of the 'self'. The authors quote Takeo Fujisawa (co-founder of Honda): 'management in Japan and management in the USA are similar up to 95 per cent, and totally different on the remaining 5 per cent, the essential 5 per cent.'

Such differences have been commented upon extensively in further research. American management produces rational tools and strategic planning in a search for coherence whereas Japanese companies (such as Canon, Komatsu, Honda, NEC) define a simple, long-term 'strategic intent', create an obsession for winning and focus on careful implementation (Hamel and Prahalad, 1989). In the United States, business schools teach professional management: 'They have perpetuated the notion that a manager with net present value calculations in one hand and portfolio planning in the other hand can manage any business anywhere' (Hamel and Prahalad, 1989). Although Japanese managers go to universities, priority there is given to on-the-job training and in-company training programmes.

The individualistic orientation of Americans and the group orientation of Japanese have several managerial consequences: for instance, there is greater loyalty to the firm in Japan (lifelong employment). Similarly, the strongly shared group values allow decisions to follow bottom-up processes in Japan compared to top-down processes in US firms (Thurow, 1991). In the US, the focus is on managers rather than on workers, the core of the enterprise is the managerial class, the manager is a cultural hero. In contrast, the core of the Japanese enterprise is the permanent worker group, decisions are taken in group consultation sessions, control is achieved by the peer group rather than by managers (Hofstede, 1993). Japanese workers do not need an American-style manager to motivate them. At the level of the firm, the concept of interdependence vs. independence also produces different organizational formulae. American firms show a tendency to segment their operations into 'strategic business units', whereas Japanese firms show more horizontal integration around core competences (Hamel and Prahalad, 1989).

Chandler (1986) put these characteristics into an historical perspective. In the US, a corporate meritocracy emerged and a new class of professional managers developed. He described this management culture as 'managerial capitalism'. Delegation of responsibility could succeed only if top management retained access to information as a means of control. Thus divisionalized structures and sophisticated management systems developed. The Japanese cultural heritage fostered a form of management that Chandler called 'group capitalism'. The homogeneity of Japanese society, its isolationism during the Tokugawa period, and the influence of Eastern religions and philosophies contributed to emphasize group behaviour and interpersonal harmony. Within the organization such values took the concrete forms of lifelong employment, information-sharing and joint decision-making ('nemawashi' and 'ringi'). Language and cultural barriers made it difficult to integrate non-Japanese. This had the effect of encouraging Japanese companies to retain decision-making and control at the centre where they could be managed by those who understood the subtleties of the system.

James C. Abbleglen and Georges Stalk (1985) used a radically different perspective in studying the Japanese corporation and comparing it to the dominant American model. They argued that market strategy and manpower strategy, *not* management style, made the Japanese world pace-setters. Japanese firms have a growth bias: 'Management with a bias towards growth have distinct mind-sets which include the expectation of continued growth, decisions and plans formulated to produce growth, and the unfaltering pursuit of growth unless the very life of the organization is threatened' (Abbleglen and Stalk, 1985). In this perspective, priority is given to the creation and ruthless exploitation of competitive advantage by creating value for the customer and superior quality.

Some recent studies seem to confirm this view. 'The world competitiveness report', produced every year by the World Economic Forum, ranks Japanese firms first in the following domains: product quality, delivery times, after-sales services and in-house training (while US firms lag behind, at around tenth place). This view is fully consistent with what Hamel and Prahalad (1989) defined as 'strategic intent': building layers of competitive advantage in order to achieve global market leadership in the long term. On the other hand, US companies are managed towards the maximization of profits and the short-term satisfaction of shareholders: managers are rewarded mainly on profitability targets and strategies are designed to improve return on investments.

Lester Thurow (1991) confirms this crucial difference in business logic: for the Americans the ultimate goal is profit, whereas for the Japanese profit is a means to build an empire and strengthen their company and 'Japan Inc'. According to him, the two *systems* are fundamentally different: US society is oriented towards consumption and the welfare of shareholders, whereas Japanese society is oriented towards savings and investments. The percentage of savings on available income is more than twice as high in Japan as in the United States. During the period 1985–90, the Japanese invested 35.6 per cent of their GNP while Americans invested only 17 per cent. Lower interest rates in Japan do not affect savings and make cheaper capital available.

Thurow (1991) also points out dramatic differences between the roles played by government in the two systems and the consequences on the structure of industry. Apart from the induced effects of the US government's defence policy, the American system is characterized by pure liberalism. The Japanese government, on the other hand, has always participated in the elaboration of national industrial strategies, indirectly protecting some domestic industries, selecting priority sectors to develop in the long term, and funding research and development related to these domains. In the 1930s, the US government initiated anti-trust legislation in order to preserve free competition on the domestic market. In contrast, the Japanese government never completely dismantled the Zaibatsus, and conglomerates survived and developed under the form of 'Keiretsus', which are absolutely legal. Mitsui, Mitsubishi, Sumitomo, Fuji, Sanwa, Daï-Ichi and Hitachi together represent an *organized* economic structure. Share-swaps between the members of a Keiretsu guarantee cheap and stable capital, both of which are needed to elaborate long-term industrial strategies. Supplier-client relationships and transfers of knowledge within the Keiretsu enhance integration.

When one considers such contrasts between the two systems, it is clear that the 5 per cent difference mentioned by Takeo Fujisawa is essential.

Top Managers' Views

Although it was not the focus of our discussions, the directors we interviewed expressed their views on the characteristics of the US and Japanese management systems (as we tried to elicit distinctive European traits). Below we briefly report the images they had of the two dominant models and check their consistency with the analyses proposed by researchers. Figure 11.6 shows a synthesis of the US system of management, and Figure 11.7 shows a synthesis of the Japanese system of management as perceived by the directors of companies established in Europe.

First it is important to note the consistency between the descriptions given by the managers and by researchers, although the labelling of concepts differs slightly. European directors depicted US management in more positive terms than researchers did; apparently they still value some key characteristics of American society such as entrepreneurship, a concept and a reality resulting from the combination of individualism, profit-orientation, and competition. Competition was identified as a basic

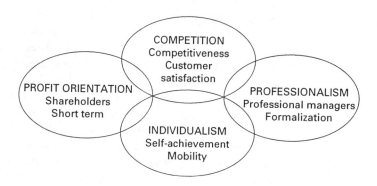

Figure 11.6 Characteristics of the US system of management

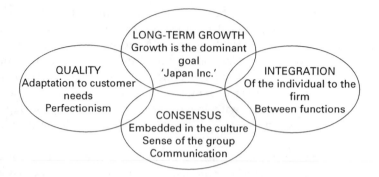

Figure 11.7 Characteristics of the Japanese system of management

characteristic, perhaps due to the contrast with Europe, where firms and markets are more protected. The directors' image of Japanese management stresses the search for quality as a fundamental characteristic; they seem to be sensitive to this as a concrete competitive challenge, and to think that Europe still has to learn from the Japanese in this domain.

The comparative analysis of US and Japanese management has led some researchers to a wider comparison between an Anglo-Saxon 'individualistic form of capitalism' (represented by the US and Great Britain) and a 'group form of capitalism' (represented by Germany and Japan), in the terms used by Georges C. Lodge (1991). In the same vein, Michel Albert (1991) differentiates between the 'Capitalisme Anglo-Saxon' and the 'Capitalisme Rhénan' which includes Germany, some of its small neighbours (Austria and Switzerland), and Japan. This extended segmentation is based on constructs which are similar to the US vs. Japan comparison. According to these authors, the UK and the US share the same paradigm: liberalism, profit orientation, short-termism, domination of finance over industry, a shareholder orientation supported by an active stock market, individualism, and high mobility of personnel . . . in brief, the 'cicada'. Germany and Japan share similar paradigms: organized competition, long-term orientation, a stakeholder orientation, high investment, stable capital structures, a sense of community, and loyalty to the firm; in brief, the 'ant-hill'.

Indeed there are striking similarities between the UK and the US on the one hand and between Germany and Japan on the other. However, some inconsistencies appear. German firms definitely belong to an occidental clan where the 'self' dominates work relationships. The German manager is a specialist, whereas the Japanese manager is a generalist. The German social market economy, and the relationships between top management and trade unions, are basically different from Japan. The differences between American and British management are more subtle. Peter Lawrence (1993) has identified some of them. In Britain management is intuitive: systems, standard operating procedures and strategic planning are much less developed than in the United States. British management is pragmatic and discretionary whereas American management is more rationalistic. In the US conflicts are considered as normal and desirable in order to bring the toughest to the front. The British view conflicts as disruptive and a sign of failure. The best British brains do not seem to favour careers in business, whereas business and business schools have a much higher status in the United States.

Among the directors we interviewed, only a few referred to the dualistic typology between 'individual capitalism' and 'group capitalism'. For the reasons listed above, we believe it is too simplistic. However, it also suggests indirectly that strong differences exist within Europe, and more precisely between the United Kingdom and Germany.

2 THE DIVERSITY OF MANAGEMENT SYSTEMS WITHIN WESTERN EUROPE

We will first review the literature proposing typologies of management systems within Western Europe, and then focus on directors' perceptions of European diversity.

Diverging conclusions from the literature

Several typologies of management systems in Europe have been proposed; the problem is that they do not really fit with each other. Laurent (1983) considers two opposite clusters of countries: France, Belgium and Italy where managers view the organization as political systems governed by hierarchical relationships and authority, and a cluster of northern European countries where managers view the organization as a network. Schneider and de Meyer (1991) also stress the difference between a Latin Europe (South) and northern Europe.

Albert (1991) contrasts the Anglo-Saxon model (the US and the UK) to the 'modèle Rhénan' (developed by the Germans), but does not characterize most of the other European countries. J. Simonet identifies four models within Europe: the German, the Latin (without France), the French, and the Anglo-Saxon (including Scandinavian countries). He differentiates by considering only two dimensions: the degree of formalization and the degree of centralization. This typology may please the French, who think they are unique, but they may be less satisfied when they discover that their uniqueness is depicted as a 'bureaucratie pyramidale'. Simonet's typology is inconsistent with the one proposed by G. Hofstede (1980). In his study of work-related values, Hofstede suggests the existence of four clusters:

Scandinavian countries, the British, a Germanic group and a group including Latin countries and Belgium.

Finally, some authors, such as Todd (1990), argue that even national boundaries are too broad and that deep regional differences exist within countries in a patchwork Europe. It should be acknowledged that the micro-regional view is well based, and that considering the nation-states as the elementary units of analysis is a simplification. For instance, Hofstede (1980) found significant differences in work-related values between the German-speaking Swiss community and the French-speaking Swiss community. In one of the cluster analyses computed in this study, Italy appears in the same cluster as Germany. Surprisingly, the author comments on this result by arguing that the people and the firm in the sample belong to *northern* Italy, which could be closer to other Alpine countries than to the Mezzogiorno!

While considering nation-states as the unit of analysis is a simplification, it is an acceptable simplification because laws and education systems are designed at the level of nation-states. Moreover, comparative analysis between nation-states can always be refined and completed by a comparison between micro-regions.

One type of research compares actual management practices across European countries such as: professional profiles of managers, reward systems, training schemes, number of hierarchical levels, etc. For instance, the yearly reports of the Price Waterhouse – Cranfield Project (1991, 1992), present a comprehensive comparison which analyzes human resource management across 10 European countries: Denmark, France, Germany, Italy, Norway, Spain, Sweden, Switzerland, the Netherlands and the United Kingdom. Aggregate analysis of the 10 main dimensions of the data base shows that each country is characterized by a specific mix of practices, i.e. no cluster of countries emerge.

Organizational structures have also been compared. Horovitz (1978), for instance, studied French, British and German firms. The British prefer a flexible decentralized structure, with few headquarters staff, and a holding form of organization. In Germany the organization is more specialized (by function), the operational units have less autonomy, decisions are made by an executive committee, and coordination is achieved through numerous headquarters staff and planning. In France organizational structures are less formal than in Germany, but specialization by function and strong roles for headquarters staff are also preferred. The role of the 'Président Directeur Général' appears to be more decisive than in the two other countries.

Peter Lawrence (1993) suggests that the orientation of the managerial profile (generalist vs. specialist), and the degree of individuals' mobility between organizations are important dimensions which characterize the manager's job. The combination of these dimensions with a measure of

Table 11.1 A comparison based on aspects of the manager's job

	Generalism	Mobility	Hierarchy
Britain	+	+	−
Germany	−	−	−
France	+	−	+
Netherlands	+	−	−

Source: adapted from Lawrence, 1993

various signs of formal authority and hierarchy (as suggested by Laurent, 1983) shows that each country is unique (cf. Table 11.1).

Another type of research has tried to capture work-related values which are ingrained in practices. The most comprehensive work of this type is the study completed by Hofstede (1980) in 53 world-wide subsidiaries of IBM. This research (based on questionnaires administered to thousands of employees) has elicited the following four dimensions which discriminate between national cultures in the work place:

1 *Power Distance* refers to the degree to which power differences are expected and, indeed, preferred by a society. A high score on this index reflects a societal belief that there 'should be' a well-defined order in which everyone has a rightful place; a low score reflects the belief that all people should have equal rights and the opportunity to change their position in society.

2 *Uncertainty Avoidance* refers to the degree to which the society willingly accepts ambiguity and risk. Nations characterized by high scores are risk-averse; they prefer certainty and security. In contrast, nations characterized by low scores are motivated by risk-taking and accept ambiguity.

3 *Individualism* and its opposite *collectivism* refer to the degree to which a society emphasizes the role of the individual versus the role of the group. In nations high on the individualism scale, every person is expected to take care of himself or herself and his or her immediate family. In contrast, nations high on collectivism show an emotional attachment to organizations and institutions. The emphasis is on 'we' and the greater good of the group.

4 *Masculinity* refers to the degree to which a society holds traditional male values, such as competitiveness, assertiveness, ambition, and the acquisition of money and other material possessions. A low masculinity score (or a high femininity score) reflects a more nurturing, caring value orientation, which emphasizes consideration of others.

National cultures in the workplace are ranked according to these four general dimensions.

From this study, we selected some results concerning European

Table 11.2 A selection of results from Hofstede's study

	Individualism	Masculinity	Power distance	Uncertainty avoidance
Austria	2	1	4	2
Germany	2	1	4	3
Switzerland	2	1	4	3
Finland	2	4	4	3
Norway	1	4	4	3
Sweden	1	4	4	4
Denmark	1	4	4	4
The Netherlands	1	4	4	3
United Kingdom	1	1	4	4
Ireland	1	1	4	4
Belgium	1	2	2	1
France	1	3	2	1
Spain	2	3	3	1
Portugal	3	4	2	1
Italy	1	1	3	2
Greece	3	2	3	1
USA	1	2	3	4
Japan	2	1	3	1

Notes:
1 signifies that the score of the country on this dimension belongs to the first (highest) quartile among the 53 countries studied.
2 signifies that the score belongs to the second quartile.
3 signifies that the score belongs to the third quartile.
4 signifies that the score belongs to the fourth quartile.

countries, and the positions of the US and Japan for purposes of comparison. Table 11.2 shows that four clusters emerge:

1 A Germanic group (Germany, Austria, Switzerland), mainly characterized by high masculinity and low power distance.
2 A Scandinavian group (Sweden, Finland, Norway, Denmark) plus the Netherlands, mainly characterized by high individualism, low masculinity and low power distance.
3 An Anglo-Saxon group (Britain and Ireland) characterized by high individualism and masculinity, and low power distance and uncertainty avoidance.
4 A relatively heterogeneous Latin group (France, Spain, Italy, Portugal, Greece) plus Belgium, which is mainly characterized by high uncertainty avoidance and high power distance.

The work by Hofstede has been criticized as being reductionist, arguing that all cultures are too complex to be captured by questionnaires and a few dimensions. Other models for cultural analysis have also been proposed, such as that by Kluckhohn and Strodbeck (1961). In spite of its biases, however, the research on work-related values by Hofstede remains the most comprehensive international field study available on this issue.

The necessary complement to the research described above is provided by a third stream of research: *rich interpretive studies of a small number of cases*. The research carried out by Philippe d'Iribarne (1989) is a good example. He studied an American, a French and a Dutch plant within the same multinational company, and provided rich comparative descriptions of practices, beliefs and basic assumptions in the three locations. We will not attempt to summarize his findings here, as no summary would do justice to his descriptions.

The first two streams of research – comparative analysis of practices, and positivistic studies of national cultures – are limited by the variables they select and measure. Different variables produce different and sometimes inconsistent typologies. Rich interpretive research is limited by the number of cases that a researcher can study in a given period of time. We believe that analysis of the content of non-directive interviews with top managers is a viable research alternative for delineating management systems in Europe. Top managers have an integrated, holistic view of the categorization based upon their expertise.

Top managers' views: the diversity of management systems across Europe

When top managers talk about the differences in Europe and delineate geographical zones, the resulting maps are even more diverse than those produced by researchers. But when the individual maps are aggregated, the final typology of management systems is instructive. Such an integrative segmentation, as presented in Figure 11.8 gives a richer picture than 'flat' typologies; one can read the dendogramme at different levels of aggregation. In the figure, the deepest differences are shown at the top. A first connection is absolutely striking: the correlation between this segmentation and geography. Four levels of segmentation are considered:

- At the first level of segmentation, the United Kingdom is an island separated from the rest of Europe. It was recognized that the UK is an exception to many possible common characteristics of management in Europe, and that British management is close to the American model of management.
- At the second level of segmentation, the north/south dichotomy of the European continent is mainly based on four dimensions:
  South more state intervention, more protectionism, more hierarchy in the firm, more intuitive (some say 'chaotic') management;
  North: less state intervention, more liberalism, more participation in the firm, more organized management.

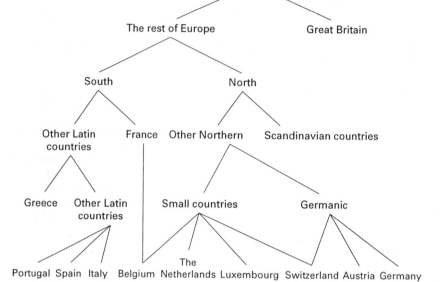

Figure 11.8 Typology of management styles systems in Europe according to top managers

- At the third level of segmentation, France is differentiated from other Latin countries mainly because it combines intuition and organization, and because the links between firms and a strong state are tight and based on a management elite produced by the 'Grandes Ecoles'. The correspondence with geography shows that more than two-thirds of France is above the 'olive tree line', which is considered as the real, but invisible, frontier between the north and the south.

  At the same level of segmentation, the northern group (which does not include the United Kingdom) splits into a subgroup of Scandinavian countries and a subgroup of other northern countries (including Germanic countries and small countries like the Netherlands and Belgium). Management in Scandinavia is differentiated from management in Germany by being less oriented towards performance, more oriented towards the quality of working life, and less favourable to status differences between people.

- At the fourth level of segmentation, the German system is the one which has been best described and has become a model. The case of the small countries, the Netherlands, Belgium and Luxembourg, calls for some comments. They fall in the middle of the segmentation dendogramme. Because of their small size and history, they opened up earlier to foreign countries and influences, and managers now consider them the best illustration of a blend of practices prefiguring a European management model:

> I think they are influenced by German practices, the Belgians may also be influenced by French practices, while the Dutch are also influenced by British practices. These small countries are melting pots. They have been more sensitive to outside influences and have integrated these influences: because of the pressures against them, because of the small base they have for recruiting and because they were forced to go outside looking for markets.

> The best examples of European companies are Shell and Unilever, who have been operating under joint Anglo-Dutch ownership for, I don't know, fifty years, more perhaps, and I suppose they are the nearest to what you might call a European company.

Switzerland also belongs to this group, thanks to diverse cultural influences.

As Figure 11.6 shows, at the fourth level of segmentation Greece is differentiated from the other Latin countries, mainly because the present situation is considered as 'chaotic'.

Managers did not explicitly mention Ireland (which probably belongs to a broader Anglo-Saxon block, but which may also share some Latin characteristics).

Of course, this picture will not satisfy a careful analyst who will argue that Catalonia, the Basque country and Andalucia are different, that Lombardy and Sicily are two different worlds, that the Alsacians and the Corsicans have little in common, and that the Walloons and the Flemish in Belgium are not the same. He or she would be right; even the most global product, Coca-Cola, has to adapt to regional differences within countries in Europe and is advertised in two languages in Barcelona. Managers have to bear in mind all the levels of differences, but they also have to simplify complexity. From this perspective, we will consider the following three types of management in Europe which correspond to the two first levels of segmentation:

1 Anglo-Saxon.
2 Latin.
3 Northern Europe, using the German model as an example.

The United Kingdom, an exception in Europe

> When you say European, you mean those who are not English?

This sentence from one of the interviewees briefly summarizes the general opinion that the United Kingdom is a case apart. Management philosophies, structures and practices in the UK are closer to the management characteristics of the United States, in the opinion of five of the directors we interviewed. For several others, the UK is (literally) 'somewhere in between' the US and the European continent:

> My first remark is: is there a European management culture? And I put a big question mark behind it ... You could also defend the thesis that there is an Anglo-Saxon, and a continental management culture, because the British in many respects have management habits which are more related to the Americans than those on the continent. They are, may be, in a sort of in-between position.

Management in the UK has the following characteristics in common with US management:

- A short-term orientation (more than continental Europe).
- A shareholder orientation (whereas the rest of Europe has more of a stakeholders' orientation).
- An orientation towards trading and finance (the importance of the stock market is more developed than in continental Europe).
- A higher turnover of managers.
- A greater liberalism towards foreigners (e.g. the Japanese).
- More freedom for top management *vis-à-vis* the workers and the government.
- More direct and pragmatic relationships between people.
- More variable remuneration.

But management in the UK generally differs from management in the United States on the following points:

- Adversarial relationships with labour.
- The tradition of the manager as a 'gifted amateur' (as opposed to the professionalism of US managers).
- The influence of class differences in the firm.

Moreover the British management system differs from the US on the common European characteristics: an orientation towards people, internal negotiation, managing international diversity, and managing between extremes. However, concerning some of these characteristics, the UK has *sometimes* been cited by the directors as a probable exception.

With regard to the importance of profits and social responsibility, and the principles involved in a 'social market economy', the UK appears to one of the managers interviewed like a separate case:

> The British, like the Americans, are more oriented towards short term and quick financial profits than, let us say, the Germans ... or even the European continent ...

In Germany, in Sweden, in Denmark, and even in France, there are a lot of checks and balances against management freedom of actions, there are supervisors' reports, there are workers' representatives on the board and there is much more government intervention, so there are many other forces acting on European continental management than there are on British management. On the other hand, British management is much more beholden to its shareholders than European management is. We have to pay far more attention to the attitude of our shareholders... This is because our market structure is different. I mean in Britain something like 80 per cent of company shares are quoted on the stock market. I think in Germany it is less than 50 per cent, and in Italy it is less than 20 per cent.

Junk bonds could never have started in Germany, it is just impossible to imagine the Germans with junk bonds. I think the UK market and the US market have more of a trading nature than Europe, which has more of an investing nature.

There is a significant degree to which the United Kingdom recognizes social responsibilities, public responsibilities, less than corporations that I know of, that we operate, and that we own in the rest of the EC. I think that we in the UK are somewhere between the European ethos and the American ethos. This is a continuum and we are a little bit out to the side towards the Americans. And indeed, you will recognize that in the last dozen years, where we have had political direction of a certain kind, this has been something which the government as a whole encouraged. I think we recognize social and public interest less than we did a dozen years ago, because the government has led us to think that it is desirable to take less interest. We have gone back nearer to the Adam Smith concept... The very fact that the government announced its intention to terminate the existence of the National Economic Development Council only a week ago is an illustration of that. That was an institutional framework that the government set up in the 1970s, so that heads of firms and the state and trade unions and communities could meet together to regulate the social market economy... So I do think that we (the UK) are different.

Management in the UK is sometimes (for two managers in our sample) an exception to the second common European characteristic: internal negotiation. In this respect also, Thatcherism has changed the power balance between the unions and management. As to a third common characteristic of management in Europe – managing international diversity – the UK is recognized as having a more global vision in the sense that they have a wider concept based on the Commonwealth and the old empire; also British managers prefer to speak English in the foreign subsidiaries of their companies.

However, these opinions are expressed by a *minority* of interviewees. For the majority, the United Kingdom shares the common European characteristics that will be developed in the next chapter.

The Latin way of doing business

Compared to the common characteristics of management in Europe, Latin (or southern) Europe has the following specificities:

- More state intervention.
- More protectionism.
- More hierarchy in the firm.
- More intuitive management.
- More family business (especially in Italy).
- More reliance on an elite (especially in France).

State intervention takes several forms. First, the state owns and manages some industrial companies and financial institutions:

> In Italy, state-owned companies were created mostly before the war, in the 1930s, when there was the great economic crisis. Many companies were close to bankruptcy, and the state created an institute to control them and to avoid plant closures. In other countries, state intervention was carried out by nationalizations ... In Italy, the state has operated as an industrial actor with a bias towards administrative [as opposed to entrepreneurial] forms of management ...

In France, the state is more firmly based, and has originated industrial policies and several 'grands projets', such as the Minitel and the Train à Grande Vitesse. Ownership of the top financial institutions is also a way in which the state influences policies.

A second form of state intervention combines regulations and attitudes towards international competition, which may be biased towards protectionism. Protectionism has been mentioned in particular by the US and Japanese managers in our sample, the latter taking the example of EC policy towards Japanese imports and car-industry transplants. In this area, France, Spain and Italy have the most protectionist positions across Europe.

Japanese managers notice that in France offices are enclosed, whereas open plan is more frequent in the UK. This is one of the many symptoms of a stronger presence of hierarchy in Latin Europe compared to northern Europe. Other symptoms are the higher number of hierarchical, organizational levels and the lower degree of participation by personnel (compared to northern Europe, excluding the UK).

Management is more personalized and the concept of leadership is better accepted in southern Europe than in Germany or in Scandinavia. This management style is more inclined to intuition and to management by 'chaos': 'Especially in southern Europe, including France, the heads of firms are suspicious about structures and procedures. They manage by pressure, intuition and chaos. They don't pay too much attention to organization charts'. Linking this view with the above-mentioned administrative style of state-owned companies gives a dual picture of management in southern Europe.

Certain characteristics are linked more specifically to some of the southern countries. In Italy, there are far more family businesses based on family ownership. As a consequence, the heads of some big firms personalize the company and management may be more paternalistic than in the north. 'I think the style of X[1] was not very different from ours. The only thing was that we were, apparently, more paternalistic than X ... Z was the owner of the whole town, public libraries, hospitals, primary schools, nurseries . . . everything was in the hands of Z who managed it for the benefit of the whole town, not only for its employees'.

A final trait of management in southern Europe is particularly developed in France: the importance of *the elite* and of the *Grandes Ecoles* which educate this elite. These alumni, with diplomas in hand, are hired to become the 'cadres dirigeants' of both private and state-owned companies: 'The French believe that they can manage any firm when they come out from l'Ecole Polytechnique or from l'Ecole Nationale d'Administration. In Germany, it is radically different; one has to go through a whole career in the company. Reaching the top depends on the person's abilities and success in the firm'.[. . .]

The German model

In the case of management in Germanic countries, some authors and a few managers use the word *model*, probably considering that German management is consistent and has proved successful enough. Michel Albert (1991) writes about 'le modèle Rhénan' with admiration.

In the broader zone that we defined as northern continental Europe (Germany, Austria, and to some extent Switzerland), the German model is close to the Scandinavian management style and to management in the small countries (Benelux), and is by far the most visible style. According to the directors we interviewed, the German model is based on three cultural and structural characteristics:

1 Strong links between banks and industry.
2 The balance between a sense of national collectivity and the Länder system.
3 The system of training and development of managers.

The model can be described by the following five components:

1 The system of co-determination with workers' representatives present on the board.
2 The loyalty of managers (and employees in general) who spend their career in a single firm, which then gives priority to in-house training.
3 The collective orientation of the work-force, which includes dedication to the company, team spirit and a sense of discipline.
4 The long-term orientation which appears in planning, in the seriousness and stability of supplier – client relationships and in the priority of industrial goals over short-term financial objectives.
5 The reliability and stability of shareholders, influenced by a strong involvement of banks in industry.

The system of co-determination, ironically implanted in the German steel industry by the Allies after World War II, certainly is a source of social cohesion and effectiveness:

> The Conseil de Surveillance (Aufsichtsrat) is composed of 50 per cent workers' representatives and 50 per cent representatives of the shareholders. Decisions cannot be blocked because the President, always named among the representatives of the shareholders, has a casting vote. This is important, parity would be disastrous. Before the Council meets, the representatives of the shareholders meet and prepare decisions and the representatives of the workers meet and prepare decisions, then the President checks if there is an agreement or not. Most of the time, there is harmony in the Council, but negotiations have taken place before. And on both sides people work hard. The workers have internal structures and are very well informed about the company. They circulate information from the top down and from the bottom up. They understand the difficulties of the company, they defend their interests but also understand the collective interest of the company. I often see real entrepreneurs among these workers, people who know what they want and who certainly are proactive and constructive... in many other countries where there is no system of co-determination, the top management makes decisions that are far from practical and is then surprised at the reaction of the workforce.

Co-determination is strengthened by the German system of a single trade union which allows easier negotiations. It seems that co-determination creates intense communication flows rather than a method of sharing power. Similar systems exist in the Netherlands and in Scandinavian countries.

The second characteristic of the German management system, loyalty to the company, may be related to participative processes, to the priority given to in-house, on-the-job training and to the team spirit in German firms.

In Germany the link between the firm and the employee is very strong, in both directions. There is a tendency to keep employees as long as possible, sometimes lifelong. The precondition for lifelong employment is strong and effective training and personal development effort by the company, both basic training and complementary training. Investment in this domain is considerable. Employees demand such support so that they can increase their knowledge and skills and keep close to the state of the art. In our firm, links with employees are very tight. The average number of years of employment is 17 . . . In Germany people spend their career in the firm and are promoted from within . . . However, the geographic mobility between sites of the same firm is not so marked; people do not like to leave Bavaria for northern Germany, or Hesse for Bavaria . . .

When common European characteristics of management philosophies, structures and practices were evoked, Germany appeared to be an exception to the general rule of low formalization:

The Germans write a lot . . . they work hard but for every one working there is somebody writing in a little book! . . .

If I invite the President of X (a big German group) to speak, three months before the meeting his secretary is already impatient to know how long he should speak . . . If no answer has been received one month before, they start to panic. The British prepare their speech two days before, and the French the week before, but the slides are ready at the last minute. When I hear the President of X talking about management in his group, there seem to be quite formal procedures, procedures that work well, by the way. We try to organize procedures but they do not work well because of our culture.

When the low customer orientation of the Europeans is discussed, Germany also appears to be a case apart for a minority of the directors interviewed.

Some similarities emerge between the German and the Japanese models of management: the loyalty of managers based on in-house training is common to the two countries. The long-term orientation is common to the two countries. However, important differences are also noted. It is true that the stability of financial resources is common to the two economies, but this stability is based on these different structures:

- the involvement of banks in industry (and vice versa) in Germany;
- the Keiretsu structure in Japan.

The participation of workers is common to the two systems but:

- it is based on negotiation in Germany;

- it is based on natural consensus in Japan.

The collective orientation of the work-force, team spirit and a sense of discipline are common to the two systems, but:

- in Japan, the individual is overshadowed by the group;
- in Germany the individual still defends his/her self-interest and originality.

Finally, German managers are 'specialists' (of a given function) whereas Japanese managers are 'generalists' who are developed through internal job rotation. For these reasons, directors do not agree with Albert's assertion that the 'modèle Rhénan' is very similar to the Japanese model (1991). Another argument is that the German model shares some characteristics with the rest of Europe, which differentiate management in Europe from that in Japan. This point will be developed in the next chapter: an orientation towards people, internal negotiation, managing international diversity, and managing between extremes.

3 CONCLUDING COMMENTS

It is tempting to view management philosophies, structures and practices in Europe as if they were stretched between three poles, as presented in Figure 11.9.

- Anglo-Saxon management to the west.
- the German model to the east and Japan to the far east.
- the Latin model to the south, based in the Mediterranean countries where occidental philosophies were born.

This is a simplified but reliable image of the diversity of management in Europe. Some believe that it is a benefit for Europe to find such diversity in such a small geographic area, and that it offers Europeans opportunities to learn complementary skills and attitudes more quickly, so that they can be more effective in a world market where two extreme models – the US and the Japanese – now compete with each other. But, citing this diversity is akin to seeing the bottle as half empty (a bottle of wine or beer,

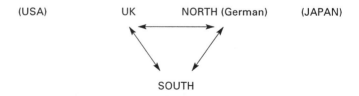

Figure 11.9 The stretching forces in European management

depending on whether you live in the south or in the north of Europe). There is also the view of the same bottle half full of some common European management characteristics. Just as statistics now show that the consumption of wine is tending to grow (relative to beer) in northern Europe, a region of brewing tradition, whereas the consumption of beer is tending to grow (relative to wine) in southern Europe, a region of wine tradition, the existence and development of common characteristics can also be reasonably expected.

The segmentation of management styles made by the directors in our study identified a cluster of 'small countries' (the Netherlands, Belgium, Luxembourg and Switzerland) as being characterized by international openness, a combination of unity and diversity, and a 'blend of practices prefiguring European management'. Study of management in the 'small countries' would be instructive with regard to an emerging European model. For instance, management in the Netherlands has been analyzed by d'Iribarne (1989) and by Lawrence (1991). d'Iribarne describes the Netherlands as a consensual society, examining facts with objectivity, moved by a desire for discussion and conciliation, with an aversion for any form of pressure from external authority. This search for pragmatic compromise between the members of a community has been described as 'Pilarisation' ('Verzuiling', cf. Lijphart, 1975). Lawrence (1991) also notes the following characteristics: mutual adjustment and cooperation, restraint, humility, heedfulness to civic values, modesty, pragmatism, informality, and a recognition of the importance of the quality of life. Most of these characteristics seem to be necessary ingredients in a process of international integration. In the past, the 'small countries' have demonstrated their ability to cooperate: in 1922 Belgium and Luxembourg created the Union Econo-mique Belgo-Luxembourgeoise', and in 1948 the Netherlands joined them to form the Benelux. So the smaller countries may well be the best source of inspiration for building distinctive managerial skills in the integrated Europe of the future.

NOTE

1 X, is a US company which merged with the Italian company whose director is speaking here; Z is another Italian company.

REFERENCES

Abbleglen, J. C. and G. Stalk (1985), *Kaisha, The Japanese Corporation*, New York: Basic Books.
Albert, M. (1991), *Capitalisme contre Capitalisme*, Paris: Seuil.
Chandler, A. D. (1986), 'The evolution of modern global competition', in Porter, M. E. (ed.) *Competition In Global Industries*, Boston, Mass: Harvard Business School Press, pp. 405–48.

d'Iribarne, P. (1989), *La Logique de l'honneur, gestion des entreprises et traditions nationales*, Paris: Editions du Seuil.

Hamel, G. and C. K. Prahalad (1989), 'Strategic intent', *Harvard Business Review*, May-June, pp. 63–76.

Hofstede, G. H. (1980), *Culture's consequences: International Differences in Work-related Values*, Beverly Hills: Sage Publications.

Hofstede, G. H. (1993), 'Cultural constraints in management theories', *Academy of Management Executive*, 7, 1, pp. 81–95.

Horovitz, J. (1978), 'Allemagne, Grande Bretagne, France: trois styles de management', *Revue Française de Gestion* 17, September-October, pp. 8–17.

Kluckhohn, F. and F. Strodbeck (1961), *Variations in Value Organizations*, New York: Row, Peterson.

Laurent, A. (1983), 'The cultural diversity of Western conceptions of management', *International Studies of Management and Organization*, XIII, 1–2, pp. 75–96.

Lawrence, P. (1991), *Management in The Netherlands*, Oxford: Basil Blackwell.

Lawrence, P. (1993), 'Through a glass darkly: towards a characterization of British management', paper presented at the *'Professions and Management in Britain' Conference*, University of Stirling, Scotland, August.

Lijphart, A. (1975), *'The Politics of Accommodation, Pluralism and Democracy in The Netherlands*, 2nd edn, Berkeley: University of California Press.

Lodge, G. C. (1991), *Perestroïka for America*, Boston, Mass.: Harvard Business School Press.

Ohmae, K. (1976), *The Mind of The Strategist: The Art of Japanese Business*, New York: McGraw Hill.

Ouchi, W. A. (1981), *Theory Z: How American Business Can Meet the Japanese Challenge*, Reading, Mass.: Addison-Wesley.

Pascale, R. T. and A. G. Athos (1981), *The Art of Japanese Management*, New York: Warner Books.

Price Waterhouse-Cranfield Project on International Strategic Human Resource Management (1991, 1992), Report, Price Waterhouse and Cranfield School of Management, UK.

Schneider, S. C. and A. de Meyer (1991), 'Interpreting and responding to strategic issues: the impact of national culture', *Strategic Management Journal*, 12, pp. 307–20.

Simonet, J. (1992), *Pratiques du management en Europe, gérer les différences au quotidien*, Paris: Les Editions d'Organisation.

Thurow, L. (1991), *Head to Head*, Cambridge, Mass.: MIT Press.

Todd, E. (1990), *L'Invention de l'Europe*, Paris: Le Seuil.

Chapter 12

Interdependence

Organizations have always needed to work with other organizations, be they suppliers, customers, collaborators, regulatory bodies or the tax authorities. The more significant those relationships for the success of the parties involved, the greater the interdependence, and the more effort the relationships require. The challenges of interdependence – of working together across boundaries – increase with the uncertainty of the task and the environment (an innovative project, a rapidly changing market); and with the extent of the differences (of outlook, of goals, of culture) among the parties involved. Different aspects of these challenges are explored in the following articles.

Chris Huxham points out that the rhetoric of collaboration is at odds with its often unproductive reality. She highlights the tensions and pitfalls inherent in cross-sector and multi-agency collaborations, especially those addressing problems beyond the scope of any particular agency or company. The second article explores the impact of information and communication technologies – until recently, deployed primarily to support the internal functions of organizations – on inter-organizational processes and how they are managed. These technologies can reduce distances and shorten time lags between geographically dispersed sites, so many types of communication processes can now be effective whether a company is located at a single site, or distributed across four continents. They also provide new possibilities for the ways in which organizations interact with each other. At the simplest level, organizations may transmit invoices or orders between each other and process these electronically. At a more ambitious level, information and communication technologies provide new possibilities for inter-organizational communication and collaboration.

Advantage or inertia? Making collaboration work

Chris Huxham

INTRODUCTION – WORKING ACROSS ORGANIZATIONAL BOUNDARIES

Organizations in all sectors are experiencing a need to work with others. In the private sector, this is evidenced in the now common currency of phrases such as *strategic alliance* and *joint venture*. The meaning attributed to these terms varies from one user to another, but most imply some form of inter-firm relationship in order to pursue a strategic purpose. Such purposes vary: marketing agreements, R & D partnerships, equity purchase and supply-chain agreements are examples. Joint ventures are generally taken to be a particular form of arrangement in which a new organization (known as the *child*) is formed and controlled by two or (rarely) more collaborating organizations (known as the *parents*) for some strategic purpose which usually involves the pooling of expertise from the parent organizations.

In the private sector, collaborative arrangements of this type are usually voluntary, though, in some countries, such as Japan, they are government-mandated. Voluntary arrangements are generally driven by economic imperative, mandated ones by nationalism or protectionism. However, it has been argued by many that even where collaboration is formally voluntary, those wishing to compete in the increasingly globalized market place have little choice but to collaborate; to compete in global markets, cross-national strategic alliances (that is, having partners in each major national market) are effectively obligatory (Lamming, 1993). The phrase 'collaborating to compete' is becoming increasingly common (Bleeke and Ernst, 1993).

Collaboration is not unique to the private sector. In recent years government policies across the world have increased the pressure for organizations in the public and community sectors to work with others. In the UK, for example, the introduction of compulsory competitive tendering and the accompanying notion that public authorities should move away from a service delivery role towards an *enabling* role, have led to a need for those contracting out services to develop effective working relationships with the contractor organizations. Local authorities have also frequently been exhorted by government ministers to tackle community development issues through encouraging collaboration with and between community organizations and through setting up *public-private partnerships* (Eisenshitz and Gough, 1993). There have also been frequent calls for *co-ordination* between public organizations in the provision of services. The US has a strong culture of inter-agency co-ordination and collaboration with 'shared power' arrangements being relatively common. Inter-governmental collaborations are also increasingly common, the European Union being a prime example.

Government policy and individual organizational gains are thus prime forces promoting organizational interdependence. At a more detailed level, it has been argued that it is usually a response to one of the following incentives: economic and technical change; declining productivity; global interdependence; blurred organizational boundaries; shrinking government funding; or dissatisfaction with legal procedures (Gray, 1989). There is, however, also a moral imperative for promoting collaboration. This stems from the view that the really big problem issues facing society – homelessness, drug addiction, poverty, crime, economic and social development and so on – fall into the *inter-organizational domain* between organizations. They are inherently unsolvable by any organization acting alone. This means that any attempt to address such issues relies, in part, on the effectiveness with which relevant organizations can work together. The role of 'third party' organizations acting as *strategic bridges* to draw organizations together may be significant here.

Managers in all sectors are therefore, for a variety of reasons, increasingly likely to find themselves in situations which involve working with people from other organizations towards apparently common goals. Unfortunately, there is ample evidence that such relationships are difficult to sustain in a way that is satisfactory to all concerned; examples of failures abound.[1] Nevertheless, the rhetoric surrounding inter-organizational relationships is so positive, emphasizing mutual benefit through co-operation and partnership, that those involved seem often to be taken by surprise when difficulties surface because they have had no warning that they have entered complex territory.

This article therefore explores issues in the management of relationships across organizational boundaries. It derives primarily from research and consultancy carried out with colleagues in public- and community-sector organizations involved in collaboration. The main focuses have been economic development, anti-poverty initiatives and community development. It thus takes its terminology and perspectives from those areas. Nevertheless, it is clear from the literature that the issues to be raised are relevant across a much wider range of organizations. Most of them are also relevant to the early stages of organizational mergers and to work that takes place across departmental boundaries within large organizations.

The main focus of the article is on the inherent complexity of collaborative situations. In the course of discussing these, a number of key concepts – collaborative advantage, collaborative inertia, meta-goals, collaborative capability, accountability and autonomy, and balancing collaborative tensions – are introduced. It will be argued that collaboration is an inherently difficult activity for which there are no easy prescriptive guidelines, but that sensitivity to the areas of difficulty and to the ways in which they can be minimized is essential.

SOME TERMINOLOGY AND KEY CONCEPTS

In order to set the scene for the rest of this article it will be useful to introduce some terminology and key concepts.

In the discussion above, inter-organizational relationships have been referred to in a number of different ways; the terms alliance, co-ordination, collaboration, network, partnership and bridge have all been used. Some authors deliberately try to use these and other terms (co-operation and coalition are two additional common ones) as ways of distinguishing between different forms of inter-organizational relationship. While such distinctions may have value in principle, there seems to be little consensus in the field about how the terms are used either in theory or practice, so they do not provide a consistent and helpful framework. In this article, therefore, the term *collaboration* will be used to refer to all kinds of inter-organizational relationships.

Given that there are a huge range of forms of inter-organizational relationship, there are also a variety of structures through which organizations can work together. It is not the intention of this article to review these differences in detail; for current purposes it is enough to note that most have in some shape or form, a working group involving one or more members of each organization which meets or communicates regularly (if in some cases infrequently) to manage or make decisions for the joint initiative. In this article, groups of this type, whatever their form, will be referred to as *core groups*.

Many benefits are often expected of collaboration. One of the most commonly cited is that collaboration is a way of reducing costs to each partner in the collaboration perhaps by taking advantage of economies of scale for, for example, joint marketing. Collaboration is also seen as a way of strengthening the partners, of reducing risk and of shaping the competition. It is also seen as a basis for drawing upon each other's expertise. This is often the rationale behind joint ventures and is the overt reason for government promotion of public-private partnerships which are intended to encourage public-sector organizations to draw upon what is viewed as the managerial 'good practice' of the private sector. Sharing different expertises is also seen as important by community organizations, as are such other potential benefits as having access to more information, being able to swap ideas, avoiding duplication and making effective use of resources.

Experience suggests, however, that these apparent benefits will not always be easy to achieve. In particular, the common notion that collaboration is a good way of reducing costs and making effective use of resources seems particularly questionable; rather, experience suggests that effective collaboration is highly resource intensive.

Nevertheless, our own perspective on the value that can be aimed for in collaboration sets, in some respects, a much more demanding expectation. Rather than focusing on particular forms of benefit, we simply pose the question, 'how can advantage be gained from collaborating?' This leads to the central concept of *collaborative advantage*.

We define collaborative advantage as being achieved in an inter-organizational relationship when:

> something unusually creative is produced – perhaps an objective is met – that no organization could have produced on its own and when each organization, through the collaboration, is able to achieve its own objectives better than it could alone.

The key point about this definition is that it focuses on outputs of collaboration that could not have been achieved except through collaborating. Not all collaborations need aim for collaborative advantage – for example, the pooling of financial resources by small businesses in the same industry towards a common marketing effort, would not, in itself lead to collaborative advantage as defined above (though pooling of expertise might well do) – but because it defines the maximum value case of collaboration, it is an appropriate focus for discussion.

In practice, many collaborations, far from achieving collaborative advantage, appear to struggle to achieve anything. We use the term *collaborative inertia* to describe the situation when the apparent rate of work output of a core group is slowed down considerably compared to what a casual observer might expect the group to be able to achieve.

It is our experience that those who have participated in collaborations recognize this phenomenon instantly. Certainly, examples of it abound. For example, Wistow and Hardy, describing joint planning arrangements for community care initiatives, argue:

> our own research for the Department of Health similarly produced evidence of limited achievement and slow progress.

> (1991:40)

And, Kanter argues that joint ventures are:

fraught with uncertainty and unexpected road-blocks.

(1994:104)

Those involved in core groups which are experiencing inertia tend to feel a great sense of frustration. Progress seems painfully slow and duty to the collaboration preys on the mind but is never prioritized high enough to generate the energy required to overcome the inertia. This article aims to explore some of the reasons why inertia is so prevalent in collaborations and some ways of thinking about collaboration which may help avoid the worst consequences of it.

WHY INERTIA? – THE COMPLEXITIES OF WORKING TOGETHER

The mechanisms contributing to a core group's arrival in a state of collaborative inertia are undoubtedly complex and subtle.[2] This section focuses on some of the main factors which practical experience of collaboration suggests contribute to the inherent slowness which is at the heart of collaborative inertia.

Multiple goals

By definition, the organizations involved in collaborative initiatives will have different aims. It is these differences which provide the basis for getting advantage from the collaboration. But these differing aims also mean that their reasons for being involved in a collaboration will differ. To succeed therefore, joint actions will have to satisfy a variety of different agendas.

The range of goals present in collaborative situations is complex; much more so than is immediately obvious. Firstly there are the *meta-goals*. These are the *goals for the collaboration* – a statement of what it is aiming to achieve. These are the apparent reason why the collaboration exists. On the face of it, meta-goals need to be stated explicitly and in detail and many authors argue that clarification of purpose is essential to progress. In practice, however, explicit definition of meta-goals can produce difficulties in itself; the more tightly meta-goals are defined, the more difficult it will be to get the participating organizations, with their different aims, to agree to them. As one partnership manager put it: 'we have to write a statement of aims to justify our existence; my job is to find a way of writing it so generally that none of the parties involved can disagree with it'.

But it is not only meta-goals that cause difficulty in collaborations. Of particular additional significance are the goals that each of the participating organizations is likely to want to achieve through the collaboration, but which are not related to the overt purpose of the collaboration. For example, an organization might wish to use the collaboration to raise its own profile in the market place or with a funding body. Similarly, individual members of the core group may have goals which can be achieved through the collaboration. These tend usually to relate to career aspirations or job security. For example, individuals may wish to gain particular forms of experience to add to their CV through participating in a collaboration, or, in the case of a voluntary organization, may see the collaborative initiative as increasing the chances of renewed funding for their own post.

Goals of this sort often form part of hidden agendas which are not brought into the public arena (Hardy, Turrell and Wistow 1992). As such, they can cause confusion and tension. However, it is these organization- and individual-specific goals – rather than just the meta-goals – that provide much of the incentive for organizations to participate in the collaboration, so it essential for core group members to be aware of their existence, even if they have not been discussed publicly.

According to our definition, achieving collaborative advantage requires that attention is paid to both meta-goals and organization-specific goals. The dilemma that core group members need to face is how much to try to bring all of these goals into the open. Core group members often express frustration about the difficulty of getting a sense of direction and often blame this for their inertia. Certainly, even if there were no hidden agendas, it is likely that, in the absence of open discussion there will be a wide variety of different assumptions about the goals of the collaboration. Confusion and counterproductive actions are likely to ensue. On the other hand, opening up discussion may itself cause inertia; even if the parties do reach agreement, this can require seemingly endless discussion and negotiation.

Culture, procedures and language

As well as differing aims, the parties will also bring to the collaboration different working cultures, ideologies and procedures. They will therefore tend to tackle tasks in different ways. Seemingly trivial or routine matters, such as what pay level or conditions of service are appropriate for a member of staff appointed to serve the collaboration, can often take a great deal of time to sort out to the satisfaction of all concerned.

As well as the practical difficulties of satisfying the norms of more than one organization, cultural and ideological differences can cause major communication problems through encouraging different interpretations of 'facts'. This problem will be exacerbated by language difficulties.

In cross-national collaborations, there is the obvious problem that participants will frequently have different first languages and even if they are relatively fluent in each other's languages, there is always the danger that the subtlety of expression and understanding essential to being sensitive to, for example, cues from others about goals and culture, will be lost. More significant (because it is generic to all collaboration and because it is less obvious) is the observation that because participants are likely to come from different professions, they are likely to use different professional language (or jargon) to frame the same situations.

To take an example, the police, social workers and educationalists – who are frequently exhorted to co-ordinate – have quite different professional languages. They also have very different aims, culture and procedures. Collaborations across different industrial sectors are likely to meet similar barriers; indeed such problems are often at the core of difficulties encountered in implementing industrial mergers. Collaborations which cross the public-private-voluntary divides can be particularly problematic. The way in which parties interpret each other's interventions will clearly be affected by all of these factors. It is not surprising therefore, if they end, at best in lengthy processes of clarification and at worst in confusion and stagnation.

Collaborative capability

Goals, language, culture and procedures will all affect an organization's ability to act as an effective collaborator with any particular other organization. Many other organizational attributes, such as those listed in Figure 12.1, may also affect the way in which an organization is likely to behave in collaborative settings. These form a part of its collaborative capability relative to another organization. For example, an organization which has its sphere of activities mandated by an external body such as an elected government – that is, which has a low degree of organizational autonomy – may have difficulty in contributing the elements of flexibility and compromise often required in collaborative settings. Managers in politically dominated local authorities may thus be unnatural collaborators for those in quangos whose links to politicians are more remote.

The point is not that a high rating on these kinds of dimensions necessarily leads to a high degree of collaborative capability *per se*, but that *at any particular time*, there are likely to be *differences* between potential collaborators over the collectivity of these dimensions. These differences are likely to affect the way in which each of the organizations reacts to the collaboration, and the ease with which particular organizations can work together.

Power and authority

There will usually also be perceived power differences between the organizations (Gray 1989). Small voluntary organizations, for example, often feel vulnerable when collaborating with statutory or large, national voluntary

```
• degree of organizational autonomy

• degree of individual autonomy

• cohesiveness of organizational structure

• development of strategic processes

• degree of elaboration of own strategy statement

• degree to which collaboration is an issue

• level of adult behaviour

• degree to which the organization has a trusting attitude
```

Figure 12.1 Example dimensions of collaborative capability
Source: Huxham (1993)

organizations which bring major resources to the collaboration. On the other hand, the larger organization may feel vulnerable if involvement of a small but entirely independent, organization is essential to achievement of its aims. This is true, for example, if they are committed to spending money in ways which involve particular organizations and need to be seen to do so. Similarly, the kind of collaborations between large multinationals and small businesses that take place, for example, when the large company develops and markets a novel technological breakthrough of the small business, are also uneasy alliances. In these situations, perceptions of where the balance of power lies may be more important than 'reality' in determining the willingness and speed with which partners may commit to action. Any perceived dependency of one organization upon another (such as between a contractor and contractee) is also likely to foster resentment.

Problems with power differences can extend beyond the organizational level to the individual members of the core group. Collaborations work best if core group members perceive themselves as being of approximately the same status (Hardy, Turrell and Wistow 1992) but this can be difficult to achieve if the organizations involved are of varied sizes or if they have aims which make the collaboration much more important to one party than another. In practice, core groups often end up involving middle

managers from large organizations and senior managers from smaller ones.
Even if senior managers from large organizations get involved at the start,
the pressure to delegate management of the collaboration to an operational
manager is large. This means that there may be imbalances in the degree
of autonomy to act that different core group members have, especially if
the larger organization is highly bureaucratic.

Interestingly, despite the genuine problems caused by power imbalances,
there is also a sense in which the parties involved are too equal. Though
some members may be seen as more senior than others in the context of
their own collaboration, there are no formal authority hierarchies within
a collaboration. This means that no one can *require* anyone else to act in
particular ways. Commitment to act thus has to be achieved entirely
through persuasion and negotiation; a time consuming business even if
eventually successful.

The tension between autonomy and accountability

Both of the previous sections have cited *autonomy* to act as a factor which
will affect the speed with which collaborative actions can take place. This
concept, together with its counter-side *accountability* appears to be central
to the creation of collaborative inertia.

Friend (1990) has argued that the need for an individual in the core
group to be accountable to their own organization often materially affects
their willingness to take particular actions in the context of the collaboration. There is frequently a process of checking back before committing
to a decision of the collaboration. By contrast, it has also been argued that
being part of a collaboration means that each organization loses the freedom to act autonomously with respect to the subject of the collaboration
(Batsleer and Randall, 1991); unless the ground rules are very clearly
understood, they may need to check back with other parties in the collaboration before they feel able to take actions.

These concepts can be seen as opposite sides of the same coin. The
individuals in the core group are accountable *both* to their organization
and to the collaboration (that is, to the other organizations). This creates
a lack of autonomy both for the individual organizations and for the
collaboration.

Clearly this creates a dilemma. If members of the core group, or other
members of their organization, do not pay serious attention to the demands
of accountability, the collaboration is likely to hit problems. Sooner or
later, someone or some organization in the collaboration will be offended
either by the actions of another organization or by what the core group
has committed it to. On the other hand, paying serious attention to
accountability, unless all involved are very clear about what the other
organizations will happily tolerate, can be almost as debilitating because it

implies a need for a continual process of checking in both directions. A likely scenario might be that someone in one organization suggests to their core group member an action relating to the collaboration's interests. This member will then check out the suggestion with other core group members who in turn will have to check with people in their organizations after which the outcome is passed back through the system. Typically, there will be difficulties in diarizing meetings, or reaching each other by telephone, at each stage in the process, particularly if – as is often the case, given the different aims of the organizations involved – the action suggested by the first person is not a high priority for other organizations. Merely getting through this checking process once can create a major time lapse. The problem will be multiplied even if there is just one negative response in the system as this would require the whole cycle to be reiterated.

Thus trying to initiate even small actions, which could be completed competently and quickly within one organization acting autonomously, or by the core group acting autonomously, can be a very frustrating experience in the context of collaboration. Unless the action is a high priority for at least someone in this system, it is likely to be put off and put off. Even if there is no actual checking as described above, a sense of what their organization or the collaboration would tolerate is likely to affect what actions core group members are willing to endorse.

One way in which people commonly try to overcome the frustrations caused by the cumbersome communication process is to bypass the core group. Members of one organization thus communicate directly with members of another. For example, in groups with which we have been involved, we have witnessed communication *upwards* from a core group member from one organization directly to the boss of another core group member who can sanction actions, *sideways* to a colleague of the core group member who can provide particular skills or other resources, and *downwards* to support staff who can take action on behalf of the core group member.

If communication is good and there is an appropriate degree of trust these direct communications can be an effective means of moving forward. On the other hand, they also provide ample scope for other problems. For example, if core group members are not informed about agreements taken outside the group, they may act inappropriately.

Alternatively, if non-core group members get involved without being fully briefed about either the aims of the collaboration or the politics of their own organization's relationship to the collaboration, they may also take inappropriate actions. Once again, autonomy taken by those interacting may be at the expense of accountability to others involved. Thus, even with the best will in the world, interactions which are aimed at getting the collaboration moving may result in damage to other relationships in the collaboration. The question of whether or not it is worth risking the damage for the sake of moving forward perhaps requires more considered judgement than it is customarily given.

Time – managing the logistics

A key thread in all this discussion has been that even if it is possible to come to terms with the difficulties inherent in collaborative situations, it will take considerable time to build mutual understanding and negotiate ways forward. In addition, the sheer logistics of collaboration tend to make it consuming of both lapsed and actual time (as well as of other resources). Core group members are likely to be based in locations which are physically remote from one another. It is not generally possible for them to meet in the corridor or arrange spontaneous meetings to deal with matters as they arise. Everything has to be planned and co-ordinated. This takes organizing time and often travel time, too. Modern technology such as electronic mail may reduce these problems but is unlikely to eliminate them.

Getting things moving – balancing tensions

The last section aimed to demonstrate some of the reasons why inertia is so common. These are summarized in Figure 12.2. It has been argued that they are inherent difficulties which will have a negative effect and which *will be present* in all collaborative situations to some degree.

In some respects, a great deal is also known about the influences which,

- multiple, often hidden goals

- differences in professional language, culture and procedures

- incompatible collaborative capability

- perceived power imbalances but no authority hierarchy

- the tension between autonomy and accountability

- time involved in managing logistics

Figure 12.2 Inherent mechanisms inducing collaborative inertia

if present, can have a positive effect on collaboration. For example, Figure 12.3 shows a list of 'success factors' compiled from a review of the conclusions of other authors. Many of these factors are cited by authors time and time again[3] so there is little doubt that they play a significant role. The difficulty for core group members is to know how to make use of these success factors. In the first place they are mostly not things that can be created instantly or, in some cases – such as having a history of collaboration or a favourable political climate – at all. Even those factors which could be addressed are rarely as simple as the list in Figure 12.3 might imply. In practice there are *tensions*, pulls and pressures to move in opposing directions.

Some such tensions have already been identified above. The dilemma about how much to bring goals out into the open is one; the tension is between the forces which suggest it is a good idea to do so and those that mitigate against it. The balance between being autonomous and being accountable is another.

An inspection of Figure 12.3 suggests that similar tensions exist for all the so-called success factors. By way of example, consider the top two factors on the list. The first of these, 'mutual respect, understanding and trust' is almost a piece of 'motherhood'; clearly respect and trust will be important. However, respect and trust can only be created as inter-organizational and inter-personal relationships develop. There is a cyclic relationship between the development of trust and taking joint action; it takes successful joint action to develop trust, but trust is required before parties will commit to joint action. Obviously, to get started in this cycle, the parties need to take a risk over their mutual trust (Ring and Venn, 1992). One tension is therefore about when and how to take this risk.

The second factor on the list in Figure 12.3, having an appropriate cross-section of members, involves a tension between the benefits of having more partners involved (fewer parties to sabotage the initiative) and the managerial benefits of having a smaller group to co-ordinate and of being able to choose partners more likely to have compatible collaborative capability.

It would be possible to make similar arguments for most of the 'success factors' cited in Figure 12.3. So learning to manage collaborative activity cannot rely on following a list of generic prescriptions. Rather, it is about being alert to the inherent difficulties and dilemmas. To take the tension surrounding goals as an example, contrary to conventional wisdom, being precisely clear about each of the goals is unlikely to be helpful. Rather, being sensitive to the possibilities is what matters. To get moving, 'enough' of a statement of meta-goals is needed, accepting that more specific goals will need to be discovered and elaborated as the collaboration evolves. Attempts to define this prematurely can be an obstacle to progress. Similarly, expecting – and respecting – that other participants will have their

- mutual respect, understanding and trust

- appropriate cross-section of members

- open and frequent communication

- sufficient funds

- skilled convenor

- members see collaboration as in their self interest

- history of collaboration or co-operation in the community

- members share a stake in both process and outcome

- multiple layers of decision making

- established informal and formal communication links

- concrete, attainable goals and objectives

- shared vision

- flexibility

- development of clear roles and policy guideline

- collaborative group seen as leader in the community

- political/social climate favourable

- ability to compromise

- adaptability

- unique purpose

Figure 12.3 Mattessich and Monsey's factors affecting the success of collaboration
Source: Mattessich and Monsey (1992)

own goals to pursue through the collaboration may be enough to avoid the worst confusions; it is not essential to know precisely what these goals are. Clearly there are no easy solutions to effective collaborative practice, but anticipating the important areas of tension (such as those identified in Figure 12.3) will help.

CONCLUSIONS – ON BEING SENSITIVE

The obvious conclusion from all of the above discussion is that in collaborative ventures more time, energy, patience, adaptability and compromise needs to be budgeted for than in individual ones. *Sensitivity* would appear to be essential to achieving collaborative advantage. This conclusion has been put eloquently by many other authors:

> Treat jointly managed schemes as fragile plants which need careful nurturing until they have taken organisational root.
>
> (Wistow and Hardy 1991:43)

> In situations involving a complex common end and/or a diversity of parties, much more self-reflective interaction will be required to develop common understandings.
>
> (Roberts and Bradley 1991:222)

> It would be misleading to imply that successful task-oriented networks do not require considerable nurturing and maintenance to survive and prosper.
>
> (Carley and Christie 1992:200)

> The ignorance that is ... exposed (when agencies are jointly exploring new ground) can only be reduced if they acknowledge it and strive for a greater clarity of purpose and procedure.
>
> (Nocon 1989:46)

> The effective management of relationships to build collaborative advantage requires managers to be sensitive to political, cultural, organisational and human issues.
>
> (Kanter 1994:108)

> Joint activities require the most competent staff and the closest attention to preparation in detail.
>
> (Webb 1991:239)

Many would agree with Webb that managerial competence and having 'robust and coherent management arrangements' are crucial to successful collaboration. Incompetence is a key factor in the collaboration – most

- an inherently easy task

- luck – things happen to go right easily

- competent individuals on the core group

- well matched individuals on the core group

- the 'level' of collaboration is near the individual end of the spectrum

- individuals on the core group are able to act autonomously on behalf

  of their own organizations; usually this means either that they are

  senior relative to the task involved, or that they are from an

  organization where responsibility is devolved and delegated

- members of the collaboration are driven by a commitment – perhaps

  to customers or other colleagues – to deliver a specific product

- a relationship exists between members of the core group beyond that

  of the group itself; this means the individuals will have obligations to

  each other in other contexts and thus need to contribute positively

  to the collaboration in order to maintain these

- an external event, such as an offer of finance, focuses attention

- the core group gets external assistance, such as a facilitator, to assist

  them to make progress towards their goals

Figure 12.4 Example factors which may prevail over collaborative inertia
Source: Huxham and Vangen (1994)

particularly in the convenor or in senior staff – can be particularly debilitating.

Collaborative inertia will not affect equally all collaborative situations.
Figure 12.4 suggests a number of mitigating circumstances which are likely
to reduce the chances of it occurring. However, in situations in which

these do not pertain, it is sensible to question whether the collaboration is worthwhile. Under these circumstances collaboration is sensible only if real collaborative advantage can be envisaged. That is, if the benefits cannot be gained in other ways. This can be an important judgement because such benefits may not necessarily related to the overt purpose of the collaboration.

ACKNOWLEDGEMENTS

The author is grateful to the many colleagues and members of the organizations with which she has worked. Especial thanks are due to Siv Vangen and Colin Eden for providing so much collaborative experience and debate.

This article is partly informed by research funded by the Economic and Social Research Council, Grant number 000234450.

NOTES

1 Chisholm (1989), Webb (1991), Himmelman (1992) and Newman (1992), for example, all emphasize the prevalence of failed collaborations.
2 Many authors have contributed to building a picture of the factors which have a negative effect on collaboration; see, for example, Gray (1989), Hardy, Turrell and Wistow (1992), Kanter (1994) and Sink (1995).
3 The importance of developing trust between participants is a prime example of a 'success factor' (Calton, 1994; Gray, 1989; Hardy, Turrell and Wistow, 1992; Koenig and Wijk, 1994; Ring and Venn, 1992; Webb, 1992).

REFERENCES

Batsleer, J. and Randall, S. (1991) 'Creating common cause: issues in the management of interagency relationships for voluntary organisations'. In Batsleer J., Cornforth C. and Paton R. (Eds) Issues in Voluntary and Non-Profit Management. Addison Wesley, Wokingham, 192–210.
Bleeke, J. and Ernst, D. (1993) Collaborating to Compete: Using Strategic Alliances and Acquisitions in the Global Marketplace. Wiley, Chichester.
Calton, J. (1994) 'Trust and Trust-building processes in networks'. Presented at the annual conference of the International Association for Business and Society at Hilton Head, SC.
Carley, M. and Christie, I. (1992) Managing Sustainable Development. Earthscan, London.
Chisholm, D. (1989) Coordination Without Hierarchy: Informal Structures in multiorganizational Systems. University of California Press, Berkeley.
Eisenshitz, A. and Gough, J. (1993) 'The Politics of Local Economic Policy; the Problems and Possibilities of Local Initiative'. Macmillan, London.
Friend, J. (1990) 'Handling organisational complexity in group decision support'. In Eden, C. and Radford, J. (Eds) Tackling Strategic Problems: The Role of Group Decision Support. Sage, London, 18–28.
Gray, B. (1989) Collaborating: Finding common ground for multiparty problems. San Francisco: Jossey-Bass.

Hardy, B., Turrell, A. and Wistow, G. (1992) *Innovations in Community Care Management*. Avebury, Aldershot.

Himmelman, A. (1992) 'Communities working collaboratively for a change'. The Himmelman Consulting Group, Minneapolis.

Huxham, C. (1993) 'Collaborative capability: An intra-organisational perspective on collaborative advantage'. *Public Money and Management*, 12, July-Sept, 21–8.

Huxham, C. and Vangen, S. (1994) 'Naivety and maturity, inertia and fatigue: are working relationships between public organisations doomed to fail?' Presented at the Employment Research Unit Conference, 'The Contract State: the Future of Public Management', University of Wales at Cardiff, September.

Kanter, R. Moss (1994) 'Collaborative advantage'. *Harvard Business Review*, July-August, 96–108.

Koenig, C. and Wijk, G. van (1993) 'Interorganizational Collaboration: Beyond Contracts'. In Pasquero J. and Collins D. (eds) International Association for Business and Society, proceedings, 96–102.

Lamming, R. (1993) *Beyond Partnership: Strategies for Innovation and Lean Supply*. Prentice Hall, London.

Mattessich, P. and Monsey, B. (1992) *Collaboration: What makes it work*. Amherst H. Wilder Foundation, St Paul, Minnesota.

Newman, W. (1992) 'Launching a viable joint venture'. *California Management Review*, 35, 73–80.

Nocon, A. (1989) 'Forms of ignorance and their role in the joint planning process'. *Social Policy and Administration*, 23, 31–47.

Ring, P. Smith and Venn, A. van de. (1992) 'Structuring co-operative relationships between organisations'. *Strategic Management Journal*, 13, 483–498.

Roberts, N. and Bradley R. (1991). 'Stakeholder Collaboration and Innovation'. *Journal of Applied Behavioural Science*, 27, 209–27.

Sink, D. (1995) 'Five Obstacles to Collaboration and Some Thoughts on Overcoming Them'. In Huxham, C. (Ed.) *Creating Collaborative Advantage*. Sage, London.

Webb, A. (1991) 'Co-ordination: A problem in public sector management'. *Policy and Politics*, 19, 229–241.

Wistow, G. and Hardy, B. (1991) 'Joint management in community care'. *Journal of Management in Medicine*, 5, 40–8.

The networked organization and the management of interdependence

John F. Rockart and James E. Short

[...]

This chapter is about one form of organizational innovation, the networked firm, and the role of IT in making the many networks operating within the firm more effective. A major premise is that IT-enabled networks permit us to more effectively manage organizational interdependence, or the firm's ability to achieve concurrence of effort along multiple dimensions of the organization.

The emergence of networks as an innovative, organizational design seems largely based on two related concepts. First, from a *design stand-point*, networked firms are usually conceived of as communication-rich environments, with information flows blurring traditional intracompany boundaries. Networks are also seen to foster and utilize important role changes in individual managers. Networks increase role complexity and require greater skill on the part of both workers and management.[1] In short, the organization is seen as information-rich, and by connecting information, people, and skill (talent) together more effectively within the firm, the firm in aggregate is more effective. Although important, these benefits [...] are not new. Galbraith, Lawrence and Lorsch, Bahrami and Evans, Child, and others have detailed the importance of enabling and enriching internal communications and information processing capability within the firm to increase performance. What is new about networks, however, is the tight meshing of the design of networks with the information technology required to enable them. In short, IT is seen as a design factor in organizational change and innovation, and not just as an enabler of more effective, organizational functioning once a given design has been put into place.[2]

Second, from a *performance standpoint*, networked organizations are seen to allow firms to retain small company responsiveness while becoming larger and more complex. All other things being equal, management practice tells us that size determines complexity. The more complex the organization, the more it has to be organized along the principle of size.[3] We have tended to build large and complex organizations to produce multiple, integrated products and services. Then, using the same organizational form, we have tried to streamline and simplify the firm's key processes to enable flexibility and responsiveness to local market needs. In short, we have typically decentralized large firms to ensure responsiveness. Conversely, very rarely have we successfully built large, complex, and flexible organizational forms. The attractiveness of the networked firm as such is that by adding IT as a design factor, we may be able to design firms that can simultaneously increase size, complexity, and responsiveness.[4]

DEFINITION AND ATTRIBUTES OF THE NETWORKED FIRM

Network concepts have been used primarily to study either inter- or intraorganizational activities.[5] In a world increasingly populated by strategic alliances, partnerships, and other forms of horizontal communications both within and between firms, however, this inter- and intraorganizational distinction is itself increasingly artificial. [. . .]

We have chosen, therefore, to think of networks more as interrelationships within or between firms to accomplish work than as 'formal' organizational designs per se. In short, we think of networks as one part of the firm's overall system of interrelationships to accomplish work. Note that this definition does not assert that networks are the *only* way in which work is done within or between firms, nor does it state how many networks operate to accomplish any specific work task. Networks may be the most effective way to design and accomplish many kinds of work, but this does not say that all work, or even most work, is done in networks.

For work that can be usefuly networked, then, what are the key attributes of the more networked approach? We see seven:

1 *Shared goals.* Networks typically organize around shared goals or objectives. (Note, however, that this does not mean people uniformly agree on how to achieve these goals.)
2 *Shared expertise.* Networks allow for the sharing of expertise and knowledge across the firm.
3 *Shared work.* Networks allow for the sharing of work across groups not normally part of the local structure.
4 *Shared decision making.* Networks allow for shared decision making, mainly through enhanced access to critical information across the firm. As a result, more expertise is brought to bear on specific decisions. Note, however, that although better-quality decisions may result, they may not be faster decisions.
5 *Shared timing and issue prioritization.* Networks allow for, and depend on, shared prioritization and time horizons for critical issues and action steps.
6 *Shared responsibility, accountability and trust.* Networks depend on the sharing of responsibility, accountability, and trust in the organization.

Trust is a critical and difficult issue. We have depended largely on face-to-face interaction to develop and solidify trust among people in most of our firms. A more IT-enabled, networked approach will eventually replace, or significantly reduce, many forms of face-to-face interaction with a technology interface (electronic mail, videoconferencing, design station to design station electronic connection, etc.). This raises serious questions about how trust will be established and developed in this kind of environment, or, conversely, the use of networks cannot be truly effective until a certain level of trust is established in the organization.[6]

7 *Shared recognition and reward.* Implicit in the effective functioning of networks is shared recognition and shared rewards for cooperative work.

A final point is that although networks depend on and enhance the sharing of work, expertise, responsibility, decision making, and so forth within the firm, a major effect of networks in many cases is to enhance internal conflict. Eccles and Crane state that 'network structures of investment banks are flexible, flat, complex, and rife with conflict'.[7] Their point about conflict echoes Lawrence and Lorsch's observation that 'recurring conflict is inevitable' in differentiated organizations. [. . .][8]

WHY NETWORKED FIRMS NOW?

[. . .] [W]e need to introduce one additional concept and a simplified framework of key points before we stop to outline our chapter. This concept will help us to address the question, Why the move to networked firms now?

We can summarize the concept as follows. In a firm's efforts to change strategic market positioning, set strategy, of increase performance, the need to manage effectively the interdependence of subunits and people within the firm is increasingly recognized. By effective management of interdependence, we mean the firm's ability to achieve concurrence of effort along multiple dimensions of the organization.[9] Our research in sixteen firms suggests that the need to manage interdependence is growing significantly. Moreover, it is a major managerial thrust today as executives cope with the demands of both managing complexity and increasing responsiveness across the organization. [. . .]

The firm's ability to continuously improve the effectiveness of managing interdependence is the critical element in product, service, or strategy innovations in the marketplace (the proactive dimension to strategy) and in effectively responding to new competitive threats (the reactive dimension). Networks, designed and enabled by information technology, are key to effectively managing this interdependence.

Figure 12.5 illustrates our points in simplified form. [. . .] The essence of the framework is outlined in five boxes, from left to right. As firms position themselves in the competitive environment, there is a need to

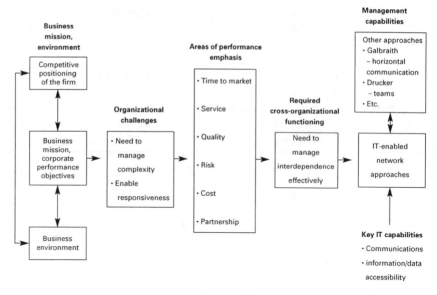

Figure 12.5 The move to networked organizations

manage the size and complexity of the organization while ensuring responsiveness and flexibility. Firms typically select areas of performance emphasis to manage this balance at the customer interface, in areas such as quality service, risk management, and cost or product quality. In order to improve performance in these emphasis areas, firms must more effectively manage interdependence across the organization. Although there are several ways to do this (examples are Galbraith's liaison roles or Drucker's team concepts, both discussed later), the key to effectively managing this interdependence is IT-enabled networks. Critical IT capabilities include advanced communications and data accessibility and the steadily improving cost-performance of the technologies themselves, leaving the machines, software, and communications more broadly available than ever before. [. . .]

THE MOVE TO NETWORKED ORGANIZATIONS

Drivers: A dynamic, global, technology-enabled, increasingly competitive business environment

The need to effectively coordinate the activities of individual organizational subunits is vastly greater [now than] it was even a few years ago. Competitive pressures are now forcing all major firms to become global in scope, to decrease time to market, and to redouble their efforts to manage risk, service, quality, and cost on a truly international scale. The dynamic, global, increasingly competitive business environment is driven by critical forces:

- *New and powerful strategies and competitors who have changed the rules of global competition.* Hamel and Prahalad argue that a small group of highly innovative firms, many of them in the Far East, have defined a whole new approach to competitive strategy and altered the rules of global competition.[10] The major impact of this has been to remove the many traditional buffers enjoyed by firms in inventory, people, space, time, quality, and lack of consumer knowledge. Removing these buffers has two direct effects. First, it reemphasizes the need to share information and to work cooperatively across the organization. Second, it prompts managers to focus on horizontal work groups, such as teams, to facilitate the required cooperation and information sharing. Both emphasize the need for increased integration of effort within the firm.
- *Information technology.* The rapid diffusion of key information technologies into the business environment has created new business markets and dramatically affected the cost structures of traditional ones. Familiar examples include airline reservation systems, cash management accounts, automated teller machines, and automated order entry systems. Technology provides firms with the technical capability to more tightly couple the firm's key internal business processes and to coordinate externally with major suppliers, customers, and other firms (alliances and so on) in new and different ways. [...]

The combined effects of new competitors and new information technologies has produced a new, dynamic, global, technology-enabled, increasingly competitive business environment (see Figure 12.6). The growing demands of this environment have dramatically affected the firm's competitive positioning and the need to increase performance against growth, profitability, quality, marketplace, and customer goals.

The need to increase organizational performance

As firms set new strategy objectives, experiment with new organizational forms, or work to improve internal performance in response to the increasingly global business environment, competitive pressures challenge firms not only to increase performance in conventional terms (marketshare, ROI, customer satisfaction, quality measures, etc.) but to reexamine how they measure performance in the first place. The network firm will require new, and perhaps unconventional, measures of firm performance. For example, individual performance measures that track span of authority and control for compensation and promotion purposes (dollar volume of business managed, number of employees) have little to do with the more diffuse,

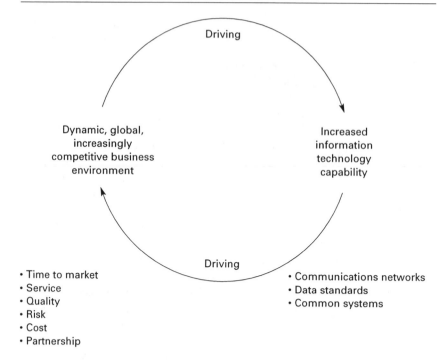

Figure 12.6 What is pushing the move to networked organizations?

cooperative, and shared work and authority environment necessary for effective networks. [. . .]

Additional significant emphasis is being placed on the following areas:

Time to market

Today's marketplace demands more rapid new-product introductions and more effective management of existing product lines. 'Time to market' refers to the firm's ability to design, produce, and bring to market new products quickly, or to better manage existing product lines. Black & Decker, for example, now brings new products to market in half the time it took before 1985. Xerox has made similar product design and manufacturing improvements in its copier division. And Ford shortened its usual product development cycle more than a year in the introduction of its Taurus/Sable vehicle line. In each case, compressing time to market required increased integration of effort among departments such as design, engineering, manufacturing, purchasing, distribution, and service.[11]

Service

Effective service to the customer requires an effective service orientation throughout the business.[12] Service, of course, is based not only on the effectiveness of a single person or team in charge of a customer account but also on organizationwide knowledge of the customer's status, current problems, and anticipated problems. The need to improve service is therefore a driver for management's increased attention to integration across many tiers of the organization.

Quality

Quality has come to mean both product and process quality. *Product quality* refers to the accuracy of the end product design and manufacturing processes (for example, the number of defects or failures in a specific part or final assembly). *Process quality*, defined in terms of customer outcomes, refers to the degree of conformance to customer needs. In short, assessing process quality is assessing how well the ultimate product or service delivered to the customer meets the customer's needs, measured in the customer's terms.[13]

Risk

Market volatility, business complexity, and competitive pressures can easily overcome a firm's ability to accurately track and manage its business risk. Merrill Lynch, for example, lost more than $250 million in less than a week when the firm failed to adequately oversee an employee trading a complex form of mortgage-backed securities.[14] [. . .]

In addition to growing business risks, the rapid development of key technologies and their effects on markets and companies carries with it growing technology risks. There are three dimensions to technology risk:

1 the risk of not keeping pace with current technologies;
2 the risk, conversely, of investing in new, unproven, or inadequately understood technologies where the payoff may never come; and
3 the risk of not understanding how the rules of competition change in electronic markets.[15]

Cost

Cost management and cost reduction are concerns for all organizations. In response to the drivers noted earlier, manufacturing firms, for example, have moved increasing amounts of manufacturing offshore in search of lower labor costs. Other firms have worked to rationalize product lines to capture global scale economies. Still others have mimicked Japanese practices, including instituting quality circles and just-in-time production techniques.

Another trend has been to consolidate shared activities across subunits within the company into one (or a very few) centralized operations to reduce costs and improve service quality. For example, several functions in auditing, cost accounting, some research activities, and some transaction processing of routine business tasks have all been candidates for consolidation into shared services organizations in firms such as Citicorp, General Electric, American Express, Dupont, Baxter Healthcare, Sun Company, and IBM. Of course, consolidating people and work to leverage expertise and to achieve economies of scale across the firm is nothing new. What is new in these cases is the role of IT in redefining what functions are consolidated and how these functions are then performed in the new services organization.

Partnership

A final area of performance emphasis is in the firm's external links with supplier, customers, and other firms. Firm-to-firm linkages through electronic data interchange (EDI), value-added networks, partnership programs, and strategic alliances have grown markedly in recent years. In the automotive industry, for example, 'arms-length' supplier relationships common just a few years ago now operate more as 'strategic partnerships', where one company may contract out part of its own value-added chain to the other. Ryder Truck, for example, now handles key pieces of Ford Motor Company's inbound and outbound logistics for vehicle assembly and distribution.

A second example is McKesson Corporation, well known to IS professionals for its successful leveraging of IT to improve customer service and cut order entry costs. As pointed out by Johnston and Lawrence, however, McKesson also transformed itself into the hub of a large value-adding partnership, successfully defending itself against its primary competition, the large vertically integrated drugstore chains.[16]

The point of the Ryder-Ford and McKesson examples, however, is that each firm's individual financial performance is increasingly tied to that of its major trading partners. For these companies, therefore, there is increasing need to develop effective internal and external procedures to define, track, and manage joint performance across these partnerships and/or strategic alliances. [...]

The need to effectively manage interdependence

As firms work to improve performance in these areas of emphasis, the need to improve work coordination and cooperation and to share information, decision making, and responsibility across many tiers of the organization is increasingly recognized. We have earlier identified this need for increased concurrence of effort along multiple dimensions of the organization as effectively managing interdependence. We asserted that the firm's ability to continuously improve the management of interdependence is the critical element in responding to new and pressing competitive forces. Unlike in previous eras, managerial strategies based on optimizing operations within functional departments, product lines, or geographical organizations simply will not be adequate in the future.

Managers, of course, oversee innumerable large and small interdependencies every day. What happens in one function or product line affects others. Specialists in one area of the company must communicate effectively with specialists in other areas of the firm: [. . .]

> Production engineers rely on product designers to design parts that can be easily and quickly fabricated. Conversely, designers depend on product engineers to implement design concepts faithfully.
> Sales representatives for a nationwide or worldwide company are also interdependent. The same large customer may be served by many sales offices throughout the world. Common discounts, contract terms, and service procedures must be maintained. Feedback can be important.

> Companies themselves rely on other companies to supply parts and services. When Toshiba faced the possibility of major economic sanctions for its sale of defense-related technologies to the Soviet Union, several U.S. computer manufacturers, including DEC and IBM, filed briefs in support of Toshiba's case. These U.S. firms feared that sanctions against Toshiba would harm them as well, given the high degree of interdependence in the industry.

In short, interdependence is a fact of organizational life. What is different today, however, is the increasing need to manage interdependence, driven by the competitive environment, and IT's role in enabling a more networked organizational approach to help meet this need.

Managing interdependence in the networked firm

How do companies today manage interdependence? Several approaches have been proposed, each with the goal of producing the concurrence of effort necessary to allow the organization to compete effectively in the marketplace. Mintzberg, for example, argues that firms coordinate work through five basic mechanisms: mutual adjustment, direct supervision, standardization of work process, standardization of work output, and standardization of worker skills.[17] Lawrence and Lorsch found that successful companies differentiated themselves into suborganizations to allow accumulation of expertise and simpler management processes driven by shared goals and objectives. Conversely, these same successful firms adopted integrating mechanisms to coordinate work activity across suborganizations. Lawrence and Lorsch postulated five mechanisms to manage the needed integration: integrative departments, whose primary activity was to coordinate effort among functional departments; permanent and/or temporary cross-functional teams; reliance on direct management contact at all levels of the firm; integration through the formal hierarchy; and integration via a 'paper-based system' of information exchange.[18]

Galbraith later expanded the intellectual understanding of managing integration through people-oriented mechanisms.[19] He noted that direct contact, liaison roles, task forces, and teams were used primarily for lateral relations, permitting companies to make more decisions and process more information without overloading hierarchical communication channels. He also introduced the concept of computer-based information systems as a vertical integrator within the firm.

The IT-enabled network has now been added to this list of approaches. Several leading-edge firms are working to redesign basic business processes through a more IT-enabled networked organizational approach with the goal of dramatically improving performance in the six emphasis areas noted earlier (market, service, quality, risk, cost, and partnership).
[...]

IT's ROLE IN ENABLING THE NETWORKED ORGANIZATION

We turn now to reviewing several of the academic literatures that discuss the impact of IT on the organization. We review how our concept of managing interdependence through IT-enabled networks expands and refocuses this earlier work, and then turn to our examples from the field. We identify five organizational contexts where IT-enabled networks have strikingly improved a company's ability to effectively manage its functional, product, or geographic subunits: in integrating across the firm's value-added chain, in within-function integration, in IT-enabled team support, in the firm's internal planning and control system, and within the IT organization itself. [...]

IT's major impacts on the firm: a brief review

We have argued earlier that a more networked organizational approach to managing interdependence is enabled by two key characteristics of IT. Vastly improved communications capabilities and more cost-effective computer hardware and software have enabled the 'wiring' together of individuals and suborganizations within the single firm, and of firms to each other. It is this multifunctional, multilevel, multiorganizational, coordinative aspect of current technology that provides managers with the capability to design networks to manage interdependence. It is the technical dimension or platform through which managers have access to the people and data they need to direct and accomplish work.[20]

The second major characteristic is management's capacity to enable and drive organizational innovation and business process redesign through IT. As Venkatraman points out, business process redesign reflects a 'conscious effort to create alignment between the IT infrastructure and the business process.... Instead of treating the existing process as a constraint in the design of the optimum IT infrastructure, the business process itself is redesigned to maximally exploit the IT capabilities.'[21]

Our research in IT-enabled networks and managing interdependence refocuses and expands several earlier IT impacts perspectives in the academic and business literatures. Although these literatures often disagree, four major classes of impact are generally posited. First, there is the view that technology changes many facets of the organization's *internal structure*, affecting roles, power, and hierarchy. A second body of literature focuses on the emergence of *team-based*, problem-focused, often-changing work groups, supported by electronic communications, as the primary organizational form. Third, there is the view that organizations today are *dis-integrating* – their borders punctured by the steadily decreasing costs of electronic interconnection between firms, suppliers, and customers. Companies, it is believed, will gradually shift to more market-based organizational forms, with specialized firms taking over many of the functions formerly performed within the hierarchical firm. Finally, a fourth view of organizational impact arises from a technical perspective. It is argued that today's improved communications capability and data accessibility will lead to *systems integration* within the business. This, in turn, will lead to vastly improved group communications and, more importantly, the integration of business processes across function, product, or geographic lines.

Major changes in managerial structure, roles, and processes

In the first class of literature, Leavitt and Whisler argued that IT would lead to a general restructing of the organization, ultimately eliminating middle management.[22] In their view, IT moved middle managers out of traditional roles and allowed top managers to take on an even larger portion of the innovating, planning, and other 'creative' functions required to run the business.

Others were quick to comment on these predictions. Some speculated that IT would lead to greater organizational centralization, greater decentralization, reduced layers of middle and upper management, and greater centralization of managerial power or, alternatively, greater decentralization of managerial power.[23] Others developed contingency-based models of organizational impact.[24] Although it is clear that IT has affected many organizations in many different ways, it is also clear that this often conflicting literature has produced very little insight into how managers should plan for IT-enabled role or structural changes within their firms. Three more recent perspectives begin to address this issue.

The team as hero

According to this second view, teams and other ad hoc decision-making structures will provide the basis for a permanent organizational form. Reich, for example, argues that a 'collective entrepreneurship', with few middle-level managers and only modest differences between senior managers and junior employees, is evolving.[25] In short, he suggests a flat organization composed of teams.

Drucker speculates that the symphony orchestra or hospital may be models of future team-based organizations.[26] Drucker sees in the emergence of teams flatter companies that will look more like an assembly of players in a symphony – each player responsible for a specific part of a larger score, with only minimal guidance from the top (the conductor). Again, the design concept is a flatter team-based organization.

The relationship between teams and technology in much of this work appears based on a technical dimension. On the one hand, this view stresses technology's role in enabling different geographically dispersed groups to better coordinate their activities through enhanced electronic communications.[27] On the other hand, some authors stress the importance of 'groupware' in facilitating teamwork through better decision-making aids and project and problem management.[28]

Unfortunately, the team-based literature to date is highly speculative. As a general model of organizational structure, it leaves many questions unanswered. Primary among these are the long-term implications of organizing in such a manner that moves primary reporting relationships away from the more usual hierarchical, functional, geographic, or product structures. These structures work to immerse employees in pools of 'front-line', continually renewed expertise. Team members separated too long from these bases tend to lose this expertise.[29]

Corporate dis-integration: more markets and less hierarchy

A third perspective argues that today's hierarchical organizations are steadily dis-integrating; their borders punctured by the combined effects of electronic communication (greatly increased flows of information), electronic brokerage (technology's ability to connect many different buyers and suppliers instantaneously through a central database), and electronic integration (tighter coupling between interorganizational processes). In this view, the main effect of technology on organizations is not just in how tasks are performed (faster, better, cheaper, etc.) but rather in how firms organize the flow of goods and services through their value-added chains.

There are two major threads to this argument. Malone, Yates, and Benjamin state that new information technologies will allow closer integration of adjacent steps in the value-added chain through the development of electronic markets and electronic hierarchies.[30] They argue that advances in IT will steadily shift firms toward proportionately more forms of market coordination, since the costs therein will gradually fall beneath those of hierarchical coordination. Johnston and Lawrence argue that IT-enabled value-adding partnerships (VAPs) are rapidly emerging.[31] Typified by McKesson Corporations' Economost drug distribution service, VAPs are groups of small companies that share information freely and view the whole value-added chain – not just part of it – as one competitive unit.

These proposals, however, are very recent and have only small amounts of sample data to support them. And the exact opposite case – the case for increased vertical integration of firms – is also being strongly propounded.[32]

Systems integration: common systems and data architecture

A fourth, more technically oriented view is that business integration is supported by systems and data integration. Here the concept of IT-enabled organizational integration is presented as a natural outgrowth of two IT properties: improved interconnection and improved shared data accessibility.[33] In this view, *integration* refers to integration of data, of organizational communications (with emphasis on groups), and of business processes across functional, geographic, or product lines.

The move to the networked firm: a descriptive framework and examples

Although each of these four perspectives offers important insights, there is a need for a fifth perspective that expands these views into a more active managerial framework. We have argued that technology's major impact on the firm will be in supporting a more networked approach to effectively managing interdependence within the firm. Technology, as we have stated, provides both the technical capacity for interconnection of people and resources and the management capacity for business process redesign.

Given pressures from the drivers noted earlier, our research has uncovered six organizational contexts where characteristics of a more IT-enabled networked approach has strikingly improved a company's ability to manage its functional, product, or geographical subunits. We focus here on five of the six, as illustrated in Figure 12.7. [...]

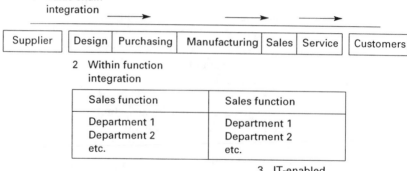

Figure 12.7 Examples of network approaches in five organizational contexts

Integration across the firm's value-added chain

Lawrence and Lorsch noted the use of 'human integrators' to manage the concurrence of effort between adjacent functions in the value-added chain (e.g., among manufacturing, distribution, and sales) more than twenty years ago.[34] Today this integration is performed increasingly through an electronic interface, via communications, computers, and databases. Firms attempt between-function integration for at least one of three reasons: to increase their capacity to respond quickly and effectively to market forces (time to market); to improve the quality of conformance to customer requirements (what we have earlier termed process quality objectives); or to reduce costs.

We have found that successful between-function integration collapses the multistage value-added chain into three major segments: producing new products, delivering products to customers, and managing customer relationships (see Figure 12.8).[35] In manufacturing companies, for example, it is clear that interdependence revolves around these three macro-organizational activities. In the insurance industry, discussions with five major companies revealed that the same three segments were targets for functional integration.

Turning to the two ends of the modified value-added chain – the product design segment on the one hand and the customer service segment on the other – the effects of a more networked technology-enabled integration are clear. To speed product development, companies such as Xerox,

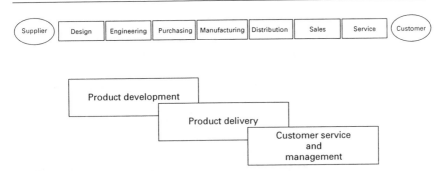

Figure 12.8 Product development, product delivery, and customer service and management: collapsing the value-added chain

Lockheed, and Digital are introducing CAD/CAM and other design aids that provide integrated support to product designers, product engineers, materials purchasing, and manufacturing personnel involved in the design-to-production process. This compression has resulted in joint 'buy-in' on new product designs, eliminating a lengthy iterative development process (which previously occurred because the designers did not take the needs and capabilities of other departments into account). Dramatically shortened product development time – a key component in improving aggregate time to market – had been a consequence of this buy-in.

At the customer service end of the chain, Otis Elevator, Digital, Xerox, and other firms have developed new service approaches based on electronic communications networks, an integrated database of customer and service history, and fault signaling that goes directly from damaged equipment to the supplier's maintenance-monitoring computer. The advantages of Otis's centrally coordinated electronic service system have been well publicized.[36] A major advantage is senior management's ability to view the status of maintenance efforts nationwide and to direct sales and service attention where needed. In addition, it is now feasible to provide the company's design, engineering, and manufacturing personnel with direct access to fault data.

In many ways, the most interesting stage of the collapsed value chain is product delivery, which requires integrating several different information systems: order entry, purchasing, materials resources planning, and distribution management. The critical business issues are to provide customers with information about when orders will be completed and to forecast and manage outside supplier, product manufacturer, and product distribution processes.

No company has yet accomplished the fully networked, large-scale integration of functions and systems required to fully manage the product delivery process. A division of the Norton Company, however, pioneered efforts in this direction in the mid-1980s. Norton initiated a set of major IT projects, ranging from the 'Norton Connection' (a computer-based telecommunications link between the company and its distributors), to a more effective order-processing system, to a series of manufacturing technologies targeted at flexible manufacturing and automated materials control.[37] More recently, Westinghouse initiated a product delivery integration process in several segments of the company. And at General Foods a series of task forces has been charged with developing a similar approach.

Most efforts, however, are more limited in scope. British Petroleum Company's chemical business has developed an integrated order management process spanning thirteen divisions. Baxter Healthcare Corporation is working to enhance its well-known ASAP order entry system to provide customers with full product line visibility to their 125,000–plus products. And a host of manufacturing integration projects have been initiated at Digital Equipment Corporation, Ford Motor, IBM, General Motors, Hewlett-Packard, and Texas Instruments, to name a few.

Within-function integration

Many companies are also recognizing the interdependence of multiple units within the same function. This recognition has prompted several actions to enhance a more network-oriented improvement of coordination and cooperation across subunits – for example, centralization of certain similar tasks or functions within the organization into the single group, central management of geographically separate units, and (in some firms) the development of common systems and/or standard data definitions to facilitate coordinating diverse organizational units.

At Sun Refining and Marketing company, for example, senior management identified crude oil trading as one of the most critical business activities in the company three years ago. At that point Sun's traders were dispersed worldwide, each acting relatively autonomously. Sun began developing a centralized on-line trading function supported by integrated market information from Reuters and other trade data sources. Today Sun recognized the importance of its integrated trading function in managing risk exposure and in developing effective pricing strategies for the volatile crude market.

Similarly, although OTISLINE can be viewed as an application enabling integration across stages of the value-added chain, it is also an integrating mechanism within the field maintenance function itself. Customers with difficult problems can be immediately directed to a specialist, not left to the limited resources of a remote branch office. Frequent trouble from a specific type of elevator can be observed as the pattern develops, and corrective action can be taken on a nationwide basis. In addition, the quality of telephone responsiveness to anxious customers can be closely monitored.

Eastman Kodak provides another example, its executive support system, which assists in the worldwide scheduling of manufacturing plants. Digital is installing common MRP systems throughout its worldwide manufacturing plants. DuPont has installed common financial systems in all of its European operations. The business drivers underscoring each of these efforts range from service to cost to time-to-market to global responsiveness – but they all recognize that no single unit within a major function is truly independent.

IT-enabled team support

Ken Olsen, chairman of Digital Equipment Corporation, believes that the ability to bring teams together electronically is one of the most important features of the company's IT capability. Ford Motor has claimed that the 'Team Taurus' approach, much of it IT-enabled, shaved more than a year off the time needed to develop, build, and bring to market the Taurus/Sable model line. In the future, as Drucker points out, many tasks will be done primarily by teams.[38]

Teamwork, of course, is not a new way to coordinate interdependent activities among separate units and people in an organization. What *is* new is that IT – chiefly electronic mail, videoconferencing, and computer-to-computer links such as those integral to CIM and EDI – is now facilitating teamwork and steadily adding capability to teams. Today, for example, it is feasible for team members to coordinate asynchronously (across time zones) and geographically (across remote locations) more easily than ever before. Teams, as such, are one part of the increasingly networked firm.

The development and use of computer software to support teams is also moving into an explosive phase. There is a growing body of software labeled 'groupware', for specialized computer aids designed to support collaborative work groups. As Bullen and Johansen point out, 'Groupware is not a thing. Rather it is a perspective on computing that emphasizes collaboration – rather than individual use'.[39] Several companies, including Xerox, General Motors, Digital, Eastman Kodak, IBM, and AT&T, are experimenting with state-of-the-art meeting and conferencing aids in addition to more 'routine' communications systems such as electronic mail or voice mail systems.

Planning and control

A fourth area where a more IT-enabled networked organizational approach is increasingly in evidence is in planning and control. [...] The major issue is how best to use IT for coordination and control of the firm's activities.

At Xerox, chairman David Kearns and president Paul Allaire have implemented an executive support system that now makes the annual planning and control process a more on-line, team-based, networked, communication- and coordination-based process. The system requires all of Xerox's thirty-four business units to submit their plans over an electronic communications network in a particular format. This allows the staff to critique the plans more effectively and to reintegrate these plans when looking for factors such as competitive threats across all SBUs, penetration into particular industries by all SBUs, and so forth.

More important, each SBU's plans can be reviewed not only by senior executives and corporate staff but also by other top officers in the firm. Each officer receiving an SBU's plans is encouraged to send corporate headquarters an electronic message raising the issues he or she sees in the plan. [. . .]

In short, Allaire's planning and control process is a computer-age process. By using a communication- and coordination-oriented network, it draws on the entire executive team for input. Understanding of the important issues facing each SBU is deeper, and its activities are therefore sometimes subtly, sometimes more precisely coordinated with the other SBUs.

A team-based networked approach to the senior executive job of managing the business is also in evidence at Philips Petroleum Company's Products and Chemicals Group. The executive vice president, Robert Wallace, is linked to his other top nine executives through an executive support system that provides on-line access not only to one another but also to varying levels of daily sales, refinery, and financial data. External news summaries relevant to the business are entered into the system three times a day. Unlike Allaire, who limits his input to planning and review meetings, Wallace has used the system to take operating command of a few critical decisions for the business. In the volatile petroleum pricing arena, Wallace believes that he and his executive team can confer with the advantage of immediate data access and can make better pricing decisions than those further down the line. He cites increased profits in the tens of millions as a result of the system.

By far the majority of senior executives today do not use their systems in nearly as dramatic a manner as Allaire and Wallace do.[40] Yet the technology provides the capability for better coordination at the senior management level. It also provides opportunities to move decisions either up or down in the organization. Team decision making is a growing reality, as geographically separated executives can concurrently access and assess data and communicate in 'real time'. Vertical on-line access to lower levels of data and text, however, violates many long-established management practices. Yet informal telephone-based systems have always provided some of this information. In an era where management is seen more as a cooperative, coaching activity than an iron-fisted one, vertical as well as horizontal networking may come of age. [...]

MANAGING INTERDEPENDENCE IN THE NETWORKED FIRM

Tomorrow's successful corporations will require increasingly effective management of interdependence to realize the performance gains made possible by a more networked organizational approach. IT-enabled changes in cross-functional integration, in the use of teams, or in within-function integration will force individual managers' agendas to change as well. In short, what managers do now and what they will do in the future are in the process of important change.

Zuboff argues that in the new 'informated' organization there is considerable interdependence among four domains of managerial activity: intellective skill development, technology development, strategy formulation, and social system development.[41] She notes that intellective skill development cannot proceed without the social system management that helps to foster roles and relationships appropriate to a new division of learning. Similarly, activity in either domain cannot proceed without technological development that supports an informating strategy. [...]

CONCLUSIONS

We believe that the IT-enabled networked organizational approach is the important design phenomenon of the 1990s. Firms increasingly will turn to network approaches with the goal of improving performance through the existing organization. In this chapter, we have identified several key characteristics of the more networked organizational approach and discussed specific areas where firms are attempting to increase performance in the business. We then argued that in their efforts to increase performance, firms are recognizing the need for more effective management of interdependence across subunits and people within the firm. IT-enabled networks are the most effective way for firms to manage this interdependence. [...]

NOTES

The authors wish to acknowledge the contributions of colleagues Christine V. Bullen, J. Debra Hofman, and John C. Henderson, Center for Information Systems Research, MIT Sloan School of Management, to the research on which this chapter is based. We are also indebted to others who read and commented on the manuscript: John Carroll, Michael S. Scott Morton, Edgar Schein, and N. Venkratraman of MIT's Sloan School; Lee Morris, CIGNA; Thomas Main, Aetna Life & Casualty; and Ron Smart, Digital Equipment Corporation.

1 S. Zuboff, *In the Age of the Smart Machine* (New York: Basic Books, 1988); R. G. Eccles, and D. B. Crane, *Doing Deals: Investment Banks at Work* (Cambridge, MA: Harvard Business School, 1988); P. F. Drucker, 'The Coming of the New Organization', *Harvard Business Review* (January–February 1988): 45–53. Also see R. K. Mueller, *Corporate Networking: Building Channels for Information and Influence* (New York: Free Press, 1986), p. 2.

2 See *California Management Review* 28, no. 3 (Spring 1986), for articles by R. E. Miles and C. C. Snow, 'Networked Organizations: New Concepts for New Forms' (pp. 62–73), and M. Tushman and D. Nadler, 'Organizing for Innovation' (pp. 74–92). Also see *California Management Review* 30, no. 1 (Fall 1987), for articles by J. Child, 'Information Technology, Organization, and Response to Strategic Challenges' (pp. 33–50), and H. Bahrami and S. Evans, 'Stratocracy in High-Technology Firms' (pp. 51–66). Also see 'A New Industrial Organization Approach' and 'The Emergence of the Network Firm' in C. Antonelli, ed., *New Information Technology and Industrial Change: The Italian Case* (Dordrecht: Kluwer Academic Publishers, 1988). On organizational innovation, see J. R. Galbraith, 'Designing the Innovating Organization', *Organizational Dynamics* (Winter 1982): 5–25; and T. Burns and G. M. Stalker, *The Management of Innovation* (London: Tavistock Publications, 1961).

3 P. F. Drucker, *Management* (New York: Harper & Row, 1973), p. 638.

4 See Child, 'Information Technology'; and Tushman and Nadler, 'Organizing for Innovation'.

5 For example, in intraorganizational, small group research, 'communications networks' are generally considered one of three variables, along with work task and leadership, which together establish norms for group interaction. As early as 1951, Bavelas and Barrett compared group performance, in their case problem-solving ability, across 'centralized' and 'decentralized' communications networks. See A. Bavelas, and D. Barrett, 'An Experimental Approach to Organizational Communication', *Personnel* 27 (1951): 366–71. Other definitions of networks and network characteristics are found in research in social psychology, organizational communications, and cognitive science. For example, see 'Communication Networks', in A. Paul Hare, *Handbook of Small Group Research* (New York: Free Press, 1976), pp. 260–77; L. K. Porter and K. H. Roberts, 'Communication in Organizations', in M. D. Dunnette, ed., *Handbook of Industrial and Organizational Psychology* (Chicago: Rand McNally, 1976), pp. 1553–89; R. L. Burgess, 'Communication Networks: An Experimental Reevaluation', in B. M. Bass, and S. D. Deep, eds., *Studies in Organizational Psychology* (Boston: Allyn and Bacon, 1972), pp. 165–79; E. P. Hollander and R. G. Hunt, eds., *Current Perspectives in Social Psychology* (New York: Oxford University Press, 1976). A more cognitive-based view is contained in T. Winograd and F. Flores, *Understanding Computers and Cognition: A New Foundation for Design* (Norwood, N.J.: Ablex Publishing, 1986).

6 In this chapter, we do not address the 'informal' organizations as such, in which trust is a key factor. The classic reference in this area is C. Barnard, *The Functions of the Executive* (Cambridge, MA: Harvard University Press, 1938).

7 Eccles and Crane, *Doing Deals*, pp. 119–46.

8 P. R. Lawrence and J. W. Lorsch, *Organization and Environment: Managing Differentiation and Integration* (Homewood, Ill. Richard D. Irwin, 1967), p. 13.

9 Researchers disagree about a precise definition of *interdependence*. An early influential view is contained in J. D. Thompson, *Organizations in Action: Social Science Bases of Administrative Theory* (New York: McGraw-Hill, 1967). Also see J. E. McCann and D. L. Ferry, 'An Approach for Assessing and Managing

Inter-Unit Interdependence – Note', *Academy of Management Journal* 4 (1979): 113–19; and B. Victor and R. S. Blackburn, 'Interdependence: An Alternative Conceptualization', *Academy of Management Journal* 12 (1987): 486–98.

10 G. Hamel and C. K. Prahalad, 'Strategic Intent', *Harvard Business Review* (May-June 1989): 63–76.

11 There are at least three key dimensions to this integration of process: shared work, shared information and expertise, and shared accountability. Getting agreement on what and how to measure joint performance across formerly independent operations is a key management issue. The dilemma is 'how joint' are the measures.

12 T. J. Peters and R. H. Waterman, Jr., *In Search of Excellence* (New York: Harper & Row, 1982), p. 156.

13 See G. A. Pall, 'Quality Process Management' (Thornwood, N.Y.: Quality Improvement Education Center, IBM, February 1988).

14 'The Big Loss at Merrill Lynch: Why It Was Blindsided', *Business Week*, May 18, 1987, pp. 112–13.

15 T. W. Malone, J. Yates, and R. I. Benjamin, 'Electronic Markets and Electronic Hierarchies', *Communications of the ACM* 30 (1987): 484–97.

16 R. Johnston and P. R. Lawrence, 'Beyond Vertical Integration – The Rise of the Value-Adding Partnership', *Harvard Business Review* (July-August 1988): 94–104.

17 H. Mintzberg, *The Structuring of Organizations* (Englewood Cliffs, N.J.: Prentice-Hall, 1979).

18 Lawrence and Lorsch, *Organization and Environment*.

19 J. L. Galbraith, *Organization Design* (Reading, Mass.: Addison-Wesley, 1977). Galbraith also introduced the concept of the organization as information processor in this work. He distinguished computer-based, vertical information systems from lateral relations and emphasized the division of organizations into suborganizations because of the need to minimize the cost of communications.

20 See R. I. Benjamin and M. S. Scott Morton, 'Information Technology, Integration, and Organizational Change', MIT Sloan School of Management, Management in the 1990s, working paper 86–017, April 1986.

21 Venkatramen, N. (1991) 'IT-Induced Business Reconfiguration', pp. 122–158 in M. S. Scott Morton *The Corporation of the 1990s*, Oxford University Press, 1991, Oxford.

22 H. J. Leavitt and T. L. Whisler, 'Management in the 1980s', *Harvard Business Review* (November-December 1958): 41–48.

23 For more on organizational centralization, see M. Anshen, 'The Manager and the Black Box', *Harvard Business Review* (November-December 1960): 85–92; T. L. Whisler, *The Impact of Computers on Organizations* (New York: Praeger, 1970); I. Hoos Russakoff, 'When the Computer Takes Over the Office', *Harvard Business Review* (July-August 1960): 102–12. Also see D. Robey, 'Systems and Organizational Structure', *Communications of the ACM* 24 (1981): 679–87. On organizational decentralization, see J. F. Burlingame, 'Information Technology and Decentralization', *Harvard Business Review* (November-December 1961): 121–26; J. L. King, 'Centralized versus Decentralized Computing: Organizational Considerations and Management Options', *Computing Surveys* 15 (1963): 319–49. On reduced layers of middle or upper management, see C. A. Myers, ed., *The Impact of Computers on Management* (Cambridge: MIT Press, 1967), pp. 1–15. On greater centralization of managerial power, see A. M. Pettigrew, 'Information Control as a Power Resource'. *Sociology* 6 (1972): 187–204; J. Pfeffer, *Power in Organizations* (Marshfield Mass.: Pitman, 1981);

and M. L. Markus and J. Pfeffer, 'Power and the Design and Implementation of Accounting and Control Systems', *Accounting, Organizations and Society* 8 (1983): 205–18. On decentralization of managerial power, see S. R. Klatsky, 'Automation, Size and the Locus of Decision Making: The Cascade Effect', *Journal of Business* 43 (1970): 141–51.

24 Carroll and Perin argue that what managers and employees *expect* from technology is an important predictor of the consequences observed. See J. S. Carroll and C. Perin, 'How Expectations about Microcomputers Influence Their Organizational Consequences', MIT Sloan School of Management, Management in the 1990s, working paper 88–044, September 1988.

25 R. B. Reich, 'Entrepreneurship Reconsidered: The Team as Hero', *Harvard Business Review* (May-June 1987): 77–83.

26 Drucker, 'The Coming of the New Organization'.

27 M. Hammer and G. E. Mangurian, 'The Changing Value of Communications Technology', *Sloan Management Review* (Winter 1987): 65–72.

28 C. V. Bullen and R. R. Johansen, 'Groupware: A Key to Managing Business Teams?' MIT Sloan School of Management, Center for Information Systems Research, working paper 169, May 1988.

29 O. Hauptman and T. J. Allen, 'The Influence of Communications Technologies on Organizational Structure: A Conceptual Model for Future Research', MIT Sloan School of Management, Management in the 1990s, working paper 87–038, May 1987.

30 T. W. Malone, J. Yates, and R. I. Benjamin, 'Electronic Markets and Electronic Hierarchies', *Communications of the ACM* 30 (1987): 484–97.

31 Johnston and Lawrence, 'Beyond Vertical Integration'.

32 T. Kumpe and P. T. Bolwijn, 'Manufacturing: The New Case for Vertical Integration', *Harvard Business Review* (March-April 1988): 75–81.

33 Benjamin and Scott Morton, 'Information Technology'.

34 Lawrence and Lorsch, *Organization and Environment*.

35 Although our three collapsed segments in the value chain are integral units, data does flow from one to another. The three segments are also interdependent but less strongly so than the functions within each segment.

36 'Otis MIS: Going Up', *Information WEEK*, May 18, 1987, pp. 32–37; J. F. Rockart, 'The Line Takes the Leadership – IS Management in a Wired Society', *Sloan Management Review* (Summer 1988): 57–64; W. F. McFarlan, 'How Information Technology Is Changing Management Control Systems', Harvard Business School, Case Note no. 9–187–139, 1987.

37 Rockart, 'The Line Takes the Leadership'.

38 Drucker, 'The Coming of the New Organization'.

39 Bullen and Johansen, 'Groupware'.

40 J. F. Rockart and D. W. DeLong, *Executive Support Systems: The Emergence of Top Management Computer Use* (Homewood, Ill.: Dow Jones-Irwin, 1988).

41 Zuboff, *In the Age of the Smart Machine*.

Acknowledgements

Chapter 1 Johnson, P. (1992) *Human Resource Management: People and Perform-ance*, chapter 3, pp. 27–36, Dartmouth Publishing Company Ltd.

Chapter 3 Lannon, J. (1994) *Journal of Brand Management*, vol. 2, 3, pp. 155–68, Henry Stuart Publications.

Chapter 4 Schlegelmilch, B. B. (1994) *Perspectives on Marketing Management*, vol. 4, pp. 55–71, John Wiley & Sons Ltd.

Chapter 5 Scott Morton, M. S. (1991) *The Corporation of the 1990s: Information Technology and Organizational Transformation*, Oxford University Press, edited version of chapter 1, pp. 3–23.

Chapter 6 Hofstede, G. (1993) *Academy of Management Executive*, vol. 7, 1, pp. 81–94.

Chapter 7 Bowen, D. E., Ledford, G. E., Jr., and Nathan, B. R. (1991) *Academy of Management Executive*, vol. 5, 4, pp. 35–51, edited version.

Chapter 8 Chernatony, L. de and McDonald, M. H. B. (1994) *Creating Powerful Brands*, edited version of chapter 2, pp. 14–54, Butterworth Heinemann.

Chapter 9 Day, G. S. (1994) *Journal of Marketing*, vol. 58, 4 October, pp. 37–52, edited version, American Marketing Association, Chicago.

Chapter 10 Davenport, T. H., Eccles, R. G. and Prusack, L. (1992) *Sloan Manage-ment Review*, vol. 34, 1, Fall, pp. 53–65, edited version, Sloan Management Association, MIT, Cambridge, Mass.
Boynton, A. C. (1993) *California Management Review*, vol. 35, 2, Winter, pp. 58–77, edited version.

Chapter 11 Pheysey, D. (1993) *Organizational Cultures*, edited version of chapter 3, pp. 43–65. Calori, R. (1994) *Common Characteristics of European Management*, chapter 1, pp. 11–30, Prentice Hall.

Chapter 12 Rockart, J. F. and Short, J. E. (1991) edited version of 'The Networked Organization and the Management of Interdependence', chapter 7, pp. 189–218, in M. S. Scott Morton, *The Corporation of the 1990s*, Oxford University Press, Oxford.

While the publishers have made every effort to contact the copyright holders of material used in this volume, they would be grateful to hear from any they were unable to contact.

Index